AMERICAN JOUR[illegible]
MATHEMATICAL AND M[illegible]
SCIENCES

VOL. 4, NOS. 3 & 4 1984

CONTENTS

AMERICAN JOURNAL OF MATHEMATICAL AND MANAGEMENT SCIENCES

MODERN STATISTICAL METHODS IN DIGITAL SIMULATION

Pandu R. Tadikamalla
Graduate School of Business
University of Pittsburgh
Pittsburgh, Pennsylvania 15260

Over the last twenty years, simulation has been increasingly employed for the solution of problems in virtually all areas of human endeavor, including business, engineering, science and social science. In the last decade, the rate of growth of simulation applications and the development of simulation methodologies has been substantial. In fact recent surveys have shown that a major portion of the articles in various math/stat and OR/MS journals are either simulation-based and/or have used simulation studies in support of their results. The purpose of this special issue is to bring together statistical methods for simulation and a state-of-the-art review of the statistical methodology in simulation in a collection. The goal of this collection of articles is to form reference and also serve as a "text book" for advanced courses in simulation. This supplements and

Key Words and Phrases: Simulation; Statistical Methods.

1984, VOL. 4, NOS. 3 & 4, 199-202
0196-6324/84/030199-4 $3.80

enhances other recent collections devoted to simulation, such as those of Nance, Adam and Sargent (1983) and Adam (1981).

This special issue contains a total of eight articles, which can conveniently be grouped into three categories: input-related, modeling-related and output-related. Obviously these groups as well as the papers are not mutually exclusive. In the input related group there are two articles: a survey article by Tadikamalla on modeling and generating univariate stochastic inputs and a similar article for multivariate stochastic inputs by Johnson, Wang and Ramberg. Tadikamalla's paper provides a state-of-the-art review of univariate random variate generation and a brief treatment of the generation of the order statistics. This paper also discusses some general systems of distributions as models to fit data when the underlying distribution is unknown. The other paper in this group by Johnson, Wang and Ramberg describes two general and several specific schemes for generating variates from continuous multi-variate distributions including the multivariate normal, Johnson system, Morgenstern, Plackett, Gumbel, Burr and other distributions. This paper also discusses the issues in designing multivariate Monte Carlo studies.

In the second group on "modeling issues", we have two articles: one by Smith and Mauro on design of experiments and the other on variance reduction techniques by Wilson. Smith and Mauro's paper discusses several topics relevant to experimental design of simulation experiments. These topics include the identification of the input variable, the statistical relation between the output and input variables, determination of the optimal combination of factor levels and the use of variance reduction techniques. The second paper in this group by Wilson is a high level state-of-the-art survey of the principal variance reduction techniques, including importance sampling, conditional Monte Carlo, stratified sampling and systematic sampling, for improving the efficiency of simulation-based performance statistics.

We have four papers in the output analysis group including Seila's paper on multivariate output analysis, Dudewicz and van der Meulen's paper on assessing the precision of simulation estimates of percentiles, Schriber and Andrew's paper on ARMA-based confidence intervals for Simulation output, and Balci and Sargent's paper on validation of simulation models. Seila's paper discusses inferential procedures for estimating multiple mean parameters in simulations with stationary multivariate output process. These techniques include classical procedures applicable to i.i.d. observations, procedures for regenerative processes and multivariate batch means. Seila also develops a new batch ratio method. Dudewicz and van der Meulen's paper reviews the approaches available for simulation estimation of a percentile of a random variable. This paper also contains a new ready-to-use procedure for percentile estimation.

Schriber and Andrews' paper presents a confidence interval procedure which is directly applicable for use with output sequences produced by stationary autoregressive moving average (ARMA) processes. The method is then applied to an ARMA model out-put sequence with an excellent performance. The proposed method seems to be promising when applied to an M/M/1 model. The last paper in this group and also in this issue is by Balci and Sargent on validation of simulation models. After presenting a state-of-the-art review, Balci and Sargent give some new results in the use of simultaneous confidence intervals and joint confidence regions for determining the operational validity of a multivariate response simulation model.

Based on the previous discussions, it can be seen than an overview of topics in the statistical methodology of simulation have been addressed in this issue. While no single issue could be exhaustive, the coverage furnishes a comprehensive state-of-the-art collection for researchers and students alike. One important area that has not been addressed is the impact of micro-computers on the simulation area. I see a great potential for "research" (tailoring existing methodologies to fit the micro-computer mold) in this area, and it could be the topic of a special work itself. Such work includes such topics as random variate generation considerations specific to micro-computers (Dudewicz, Karian, and Marshall (1985)).

I take this opportunity to thank all of the authors for their contributions and for their patience with the lengthy review process. I also wish to thank all fifteen referees for their conscientious and timely efforts; without their work, the quality of the papers could not have been achieved, and we owe them a great debt. The referees are: R. W. Andrews (University of Michigan), W. E. Biles (Louisiana State University), R. C. H. Cheng (UWIST, United Kingdom), A. V. Gafarian (University of Southern California), D. Goldsman (Georgia Institute of Technology), W. D. Kelton (University of Michigan), A. J. Kinderman (California State University, Northridge), A. M. Law (University of Arizona), B. L. Nelson (Ohio State University), J. W. Schmidt (Virginia Polytechnic Institute & State University), T. J. Schriber (University of Michigan), A. F. Seila (University of Georgia), M. A. Stephens (Simon Fraser University), J. J. Swain (Georgia Institute of Technology), and J. R. Wilson (Purdue University). Finally, I extend my appreciation and thanks to Edward Dudewicz for the opportunity and the encouragement in preparing this volume.

REFERENCES

Adam, N. R. (Eds.) (1981). Communications of the ACM. A Special issue on Simulation, Vol. 24.

Dudewicz, E. J., Karian, Z. A., and Marshall, R. J. III (1985). Random number generation on microcomputers. Modeling and Simulation on Microcomputers: 1985, The Society for Computer Simulation, LaJolla, California, pp. 9-14.

Nance, R. E., Adam, N. R., and Sargent, R. G. (Eds.) (1983). Operations Research, A Special Issue on Simulation, Vol. 31, No. 6.

Received 2/28/85; Revised 3/18/85.

AMERICAN JOURNAL OF MATHEMATICAL AND MANAGEMENT SCIENCES

MODELING AND GENERATING STOCHASTIC INPUTS FOR SIMULATION STUDIES

Pandu R. Tadikamalla
Graduate School of Business
University of Pittsburgh
Pittsburgh, Pennsylvania 15260

SYNOPTIC ABSTRACT

The problem of modeling and generating stochastic inputs for simulation studies is reviewed. A state-of-the-art review of univariate random variate generation is provided. A brief treatment of the generation of order statistics is also given. Some general systems of distributions are discussed as models to fit data when the underlying distribution is unknown. A comprehensive list of references is included.

Key Words and Phrases: stochastic inputs; random variate generation; univariate continuous and discrete distributions; general systems of distributions; order statistics.

1984, VOL. 4, NOS. 3 & 4, 203-223
0196-6324/84/030203-21 $7.20

1. INTRODUCTION

The purpose of this article is to present an overview and a state-of-the-art survey of modeling and generating univariate stochastic inputs for simulation studies. For various univariate distributions (both continuous and discrete), we provide a state-of-the-art review of random variate generation with specific recommendations. A comprehensive list of references is included.

A variety of situations exist in simulation experiments where an investigator needs stochastic events. In queueing models, the interarrival times and service times are often stochastic. In inventory models, the times between the demands and demand quantities may be stochastic. In reliability models, the times to failure are usually stochastic. Persons desiring to use computer simulation models to solve these problems must first model the stochastic phenomena (e.g., specify an underlying probability distribution). Next they must determine a method of generating data from the specified model.

The state of knowledge of the investigator, with regard to these probability distributions, can be divided into two classes: 1) The distribution is known, and 2) the distribution is unknown.

1) The distribution is known: This case can be further divided into two categories, parameters known and parameters unknown.

1.a) Parameters known: This situation arises when the investigator wants to study the properties of a new statistical procedure using Monte Carlo techniques. In this case, the problem is to find a "suitable method" for generating random variates from a known distribution.

1.b) Parameters unknown: This situation arises when the investigator knows the distribution of the input process, but for a given design the parameters are unknown. In queueing models the interarrival times are often assumed to be exponentially distributed, but for many situations the parameter is unknown and hence must be estimated. Once the parameters are estimated, the unknown parameters case can be treated in the same manner as the known parameters case.

2) The distribution is unknown: Often the investigator does not know the distribution of the input process. He may have some data available and wish to generate "similar" data for the simulation model. One approach to this problem is to employ a system of distributions which covers a wide variety of commonly occurring shapes. Such systems of distributions, including the Pearson, the Johnson, the Burr, the Tadikamalla-Johnson and the Generalized Lambda, are discussed in this paper.

Section 2 discusses criteria for judging variate generation algorithms. Section 3 describes the state-of-the-art for generating univariate continuous and discrete distributions. Section 4 gives a brief treatment of the generation of order statistics. Section 5 contains a brief description of some general systems of distributions useful for modeling in simulation studies.

2. METHODS; CRITERIA FOR ALGORITHM EVALUATION AND COMPARISONS

The most common techniques for random variate generation are those of: (i) inverse transformation, (ii) special transformations, (iii) rejection, and (iv) mixtures. A brief description of these methods can be found in Tadikamalla and Johnson (1981), among other places.

The important criteria used in judging random variate generation algorithms are speed, simplicity, accuracy, and generality of the technique. Speed can be measured in terms of the marginal CPU time required for generating one variate from a distribution for a given set of parameters. The set-up time required when a change in the parameters occurs should be taken into consideration in comparing algorithms. It is difficult to measure simplicity, but it can be viewed as a combination of ease of implementation (which in turn can be considered in terms of program length, portability, and special functions or subprograms required, if any) and the core storage required for the algorithm.

Random variate generation algorithms can be approximate or exact, theoretically. We will limit the discussion to exact methods, since the leading algorithms in all cases are exact. These methods are exact, subject only to the accuracy of the machine and of the standard machine functions logarithm, exponential, and square root. A technique used for obtaining an algorithm can be general (such as the rejection technique), or it can be specific for a given situation (such as the Box-Muller (1958) transformation for obtaining normal variates).

3. SURVEY OF ALGORITHMS

In this section, we discuss the state-of-the-art in random variate generation for continuous and discrete univariate distributions.

All random variate generation algorithms are based on the transformation of uniform (0,1) random numbers. A comprehensive treatment of uniform random number generation is given by Dudewicz and Ralley (1981). For our purposes we assume the availability of a good uniform random number generator. Throughout this paper, U_1, U_2,... represent independent uniform (0,1) random numbers.

3.1. Continuous Univariate Distributions.

Continuous univariate distributions have received a great deal of attention in the literature of random variate generation. Within this group, the normal, the gamma and the beta distributions have received the most attention.

The Normal Distribution. A number of algorithms are available for generating normal variates. The first exact method for normal variates was given by Box and Muller (1958). This method yields a pair of independent normal variates X_1, X_2 through the transformation $X_1 = (-2\ln(u_1))^{\frac{1}{2}} \sin(2\Pi u_2)$ and $X_2 = (-2\ln(u_1))^{\frac{1}{2}} \cos(2\Pi u_2)$. This method, although very simple, is somewhat slow and also has problems with certain types of uniform generators (see Chay, Fardo and Mazumdar (1975)). A slight modification of this method using trigonometric transformations (called the Polar method) yielding a slightly faster algorithm is discussed in Marsaglia and Bray (1964). Apart from these two algorithms, the later algorithms have been primarily rejection and composition based. At the assembly language level, where bit manipulation is easy, Marsaglia, MacLaren and Bray's (1964) algorithm (available in the "SUPER-DUPER" package and in Dudewicz and Ralley (1981)) is probably the fastest. Among other algorithms which are easy to implement and require no bit manipulation, Kinderman and Ramage's (1976) KR, Kinderman and Monahan's (1977) RU, and Deak's (1981) ET are fast. Among all these algorithms Kinderman and Monahan's (1977) RU is probably the simplest and yet reasonably fast.

The Gamma Distribution. The probability density function (pdf) of the standard gamma distribution can be written as $f(x) = x^{\alpha-1} \cdot e^{-x}/\Gamma(\alpha)$, $x \geq 0$, $\alpha > 0$. Considerable attention has recently been directed at developing simpler and faster algorithms for generating gamma random variates with arbitrary shape parameter α. Recently, Tadikamalla and Johnson (1981) provided a complete guide to gamma variate generation. Most of gamma algorithms are based on the rejection and composition techniques. Based on the criteria discussed above, Tadikamalla and Johnson (1981) make the following recommendations. For $\alpha < 1$, algorithm GS given by Ahrens and Dieter (1974) is recommended. Recently, Best (1983) modified GS to yield a faster algorithm RGS. For $\alpha > 1$ and for the situations where α changes frequently algorithm GKM3 by Cheng and Feast (1979) is suggested. If a large number of variates are required for a given value of α, algorithm G4PE by Schmeiser and Lal (1980) is recommended along with Cheng and Feast's (1980) GT and GBH. The later two are attractive because of their simplicity over G4PE.

The Beta Distribution. The density function of the standard beta distribution is given by $f(x) = x^{a-1}(1-x)^{b-1}/\beta(a,b)$, $0 \lesssim x \lesssim 1$, where $\beta(a,b) = \int_0^1 y^{a-1}(1-y)^{b-1}dy$. Considerable attention has been given to the beta variate generation. The state-of-the-art in beta variate generation is presented by Schmeiser and Babu (1980). For $a < 1$ and/or $b < 1$, Cheng's (1978) switch algorithm BC is recommended. Schmeiser and Babu's (1980) B4PE is uniformly faster than all other algorithms for all parameter combinations, $a > 1$ and $b > 1$. However, Cheng's (1978) algorithm BB should also be considered in light of its simplicity and smaller set up cost for the case of $a > 1$ and $b > 1$.

The Student's t Distribution. The density function of a t variate with α degrees of freedom is given by $f(x)= C_\alpha/(1+x^2/\alpha)^{(\alpha+1)/2}$ for $\alpha > 0$ where $C_\alpha = \Gamma((\alpha+1)/2)/(\sqrt{(\Pi\alpha)}\ \Gamma(\alpha/2))$. The t family is a special form of Pearson type VII distributions, and includes the Cauchy distribution ($\alpha = 1$), and the normal distribution ($\alpha \to \infty$) as a limiting case. Kinderman, Monahan and Ramage (1977) presented several new algorithms for sampling from the t family. Later Best (1978) and Marsaglia (1980) presented two algorithms for sampling from the t distribution applicable when $\alpha \geq 3$ and $\alpha \geq 2$, respectively. Recently Kinderman and Monahan (1980) and Stadlober (1981) presented two algorithms for sampling from the t distribution when $\alpha \geq 3$. Marsaglia's algorithm requires a normal variate generator. Subject to the availability of a fast normal variate generator (such as the one in "SUPER-DUPER"), Marsaglia's algorithm could be a contender. Stadlober's (1981) algorithm TD requires very little set-up time and is slightly faster than Kinderman and Monahan's (1980) algorithm TROU. However, we recommend Kinderman and Monahan's (1980) algorithm TROU because of its simplicity for all applicable values of $\alpha \geqslant 3$.

"Other" Distributions. In addition to the four distributions discussed above, we now briefly discuss several other continuous distributions and the leading algorithms in each case.

The Lognormal Distribution. If X has the normal distribution with mean μ and variance σ^2, then $Y = e^X$ has the lognormal distribution.

The Weibull Distribution. The cumulative distribution function of the three-parameter Weibull distribution is given by $f(x) = 1-\exp((-(x-a)/b)^c)$, $x \geq a$, $a,b,c>0$. Since the F^{-1} exists in a simple closed form, Weibull variates can be generated by $X = a+b\{-\ln U\}^{1/c}$. Also note that the exponential is a special case (with $c = 1$ and (often) $a = 0$).

The Inverse Gaussian Distribution. The probability density function of the inverse Gaussian distribution is given by $f(x) = (\sqrt{\lambda/2\Pi x^3}) \exp(-\lambda(x-\mu)^2/2\mu^2 x)$, $x > 0$, λ, $\mu > 0$. Michael, Schucany and Haas (1976) present a simple, and the only available exact algorithm for sampling from the inverse Gaussian distribution.

The Generalized Gamma Distribution. If X has the gamma distribution, then $Y = X^{1/c}$ has the generalized gamma distribution as defined by Stacy (1962). Random variates from the distribution can be generated by generating random variates X from the gamma distribution and making the transformation $Y = X^{1/c}$. Tadikamalla (1979) proposed a simple method to obtain generalized gamma variates without having to generate gamma variates.

The Exponential Power Distribution (EPD). The density function of the standard EPD can be written as $f(x) = \exp(-|x|^{\alpha})/(2\Gamma(1+1/\alpha))$, $\alpha \geq 1$. This family of distributions is symmetric about zero and includes the uniform distribution ($\alpha \to \infty$), the normal distribution ($\alpha = 2$), and the double exponential distribution ($\alpha = 1$). If X has the density function given above, then $Y = |X|^{\alpha}$ has the gamma distribution with shape parameter α. The method of generating EPD variates would be to generate a gamma variate with shape parameter $1/\alpha$, raise it to the $1/\alpha$ power, and attach a random sign (Johnson (1979)). Recently, Tadikamalla (1980a) proposed two algorithms (ED and EN) for generating EPD variates with $\alpha \geq 1$ and $\alpha \geq 2$ respectively. Both of these algorithms are faster than

Johnson's (1979) algorithm for $\alpha \leq 6$.

Other less well known distributions have received little attention. The relevant references for some of these distributions are:

Von Mises Distribution: Best and Fisher (1979)

Stable Distributions: Bartels (1978) and Chambers, Mallows and Stuck (1976)

Cauchy Distribution: Arnason (1974) and Monahan (1979)

Kolmogrov-Smirnov Statistics: Devroye (1981)

Extreme Value Distribution: Goldstein (1963)

3.2. Discrete Univariate Distributions.

Recently two new techniques, called the acceptance/complement method and aliasing, have been used in developing algorithms for discrete variate generation. Both of these techniques are based on the fundamental ideas of the probability mixing and rejection methods. The acceptance/complement method has been proposed and developed by Ahrens and Dieter (1982), Deak (1981) and Kronmal and Peterson (1981). The alias method was proposed by Walker (1974, 1977) and was further developed by Kronmal and Peterson (1979). For a brief discussion of these methods, also see Schmeiser (1983). Of all discrete univariate distributions, the Poisson and the Binomial have received the most attention.

The Poisson Distribution. The probability mass function of the Poisson is given by $P(X=x) = e^{-\mu}\mu^{x}/x!$, $x = 0,1,2,\ldots$ where $\mu > 0$ is the mean of the distribution. In a recent article, Schmeiser and Kachitvichyanukul (1983) provide a survey of Poisson algorithms and also present a new algorithm PTPE applicable for $\mu \geq 10$. Among the several algorithms available for Poisson variate generation, algorithm PINV (Fishman (1976), Schmeiser (1983)) is recommended for small values of μ ($\mu \leq 5$). For small to medium values of μ ($5 < \mu < 15$), algorithm PIF given by Fishman (1976) is recommended. For large values of μ, the two contenders are Schmeiser and Kachitvichyanukul's (1983) PTPE and Ahrens and Dieter's (1982) KPOISS. Algorithm KPOISS requires a normal variate generator. <u>If a fast normal variate generator is available and/or the mean μ changes frequently, algorithm KPOISS is recommended</u>. <u>If a large number of variates are required for a given mean, algorithm PTPE is faster</u>.

<u>The Binomial Distribution</u>. The probability mass function of the binomial is given by $P(X=x) = \binom{n}{x} p^x (1-p)^{n-x}$ for $x=0,1,2,\ldots,n$. When n is small, summing up n Bernoulli trials with probability of success p works well. Relles (1972) and Ahrens and Dieter (1974) give algorithms whose execution times increase slowly (proportional to ln n) with the mean (np), based on the binomial distribution's relationship with the beta distribution. Fishman (1979) presents an algorithm using a Poisson majorizing function with mean 15. Fishman recommends Relle's (1972) algorithm RBINOM for $n \leq 30$ and his algorithm for $n \geq 30$. <u>The more recent algorithms of Devroye (1980) and Ahrens and Dieter (1980) are much faster</u>. <u>Kachitvichyanukul (1982) describes binomial algorithm BTPE, similar to Poisson algorithm PTPE</u>, which is the fastest of all the binomial algorithms, except when the mean is small.

<u>The Negative Binomial Distribution</u>. The probability mass function of the negative binomial distribution is $P(X=x) = \binom{n+x-1}{x} p^x (1-p)^x$ for x=0,1,....The <u>geometric distribution</u> is the special case n = 1. For integer n, (which usually is the case), the negative binomial distribution is also called the <u>Pascal distribution</u> in which case it can be viewed as the sum of n geometric random variables with probability of success p and X is the number of failures before n successes.

The geometric distribution is a discrete analogue of the exponential distribution. <u>Geometric random variables may be generated directly using the inverse transformation $x = \lfloor \ln(1-u)/\ln(1-p) \rfloor$, where $\lfloor y \rfloor$ denotes the largest integer less than or equal to y</u>.

If X is a Poisson random variable with mean θ and if θ is gamma distributed with parameters α and β ($\alpha = n$ and $\beta = (1-p)/p$))

then X has a negative Binomial distribution with parameters n and p (see Johnson and Kotz (1969)). Thus, a negative binomial variate can be generated by generating a gamma (α,β) variate y and then generating a Poisson variate with mean y. Johnson and Kotz (1969) present several compound discrete distributions by "mixing" various discrete and continuous distributions as described in the case of the negative binomial distribution; similar generation methods can be used in such cases.

4. ORDER STATISTICS

If $X_1, X_2, \ldots, X_n$ denote a random sample from a distribution with distribution function (df) F(x) and $X_{(1)} \leq X_{(2)} \leq \ldots \leq X_{(n)}$ are the ordered X's, then $X_{(1)}, X_{(2)}, \ldots, X_{(n)}$ are called the order statistics corresponding to $X_1, X_2, \ldots, X_n$. Order statistics play an important role in statistical inference and in simulation studies for a number of reasons. For example, some of the properties of order statistics do not depend upon the distribution from which the random sample is obtained. (In some simulation studies, only a portion of the order statistics is of interest.)

Suppose we are interested in generating order statistics from a continuous distribution with df, F(.). If the inverse transformation method is used to generate the random sample, there is a direct correspondence between the order statistics of $(X_1, X_2, \ldots, X_n)$ and the order statistics of the associated uniform sample $(U_1, U_2, \ldots, U_n)$. Since F^{-1} is a monotonic function, $Y_i = F^{-1}(U_{(i)})$, i = 1,2,...,n, represent the order statistics from the distribution with df, F(.), where $U_{(1)} \leq U_{(2)} \leq \ldots U_{(n)}$ are the order statistics from the uniform (0,1) distribution. Thus if the inverse transformation method is used to sample from the df F(.), the problem of generating order statistics reduces to the problem of generation of order statistics from the uniform (0,1) distribution.

A straightforward approach to the generation of order statistics is to generate a sample of size n and then sort the sample to obtain the desired order statistics. For medium and large values of n this sorting procedure can be very time consuming relative to a direct method for the generation of observations from the joint distribution of the extreme values. Now we discuss the generation of certain sets of order statistics from the uniform (0,1) distribution.

Hogg and Craig (1970) discuss the marginal and joint probability densities of order statistics from a continuous distribution with pdf f(x) and df F(x). These results take a simple form in the case of the uniform (0,1) distribution, yielding some simple methods for sequential generation of order statistics. (Also see Lurie and Hartley (1972).) Let $V_1, V_2, V_3 \ldots$ be observations from the uniform (0,1) distribution.

Then

$$U_{(1)} = 1 - V_1^{1/n}$$

$$U_{(2)} = 1 - (1-U_{(1)})V_2^{1/(n-1)}$$

$$\vdots$$

$$U_{(i+1)} = 1- (1-U_{(i)})\, V_{i+1}^{1/(n-i)} .$$

Lurie and Hartley (1972) showed that $U_{(1)}$, $U_{(2)}, \ldots$ are distributed as the order statistics from the uniform (0,1) distribution and proposed this method of generation. Later, Schucany (1972) used a similar approach to generate the order statistics in descending order, without sort, with $U_{(n)}$, as follows:

$$U_{(n)} = V_1^{1/n}$$

$$\vdots$$

$$U_{(n-i)} = U_{(n-i+1)}\, V_{i+1}^{1/(n-i)} \qquad (i = 1,2,\ldots,n-1).$$

Reeder (1972) suggested that generating order statistics in descending order is faster than that in ascending order, and Lurie and Mason (1973) confirmed this claim. Both of these methods of generating order statistics are particularly useful when a subset of the order statistics starting from one extreme are needed, e.g. the largest 5 or the smallest 5 of a sample size of 40. Ramberg and Tadikamalla (1978) suggest generating U_i as a beta variable (U_i is beta (i,n-i+1)) and generating U_{i-1}, U_{i-2} using the above recursion algorithm suggested Schucany by (1972). This approach will probably be faster in generating a subset of order statistics when the required subset is somewhere in the middle of the sample of size n.

Devroye (1980) considers the case of $U_{(n)}$ when n is very large and evaluation of $U_{(n)} = V_1^{1/n}$ may cause numerical problems. Schmeiser (1978b) considers the generation of $X_{(1)}$ or $X_{(n)}$ when the observations are not identically distributed, but $F^{-1}(.)$ is available for each distribution. Gerondtidis and Smith (1982) review the inversion method and the grouping method for generating order statistics from a general distribution. The grouping method can briefly be described as follows. Given an integer k (a suggested value is n/4), divide the range of the distribution into k equal probability intervals. Next generate a multinomial vector $(m_1, m_2, \ldots, m_k)$ corresponding to the division of n objects independently among k equally likely cells. (See Fishman (1978) and Ho, Gentle and Kennedy (1979).) Then draw m_j variables (from the specified general distribution) from the jth interval for $1 \leq j \leq k$, and sort each group of m_j variables directly and put the k groups together to obtain a complete ordered sample. Gerontidis and Smith (1982) recommend the inversion method if F^{-1} exists in simple closed form. In other cases and in large scale simulations the grouping method may well offset the greater initial programming effort and the time required to calculate the interval end points.

5. GENERAL SYSTEMS OF DISTRIBUTIONS

Often an investigator has insufficient theoretical grounds for selecting a theoretical distribution such as the normal, the gamma, or the Weibull, to model the stochastic process of interest. He has data available (or can obtain data) and by empirical methods must draw conclusions concerning the process under study. One approach to this problem may be to fit a general system of distributions to the data and use that distribution as the underlying model of the process. We consider five different systems of distributions namely the Johnson system (Johnson (1947)), Tadikamalla-Johnson system (Tadikamalla and Johnson (1982)), the Generalized-Lambda distribution (Ramberg and Schmeiser (1974)), the Schmeiser-Deutch system (Schmeiser and Deutch (1977)), and the Burr Type XII distributions (Burr (1942)). Recently Tadikamalla (1980c) provided a review of these distributions from the simulation point of view. The inverse of the cumulative distribution function for all five systems exists in simple closed form, making random variate generation simple. The Johnson system is based on the transformation of a normal variate and thus requires the use of a normal random variate. The Pearson system (Pearson (1895)) of distributions, widely mentioned in the statistics literature for fitting data, has a limited appeal in simulation modeling because of the complexity of random variate generation. However, the commonly used normal, gamma, beta and t-distributions are all part of the Pearson system. Figure 1 shows the regions in the (β_1, β_2) plane covered by several of the distributions discussed in this paper. Here $\sqrt{\beta_1}$ is the skewness (third standarized moment) and β_2 is the kurtosis (fourth standardized moment). Note that a distribution with no variable shape parameters (such as the normal) is represented in the (β_1, β_2) plane as a point, a distribution with one shape parameter (such as the gamma) is a line, and a distribution with two shape parameters (such as the Burr) as a region. The Johnson, the Tadikamalla-Johnson, and the Schmeiser-Deutch distributions cover the entire possible region in the (β_1, β_2) plane.

In the absence of any theoretical background for the process, which distribution should be used for modeling the stochastic pro-

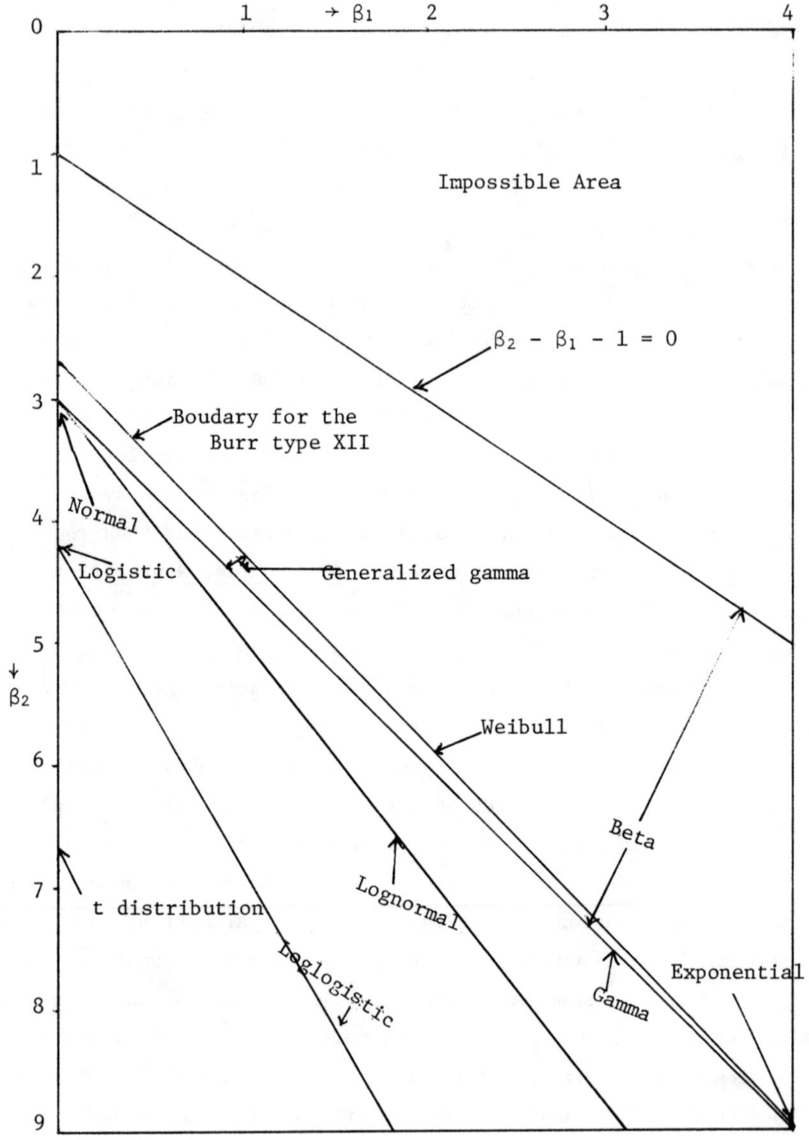

Figure 1. Various Distributions in the (β_1, β_2) Plane.

cess under consideration? The Schmeiser-Deutch distributions have a "cusp" like the double-exponential distribution and are truncated which may be undesirable. The Generalized Lambda and the Burr distributions cover almost the same region in the (β_1,β_2) plane. For random variate generation, the Generalized Lambda algorithm is slightly faster than the Burr algorithm. However the pdf and the cdf do not exist in simple closed form for the Generalized Lambda distribution, though this causes no problems to computer plotting. (See Ramberg, Tadikamalla, Dudewicz, and Mykytka (1979)). Both the Johnson and the Tadikamalla-Johnson systems of distributions use more than one functional form. Between the two, the later yields simpler & faster algorithms for random variate generation. However, the Johnson system has been in use for a long time. The estimation of parameters for all these five systems of distributions is limited to the method of moments and in some cases to the methods based on percentiles. For all these distributions the maximum likelihood estimation procedures are rather lengthy, but not impracticably so.

If what is needed is a distribution to fit the data and generate random observations without much difficulty, the Generalized Lambda distribution (with limited coverage) and the Tadikamalla-Johnson system seem to be attractive. If the analysis of the sample observations requires a comparison and/or the use of some properties of the parent population, the Burr distribution (with limited coverage), the Johnson system and the Tadikamalla-Johnson system seem to be competitive.

REFERENCES

Ahrens, J. H. and Dieter, U. (1974). Computer methods for sampling from gamma, beta, Poisson and binomial distributions. Computing, 12, 223-246.

Ahrens, J. H. and Dieter, U. (1980). Sampling from binomial and Poisson distributions. A method with bounded computational times. Computing, 25, 193-208.

Ahrens, J. H. and Dieter, U. (1982). Computer generation of Poisson deviates from modified normal distributions. ACM Transactions on Mathematical Software, 8, 163-170.

Arnason, A. N. (1974). Computer generation of Cauchy variates. Proceedings of the Fourth Manitoba Conference of Numerical Mathematics, edited by H. C. Williams and B. L. Harkness. Utilitas Mathematica Publishing, Winnipeg, Canada, 177-199.

Bartels, R. (1978). Generating non-normal stable variates using limit theorem properties. Journal of Statistical Computation and Simulation, 7, 199-212.

Best, D. J. (1978). A simple algorithm for the computer generation of random samples for a student's t or symmetric beta distribution. COMPSTAT, Physical-Verlog, Vienna, 341-347.

Best, D. J. (1983). A note on gamma variate generators with shape parameters less than unity. Computing, 30, 185-188.

Best, D. J. and Fisher, N. I. (1979). Efficient simulation of the Von Mises distribution. Applied Statistics, 28, 152-157.

Box, G. E. P. and Muller, M. E. (1958). A note on the generation of random normal deviates. Annals of Mathematical Statistics, 29, 610-611.

Burr, I. W. (1942). Cumulative frequency functions. Annals of Mathematical Statistics 13, 215-232.

Chambers, J. M., Mallows, C. L. and Stuck, B. W. (1976). A method for simulating stable random variables. Journal of the American Statistical Association, 71, 340-344.

Chay, S. C., Fardo, R. D. and Mazumdar, M. (1975). On Using the Box-Muller transformation with multiplicative congruential pseudo-random number generators. Applied Statistics, 24, 132-135.

Cheng, R. C. H. (1978). Generating beta variates with non-integral shape parameters. Communications of the ACM, 21, 317-322.

Cheng, R. C. H. and Feast, G. M. (1979). Some simple gamma variate generators. Applied Statistics, 28, 290-295.

Cheng, R. C. H. and Feast, G. M. (1980). Gamma variate generators with increased shape parameter range. Communications of the ACM, 23, 389-393.

Deak, I. (1981). An economical method for random number generation and a normal generator. Computing, 27, 113-121.

Devroye, L. (1980). Generating the maximum of independent identically distributed random variables. Computers and Mathematics with Applications, 6,305-315.

Devroye, L. (1981). The series method for random variate generation and its application to the Kolmogorov-Smirnov distribution. American Journal of Mathematical and Management Sciences, 1, 359-379.

Devroye, L. and Naderisamai, A. (1980). A binomial random variate generator. Technical Report, McGill University.

Dudewicz, E. J. and Ralley, T. G. (1981). The handbook of random number generation and testing with TESTRAND computer code. American Science Press, Columbus, Ohio, U.S.A.

Fishman, G. S. (1976). Sampling from the Poisson distribution on a computer. Computing, 17, 147-156.

Fishman, G. S. (1978). Sampling from the multinomial distribution on a computer. Technical Report # 78-5, curriculum in operations research and systems analysis. University of North Carolina, Chapel Hill.

Fishman, G. S. (1979). Sampling from the binomial distribution on a computer. Journal of the American Statistical Association, 74, 418-423.

Gerontidis, I. and Smith, R. L. (1982). Monte carlo generation of order statistics from general distributions. Applied Statistics, 31, 238-243.

Goldstein, N. (1963). Random numbers from the extreme value distribution. Publications de l'Institut Statistique de l' Universite' de Paris, 12, 137-158.

Ho, F. C. M., Gentle, J. E., and Kennedy, W. J. (1979). Generation of random variates from the multinomial distribution.

Proceedings of the statistical computing section, American Statistical Association, 336-339.

Hogg, R. V. and Craig, A. T. (1970). Introduction to Mathematical Statistics, 3rd Ed. MacMillam Publishing Company, New York

Johnson, M. E. (1979). Computer generation of the exponential power distributions. Journal of Statistical Computation and Simulation, 9, 239-240.

Johnson, N. L. (1947). Systems of frequency curves generated by methods of translation. Biometrika, 36, 149-176.

Johnson N. L. and Kotz, S. S. (1969). Discrete Distributions, Houghton-Mifflin Company, Boston.

Kachitvichyanukul, V. (1982). Computer generation of Poisson, binomial, and hypergeometric random variates. Ph.D. Thesis, School of Industrial Engineering, Purdue University.

Kinderman, A. J. and Monahan, J. F. (1977). Computer generation of random variables using the ratio of uniform deviates. ACM Transactions on Mathematical Software, 3, 257-260.

Kinderman, A. J. and Monahan, J. F. (1980). New Methods for generating student's t and gamma variables. Computing, 23, 369-377.

Kinderman, A. J. and Ramage, J. G. (1976). Computer generation of normal random variables. Journal of the American Statistical Association, 71, 893-896.

Kinderman, A. J., Monahan, J. F. and Ramage, J. G. (1977). Computer methods for sampling from student's t distribution. Mathematics of Computation, 31, 1009-1018.

Kronmal, R. A. and Peterson, Jr., A. V. (1979). On the alias method for generating random variables from a discrete distribution. American Statistician, 33, 214-218.

Kronmal, R. A. and Peterson, Jr., A. V. (1981). A variant of the acceptance-rejection method for computer generation of random variables. Journal of the American Statistical Association, 76, 446-451.

Lurie, D. and Hartley, H. O. (1972). Machine generation of order statistics for monte carlo computations. American Statistician, 26, 26-27.

Lurie, D. and Mason, R. L. (1973). Empirical investigation of general techniques for computer generation of order statistics. Communications in Statistics, 2, 363-371.

Marsaglia, G. (1980). Generating random variables with a t distribution. Mathematics of Computation, 34, 235-236.

Marsaglia, G. and Bray, T. A. (1964). A convenient method for generating normal variables. SIAM Review, 6, 260-264.

Marsaglia, G., MacLaren, M. D. and Bray, T. A. (1964). A fast procedure for generating random normal variables. Communications of the ACM, 7, 4-10.

Michael, J. R., Schucany, W. R. and Haas, R. W. (1976). Generating random variates using transformations with multiple roots. The American Statistician, 30, 88-90.

Monahan, J. F. (1979). Extensions of von Neumann's method for generating random variables. Mathematics of Computation, 33, 1065-1069.

Pearson, K. (1895). Contributions to the mathematical theory, of evolution, II, skew variations in homogeneous material. Philosophical Transactions of the Royal Society, London, Series A, 186, 343-414.

Ramberg, J. S., Tadikamalla, P. R., Dudewicz, E. J. and Mykytka, E. F. (1979). A probability distribution and its uses in fitting data. Technometrics, 21, 201-214.

Ramberg, J. S. and Schmeiser, B. W. (1974). An approximate method for generating asymmetric random variables. Communications of the ACM, 17, 78-82.

Ramberg, J. S. and Tadikamalla, P. R. (1978). On generation of subsets of order statistics. Journal of Statistical Computation and Simulation, 6, 239-241.

Reeder, H. A. (1972). Machine generation of order statistics. American Statistician, 26, 56-57.

Relles, D. (1972). A simple algorithm for generating binomial random variables when N is large. Journal of the American Statistical Association, 67, 612-613.

Schmeiser, B. W. (1978a). Order statistics in digital computer simulation. A survey. Proceedings of the 1978 Winter Simulation Conference. 136-140.

Schmeiser, B. W. (1978b). Generation of the maximum (minimum) value in digital computer simulation. Journal of Statistical Computation and Simulation, 8, 103-115.

Schmeiser, B. W. (1980). Random variate generation. A survey. Proceedings of the 1980 Winter Simulation Conference. 79-104.

Schmeiser, B. W. (1983). Recent advances in generating observations from discrete random variables. Proceedings of Computer Science and Statistics 15th Symposium, Interface, North-Holland (forth coming).

Schmeiser B. W. and Babu, A. J. G. (1980). Beta variate generation via exponential majorizing functions. Operations Research, 28, 917-926.

Schmeiser, B. W. and Deutch, S. J. (1977). A versatile four parameter family of probability distributions suitable for simulation. AIIE Transactions, 9, 176-182.

Schmeiser, B. W. and Kachitvichyanukul, Voratas. (1983). Poisson random variate generation. Technical Report, School of Industrial Engineering, Purdue University

Schmeiser, B. W. and Lal, R. (1980). Squeeze methods for generating gamma variates. Journal of the American Statistical Association, 75, 679-682.

Schucany, W. R. (1972). Order Statistics in Simulation. Journal of Statistical Computation and Simulation, 1, 281-286.

Stacy, A. W. (1962). A generalization the gamma distribution. Annals of Mathematical Statistics, 33, 1187-1192.

Stadlober, E. (1981). Generating Student's t variates by a modified rejection method. Proceedings of 2nd Pannonian Symposium on mathematical statistics, June 14-20.

Tadikamalla, P. R. (1979). Random sampling from the generalized gamma distribution. Computing, 23, 199-203.

Tadikamalla, P. R. (1980a). Random sampling from the exponential power distribution. Journal of the American Statistical Association, 75, 683-686.

Tadikamalla, P. R. (1980b). A look at the Burr and related distributions. International Statistical Review, 48, 337-344.

Tadikamalla, P. R. (1980c). On simulating non-normal distributions. Psychometrika, 45, 273-279.

Tadikamalla, P. R. and Johnson, M. E. (1981). A complete guide to gamma variate generation. American Journal of Mathematical and Management Sciences, 1, 213-236.

Tadikamalla, P. R. and Johnson, N. L. (1982). Systems of frequency curves generated by transformations of logistic variables. Biometrika, 69-461-465.

Walker, A. J. (1974). New fast method for generating discrete random numbers with arbitrary frequency distribution. Electronic Letters, 10, 127-128.

Walker, A. J. (1977). An efficient method for generating discrete random variables with general distributions. ACM Transactions on Mathematical Software, 3, 253-256.

Received 9/21/83; Revised 5/7/84.

AMERICAN JOURNAL OF MATHEMATICAL AND MANAGEMENT SCIENCES

GENERATION OF CONTINUOUS MULTIVARIATE DISTRIBUTIONS FOR STATISTICAL APPLICATIONS

Mark E. Johnson, Chiang Wang and John S. Ramberg
Systems and Industrial Engineering Department
The University of Arizona
Tucson, Arizona 85721

SYNOPTIC ABSTRACT

Two general and several specific schemes are described for generating variates from continuous multivariate distributions. Algorithms are provided for the multivariate normal, Johnson system, Cauchy, elliptically contoured (including Pearson Types II and VII), Morgenstern, Plackett, Ali, Gumbel, Burr (and related), Beta-Stacy and Khintchine distributions. Issues in designing multivariate Monte Carlo studies are discussed.

Key Words and Phrases: Cauchy, elliptical distributions, Morgenstern, Plackett, Ali, Gumbel, Burr, Beta-Stacy, Khintchine.

1984, VOL. 4, NOS. 3 & 4, 225-248
0196-6324/84/030225-24 $7.80

1. INTRODUCTION.

Many multivariate procedures suffer from a lack of empirical testing outside the realm in which they were originally designed -- frequently the multivariate normal distribution context. This deficiency is due not so much to negligence but rather to a lack of suitable and available distributions for Monte Carlo studies. Very little attention has been devoted to the generation of multivariate random vectors, so it seems that every investigator who decides to conduct empirical tests must effectively start from scratch. The purpose of this paper is to ease this burden by providing generation algorithms for a variety of distributions in multivariate Monte Carlo studies. This treatment is set initially in a general context so that algorithms for multivariate distributions not covered in this paper specifically may be developed along similar lines.

Aside from the issue of what multivariate distributions can be generated, a more pertinent question relates to what distributions should be generated. The answer to this question depends heavily on the particular multivariate procedure under investigation. Thus, at most only general guidelines can be given. A brief discussion of two research areas may serve to identify for the reader some possible uses of the distributions described in this paper.

Tests for multivariate normality provide a mechanism for assessing the appropriateness of this common distributional assumption. For associated references and specific tests, see Malkovich and Afifi (1973) and Hawkins (1981). The better tests have not been extensively scrutinized with respect to power as a function of (small) sample size, dimension, and (of course) the non-normality. The results given in this paper should provide a convenient starting point for pursuing such investigations.

Intuitively appealing classification rules are readily derived in discriminant analysis applications (Beckman and

Johnson (1981)). Detailed study of new classification rules invariably necessitates a Monte Carlo study, in which case the algorithms given herein can be exploited. In the classification rule context the multivariate normal distribution need not be the baseline case for comparison. Simulation studies with multivariate distributions in discriminant analysis have been conducted, although additional areas warrant attention (Johnson, Ramberg and Wang (1982)).

These two examples suggest the types of studies we have in mind in terms of the distributions to be covered below. For some investigations, our coverage of distributions may be inadequate. In such situations, the general methods described in Section 2 may be used to develop specific algorithms. In Section 3 algorithms are given for the multivariate normal, Johnson system, Cauchy, elliptically contoured (including Pearson Types II and VII), Morgenstern, Plackett, Ali, Gumbel, Burr (and related), Beta-Stacy and Khintchine distributions. A limited comparison of some of these distributions, which can have normal marginal distributions, is also provided by means of contour plots. More detailed comparisons of these distributions will be available in a forthcoming monograph (Johnson (1986)). The issue of distribution selection in Monte Carlo studies is addressed in Section 4.

2. GENERAL METHODS.

To establish a framework for the specific generation algorithms (given in Section 3 below), a discussion of two general methods, the transformation and conditional distribution techniques, will now be given. Strictly speaking, the conditional distribution method is a special case of transformation, since it involves a function of certain univariate random variables. However, because of its many successful applications (illustrated in Section 3) this special designation seems appropriate. On the other hand, "acceptance-rejection" (AR) methods, which are extensively used in univariate generation, are not examined here. Although in theory the AR method applies in multivariate situations, practical difficulties have stifled its use. In the parlance of AR methodology, these difficulties include a lack of suitable dominating functions, complications in optimizing the choice of parameters in the dominating function, and low efficiencies. The conditional distribution and transformation methods will now be described.

The Conditional Distribution Method reduces the multivariate generation problem to a sequence of univariate generation problems. Let $\underline{X} = (X_1,\ldots,X_p)'$ be a p-dimensional random vector distributed according to probability density function (pdf) $f(\underline{x})$. Rosenblatt (1952) and many subsequent authors suggest the following conditional distribution method for generating a random vector $\underline{X}$ having density f:

1. Generate $X_1 = x_1$ from the marginal distribution of X_1.
2. Generate $X_2 = x_2$ from the conditional distribution of X_2 given $X_1 = x_1$.
3. Generate $X_3 = x_3$ from the conditional distribution of X_3 given $X_1 = x_1$ and $X_2 = x_2$.

$$\vdots$$

p. Generate $X_p = x_p$ from the conditional distribution of X_p given $X_1 = x_1$, $X_2 = x_2,\ldots,$ $X_{p-1} = x_{p-1}$.

Therefore, two major tasks must be performed to generate random vectors using the conditional distribution method. First, the marginal distribution of X_1 and each of the above conditional univariate distributions must be derived. Second, a generation procedure for each of the univariate distributions must be determined. The efficiency of this method for a given multivariate distribution depends on how the univariate distributions needed can be generated. This method can be considered as a "transformation" method in the sense that the multivariate distribution is obtained by a transformation of specified univariate distributions. Eight examples of this approach are illustrated in Section 3.

The Transformation Method. The basic concept of the transformation method is as follows. Let $\underline{X} = (X_1, X_2, \ldots, X_p)'$ be a p-dimensional random vector to be generated having a certain multivariate distribution. Also, let $\underline{Y} = (Y_1, Y_2, \ldots, Y_q)'$ be a q-dimensional $(q \geq p)$ random vector having a different distribution than $\underline{X}$. If there exists a function $g(\underline{Y}) = (g_1(\underline{Y}), \ldots, g_p(\underline{Y}))'$ such that $g(\underline{Y})$ has the same distribution as $\underline{X}$, then the random vector $\underline{X}$ can be generated directly by first generating the random vector $\underline{Y}$ and then evaluating $g(\underline{Y})$.

The transformation method is most attractive when the specific transformation is already "known." For a variety of distributions, this is the case (see Section 3). Given an arbitrary multivariate density $f(\underline{x})$, it is rarely obvious what transformations of easy-to-generate random vectors will lead to this distribution. The following guidelines may facilitate the effort:

1. Conduct a thorough literature search for an appropriate construction scheme in one of the references to the distribution.
2. Attempt (invertible) transformations to $\underline{X}$. Is it possible to obtain a recognizable result? Start with component transformations such as the probability integral transformation.
3. If 1 and 2 are unsuccessful, look again at the conditional distributions.

3. EXAMPLES.

This section describes specific generation algorithms for a variety of bivariate and multivariate distributions using the conditional distribution and transformation methods of Section 2. More detailed treatments of the distributions themselves can be found in the cited references. Johnson (1986) provides a unified treatment for Monte Carlo applications.

Multivariate Normal Distribution. The use of the conditional distribution and the transformation approaches for generating the multivariate normal distribution has been available for some time (Scheuer and Stoller (1962)). Let $\underline{X} \sim N_p(\underline{\mu},\Sigma)$ denote a p-dimensional multivariate normal random vector with mean vector $\underline{\mu}$ and covariance matrix Σ. Let L be the lower triangular (Choleski) decomposition of Σ, that is a matrix such that $LL' = \Sigma$. Given p-independent univariate standard normals, $\underline{Y}' = (Y_1, Y_2, \ldots, Y_p)$, transform them via $\underline{X} = L\,\underline{Y} + \underline{\mu}$ to achieve the desired $N_p(\underline{\mu},\Sigma)$ distribution. Simple formulas for determining the components of L are available in Kennedy and Gentle (1980, pp.294-296). The computer package LINPACK (Dongarra, Moler, Bunch and Stewart (1979)) also contains the subroutine SCHDC which can compute L.

In many situations, consideration of 2 or 3 dimensions will suffice. Here, the entries of L can be given explicity. Suppose the covariance matrix of $\underline{X}$ is given by

$$\Sigma = \begin{bmatrix} \sigma_1^2 & \rho_{12}\sigma_1\sigma_2 & \rho_{13}\sigma_1\sigma_3 \\ \rho_{12}\sigma_1\sigma_2 & \sigma_2^2 & \rho_{23}\sigma_2\sigma_3 \\ \rho_{13}\sigma_1\sigma_3 & \rho_{23}\sigma_2\sigma_3 & \sigma_3^2 \end{bmatrix}.$$

The Choleski decomposition of Σ is

$$L = \begin{bmatrix} \sigma_1 & 0 & 0 \\ \sigma_2\rho_{12} & \sigma_2\sqrt{(1-\rho_{12}^2)} & 0 \\ \sigma_3\rho_{13} & \dfrac{\sigma_3(\rho_{23}-\rho_{12}\rho_{13})}{\sqrt{(1-\rho_{12}^2)}} & \dfrac{\sigma_3\sqrt{[(1-\rho_{12}^2)(1-\rho_{13}^2)-(\rho_{23}-\rho_{12}\rho_{13})^2]}}{\sqrt{(1-\rho_{12}^2)}} \end{bmatrix}$$

Note that the submatrix obtained by deleting the third row and column of L is the Choleski decomposition of the covariance matrix for the first two components of $\underline{X}$. Univariate normal generators are widely available (two methods are given below when we consider elliptically contoured distributions).

Johnson Translation System. Johnson's (1949) system of distributions is easy to generate on a computer. Given a multivariate normal random vector $\underline{X}' = (X_1,\ldots,X_p)$, simply apply one of the following transformations to each component

lognormal:	$Y_i = \exp(X_i)$
$\sinh^{-1}$-normal:	$Y_i = [\exp(X_i) - \exp(-X_i)]/2$
logit-normal:	$Y_i = [1 + \exp(X_i)]^{-1}$.

This scheme is so simple that frequently researchers have adapted it (especially in discriminant analysis Monte Carlo studies) without giving its implications much thought. In particular, the moment structure of $\underline{Y}$ will be considerably different from the moments of $\underline{X}$. Johnson, Ramberg and Wang (1982) derive some results for controlling such characteristics with the Johnson system and redo parts of previous simulation studies which had confounded the effects of non-normality and moment structure.

Multivariate Cauchy. Consider a multivariate Cauchy distribution having density (Johnson and Kotz (1972), p. 294)

$$f(\underline{x}) = \pi^{-(p+1)/2}\Gamma[(p+1)/2]\ [1+\underline{x}'\underline{x}]^{-(p+1)/2}\ . \qquad (1)$$

Variates having density (1) are readily generated using the conditional distribution approach since: the distribution of X_1 is Cauchy and can be obtained as $X_1 = \tan(\pi(U-0.5))$ where U is uniform 0-1 (see Dudewicz and Ralley, 1981); and the conditional distribution of $[m^{1/2}(1 + \sum_{j=1}^{m-1} x_j^2)^{-1/2}]\cdot X_m$ given $X_1 = x_1$, $X_2 = x_2,\ldots, X_{m-1} = x_{m-1}$ is univariate Student's t with m degrees of freedom. The $t_{(m)}$ distribution can be readily sampled from $Y/\sqrt{(Z/m)}$ where Y is standard normal and Z is chi-square with m degrees of freedom (see Tadikamalla and Johnson (1981)) or by the "ratio-of-uniforms" technique (Kinderman, Monahan and Ramage (1977)).

The distribution as given in (1) is a multivariate t with 1 degree of freedom and can be alternately generated, as follows: Generate $\underline{Y} \sim N_p(\underline{0}, I)$, where I is the pxp identity matrix, and take $\underline{X} = (Y_1/Z, Y_2/Z, \ldots Y_p/Z)'$ where Z is an independent $\chi^2_{(1)}$ variate. More generally, a multivariate t with k degrees of freedom is obtained if Z is $\chi^2_{(k)}$. These multivariate Cauchy and t distributions are special cases of elliptically contoured distribution for which some convenient methods of generation are given next.

Elliptically Contoured Distributions. An interesting and useful class of multivariate distributions, including the multivariate normal as a special case, is the set of elliptically contoured distributions. A valuable mathematical treatment of these distributions is given by Cambanis, Huang and Simons (1981). Before considering their approach, we set the stage by describing two simple methods for generating independent normal variates; the underlying principle of these two techniques is a precursor to the representation of the elliptically-contoured distributions given by Cambanis, Huang and Simons.

The well-known Box-Muller (1958) method for generating two independent standard normals X_1 and X_2 from two independent uniform 0-1's U_1 and U_2 sets

$$X_1 = (-2 \ln U_1)^{1/2} \cos(2\pi U_2)$$
$$X_2 = (-2 \ln U_1)^{1/2} \sin(2\pi U_2). \tag{2}$$

This method can be verified using standard change-of-variable arguments (e.g., Hogg and Craig (1978), p. 141). As an informal argument note that the point ($\cos 2\pi U_2$, $\sin 2\pi U_2$) is uniformly distributed on the boundary of the unit circle. Also, if X_1 and X_2 are independent standard normals, $X_1^2 + X_2^2$ is distributed $\chi^2_{(2)}$. From (2)

$$X_1^2 + X_2^2 = (-2\ \ell n\ U_1)\cos^2(2\pi U_2)+(-2\ \ell n\ U_1)\sin^2(2\pi U_2)$$
$$= -2\ \ell n\ U_1,$$

which is distributed $\chi^2_{(2)}$ (an exponential with scale parameter 2).

A modification of (2) can be used to avoid trigonometric evaluations. This technique (Marsaglia and Bray (1964)) sets

$$X_1 = \left(\frac{-2\ \ell n\ W}{W}\right)^{1/2} U_1$$
$$X_2 = \left(\frac{-2\ \ell n\ W}{W}\right)^{1/2} U_2,$$

where U_1 and U_2 are independent uniform 0-1′s constrained by $W \equiv U_1^2 + U_2^2 \leq 1$. This method is quite similar to the Box-Muller transformation. A simple change-of-variable argument shows that W is distributed uniform 0-1, and hence $-2\ \ell n\ W$ is $\chi^2_{(2)}$ as above. Also, $(U_1/W^{1/2}, U_2/W^{1/2})$ is the projection of the point (U_1,U_2) from the interior of the unit circle to the boundary of the unit circle. Thus, both methods (eventually) sample uniformly from the boundary of the unit circle and then adjust the generated point′s distance from the origin according to the square root of a $\chi^2_{(2)}$ distribution.

More generally, Cambanis, Huang and Simons gave a useful representation of p-dimensional elliptically contoured distributions using some fundamental results of Schoenberg (1938). For notation, let L be a p x p lower triangular factorization of Σ, $\underline{U}^{(p)}$ denote a random vector with a uniform distribution on the surface of the p-dimensional unit hypersphere, and R be a positive random variable independent of $\underline{U}^{(p)}$. A p-dimensional random vector $\underline{X}$ is <u>elliptically contoured</u> with scaling matrix Σ and location vector $\underline{\mu}$ if

$$\underline{X} = R \cdot L \cdot \underline{U}^{(p)} + \underline{\mu}. \tag{3}$$

The random variable R^2 has the distribution of $(\underline{X}-\underline{\mu})'\Sigma^{-1}(\underline{X}-\underline{\mu})$. In some cases of practical interest, R^2 has a recognizable, easy-to-generate distribution. These cases include the Pearson Type II and Pearson Type VII multivariate distributions.

The generation of $\underline{U}^{(p)}$ is straightforward. First, generate $Z_1, Z_2, \ldots, Z_p$ independent standard normals and let $Z_0 = (Z_1^2 + Z_2^2 + \ldots + Z_p^2)^{1/2}$. Set the ith component of $\underline{U}^{(p)}$ to be Z_i/Z_0, $i = 1,2,\ldots,p$. (This method is generally credited to Muller (1959)). Alternate methods for generating $\underline{U}^{(p)}$ have been surveyed recently by Tashiro (1977).

The Pearson Type II distribution has density function

$$f(\underline{x}) = \frac{\Gamma(p/2 + m+1)}{\Gamma(m+1)\pi^{p/2}} |\Sigma|^{-1/2} [1-(\underline{x}-\underline{\mu})'\Sigma^{-1}(\underline{x}-\underline{\mu})]^m \tag{4}$$

where the support of the distribution is restricted to the region $(\underline{x}-\underline{\mu})'\Sigma^{-1}(\underline{x}-\underline{\mu}) \leq 1$; $\underline{\mu}$ is a location vector; Σ is the scaling matrix; the additional parameter $m > -1$; and, p is the dimension. Variate generation is quite easy since the distribution of the quadratic form $R^2 = (\underline{X} - \underline{\mu})'\Sigma^{-1}(\underline{X} - \underline{\mu})$ is beta with parameters p/2 and m+1. (Beta generation is described later in the discussion of the Beta-Stacy distribution.)

The Pearson Type VII distribution has density function:

$$f(\underline{x}) = \frac{\Gamma(m)}{\Gamma(m-p/2)\ \pi^{p/2}} |\Sigma|^{-1/2} [1+(\underline{x}-\underline{\mu})'\Sigma^{-1}(\underline{x}-\underline{\mu})]^{-m} \quad , \tag{5}$$

where $\underline{\mu}$ is a location vector; Σ is the scaling matrix; and, m is an additional parameter restricted by $m > p/2$ with p the dimension. Variate generation is slightly less apparent here than for the Pearson Type II. The distribution of $Z=R^2$ corresponding to (5) has density function

$$f(z) = \frac{\Gamma(m)}{\Gamma(p/2)\ \Gamma(m-p/2)} z^{p/2-1} (1+z)^{-m}, \ z>0 \quad . \tag{6}$$

This density is that of a Pearson Type VI distribution, and can be generated via $Z = Y/(1-Y)$, where Y is beta with parameters p/2 and m-p/2. If $m = (p+1)/2$, Σ is an identity matrix and $\underline{\mu}=\underline{0}$, then the density in (5) reduces to the multivariate Cauchy in (1).

In the bivariate case (p=2), explicit generation formulas for the Pearson II and VII distributions can be given (Johnson and Ramberg (1977)). Let U_1 and U_2 be independent uniform 0-1 variates. Then

$$\text{Pearson II:} \quad X_1 = (1-U_1^{1/(m+1)})^{1/2} \cos(2\pi U_2)$$
$$X_2 = (1-U_1^{1/(m+1)})^{1/2} \sin(2\pi U_2)$$

$$\text{Pearson VII:} \quad X_1 = (U_1^{\frac{1}{1-m}}-1)^{1/2} \cos(2\pi U_2)$$
$$X_2 = (U_1^{\frac{1}{1-m}}-1)^{1/2} \sin(2\pi U_2)$$

$$\text{Cauchy:} \quad X_1 = (U_1^{-2}-1)^{1/2} \cos(2\pi U_2)$$
$$X_2 = (U_1^{-2}-1)^{1/2} \sin(2\pi U_2)$$

The resulting distributions have location vectors at the origin and identity matrix as scaling matrices.

These schemes for generating elliptically contoured distributions are easy to implement and have been used by Chmielewski (1981a) in a study of tests for normality. A guide to references on these distributions has also been published by Chmielewski (1981b).

Morgenstern's Bivariate Uniform Distribution. This distribution, which could be credited to Eyraud (1936), has the simple density function

$$f(x_1,x_2) = 1 + \alpha(2x_1-1)(2x_2-1), \quad 0\leq x_1,x_2\leq 1, \quad -1\leq\alpha\leq 1. \tag{7}$$

Each of the components of (X_1,X_2) has uniform 0-1 distribution so that the functional form of the density of $X_2|X_1 = x_1$ is also given by (7). Since this function is linear in x_2, the corresponding distribution function is quadratic in x_2. Setting the conditional distribution function equal to a generated uniform 0-1, say U_2, and solving for X_2, is the basis of the following algorithm.

1. Generate U_1, U_2 independent uniform 0-1 and set $X_1 = U_1$.
2. Compute:

$$A = \alpha(2U_1-1)-1$$
$$B = [1-2\alpha(2U_1-1) + \alpha^2(2U_1-1)^2 + 4\alpha U_2(2U_1-1)]^{1/2}$$

3. Set $X_2 = 2U_2/(B-A)$.

Multivariate extensions of (7) have been explored, although this distribution can model only weak dependencies. Johnson (1982) cites some relevant papers and describes the generation of multivariate forms of (7). The recent work of Cambanis (1977) may also be of interest.

Plackett's Bivariate Uniform Distribution. Plackett's (1965) distribution is given by the density function

$$f(x_1,x_2) = \frac{\alpha(\alpha+1)(x_1+x_2-2x_1x_2) + 1}{[\{1+(\alpha-1)(x_1+x_2)\}^2 - 4\alpha(\alpha-1)x_1x_2]^{3/2}} \qquad (8)$$

$$\alpha > 0,\ 0 < x_1,\ x_2 < 1.$$

The components X_1 and X_2 are marginally uniform 0-1. For a detailed description of distribution (8), see Mardia (1970); for a recent application, see Wahrendorf (1980). Mardia (1967) developed the conditional distribution approach for sampling from (8) which is summarized, as follows:

1. Generate U_1, U_2 independent uniform 0-1 variates.
2. Set $X_1 = U_1$.
3. Set $X_2 = [B-(1-2U_2)C]/2A$, where

$$A = \alpha + (\alpha-1)^2\, U_2\,(1-U_2)$$

$$B = 2\,U_2(1-U_2)(\alpha^2U_1-U_1+1) - 2\alpha U_2(1-U_2) + \alpha$$

$$C = [\alpha^2 + 4\alpha(1-\alpha)^2U_1U_2(1-U_1)(1-U_2)]^{1/2}.$$

Then the pair (X_1,X_2) is distributed according to (8).

Ali's Bivariate Distribution. A recently developed distribution due to Ali, Mikhail and Haq (1978) can be easily generated via the conditional distribution approach. A simple representation of this bivariate distribution is given by its distribution function

$$F(u_1,u_2) = u_1u_2/[1-\alpha(1-u_1)(1-u_2)],\quad 0\leq u_1,u_2\leq 1,\ -1\leq\alpha\leq 1. \qquad (9)$$

The pair (U_1,U_2) with this distribution function has uniform 0-1 marginal distributions. The equation $F(u_2|U_1=u_1) = p$, $0 < p < 1$, is quadratic in u_2 which leads to the following straightforward algorithm for sampling from (9):

1. Generate independent uniform 0-1 variates V_1, V_2, and set $U_1 = V_1$.
2. Compute

$$b = 1 - V_1$$

$$A = \alpha(2bV_2 + 1) + 2\alpha^2 b^2 V_2 + 1$$

$$B = \alpha^2(4b^2 V_2 - 4bV_2 + 1) + \alpha^2(4V_2 - 4bV_2 - 2) + 1$$

3. Set $U_2 = 2V_2(\alpha b - 1)^2/(A + \sqrt{B})$.

Gumbel's Bivariate Exponential Distribution. The following bivariate density is due to Gumbel (1960):

$$f(x_1, x_2) = [(1+\theta x_1)(1+\theta x_2) - \theta] e^{-x_1 - x_2 - \theta x_1 x_2}, \quad x_1, x_2 > 0,\ 0 \leqslant \theta \leqslant 1. \tag{10}$$

The pair (X_1, X_2) distributed as (10) has standard exponential components. The conditional distribution of X_2 given $X_1 = x_1$ has density

$$f(x_2 | X_1 = x_1) = e^{-x_2(1+\theta x_1)} [(1+\theta x_1)(1+\theta x_2) - \theta],$$

which can be rewritten as

$$f(x_2 | X_1 = x_1) = p\beta e^{-\beta x_2} + (1-p)\beta^2 x_2\, e^{-\beta x_2}, \tag{11}$$

where $\beta = 1 + \theta x_1$ and $p = (\beta - \theta)/\beta$. The form in (11) admits an immediate probabilistic interpretation: a variate with density (11) arises with probability p as exponential with mean $1/\beta$, and with probability 1-p the variate is the sum of two independent exponentials each with mean $1/\beta$. Generation is therefore immediate since these exponentials can be obtained as $-\beta^{-1} \ell n(U)$, where U is uniform 0-1.

Multivariate Burr (and Related) Distributions. Takahasi (1965) describes the multivariate Burr distribution having the density function

$$f(\underline{x}) = \frac{\Gamma(k+p)}{\Gamma(k)} \left(1 + \sum_{i=1}^{p} \alpha_i x_i^{c_i}\right)^{-(k+p)} \prod_{i=1}^{p} \left(\alpha_i c_i x_i^{c_i - 1}\right), \tag{12}$$

$$x_i, \alpha_i, c_i > 0, \ i=1,2,\ldots,p.$$

The marginal distribution functions are

$$F(x_i) = 1 - [1+(\alpha_i x_i)^{c_i}]^{-k}, \ i = 1,2,\ldots,p, \tag{13}$$

which corresponds to Burr's (1942) distribution. This distribution can also be viewed as a power of an $F_{2,k}$ variate. The form in (13) is ideally suited for variate generation -- the equation $F(x_i) = U$ is readily solved for x_i, where U is uniform 0-1. Also, the conditional distributions in (12) are themselves distributed as scaled Burr variates. Thus, a scheme based on the conditional distribution approach for sampling from (12) could be developed (see Johnson and Kotz (1972), p. 288-290 for details).

Following Cook and Johnson (1981), a direct transformation approach will be described. The distribution in (12) can be constructed via $X_i = (\alpha_i^{-1} Y_i/Z)^{1/c_i}$, i=1,2,...,p, where $Y_1, Y_2, \ldots, Y_p$ are independent standard exponentials and Z is an independent gamma variate with shape parameter k and unit scale parameter. Similarly, using the same Y_i's and Z, a multivariate Pareto (Johnson and Kotz (1972), p. 286) and a multivariate logistic (Johnson and Kotz (1972), p. 291) can be constructed:

$$\text{Pareto:} \quad X_i = \theta_i(1+Y_i/Z)$$
$$\text{logistic:} \quad X_i = -\ln(Y_i/Z)$$

It should be evident that the multivariate Burr, Pareto and logistic distributions are intrinsically related. Cook and Johnson (1981) identified the standard form density

$$f(u_1,u_2,\ldots,u_n) = \frac{\Gamma(\alpha+n)}{\Gamma(\alpha)\alpha^n} \prod_{i=1}^{n} u_i^{-(1/\alpha)-1} \left[\sum_{i=1}^{n} u_i^{-1/\alpha} - n + 1\right]^{-(\alpha+n)},$$

$$0 < u_i < 1, \ i=1,2,\ldots,n,$$

which has uniform 0-1 marginals. The three special cases are obtained by applying the appropriate inverse distribution function transformation to each component.

Beta-Stacy Bivariate Distribution. Mihram and Hultquist (1967) developed a distribution whose actual construction follows the conditional distribution approach. The first component X_1 has Stacy's (1962) generalized gamma distribution (a gamma $(\alpha,1)$ variate raised to the power $1/c$). The conditional distribution of X_2 given $X_1 = x_1$ is then specified as beta with parameters θ_1 and θ_2 on the interval $(0,x_1)$. Thus, both X_1 and $X_2|X_1 = x_1$ can be generated by use of a gamma generator, as follows:

1. Generate Y_1 having a $\Gamma(\alpha,1)$ distribution.
2. Set $X_1 = Y_1^{1/c}$.
3. Generate Z_i having a $\Gamma(\theta_i,1)$ distribution, $i = 1, 2$.
4. Set $X_2 = X_1[Z_1/(Z_1+Z_2)]$.

The resulting (unconditional) joint distribution of (X_1,X_2) has density

$$f(x_1,x_2) = \frac{c\Gamma(\theta_1+\theta_2)x_1^{\alpha c-\theta_1-\theta_2}x_2^{\theta_1-1}(x_1-x_2)^{\theta_2-1}}{\Gamma(\alpha)\Gamma(\theta_1)\Gamma(\theta_2)a^{\alpha c}}\exp[-(x_1/a)^c]$$

$$0 < x_2 < x_1 \quad .$$

Khintchine-Normal Distribution. Bryson and Johnson (1982) derived a variety of multivariate distributions by appealing to a theorem of Khintchine (1938) on the unimodality of continuous univariate distributions. One form of potential value to Monte Carlo work has density function

$$f(x_1,x_2) = \frac{\alpha x_1x_2}{2A}\phi(A) + \frac{1-\alpha x_1x_2}{2}\Phi(A),$$

where $A = \max\{|x_1|,|x_2|\}$, $\phi(x) = (2\pi)^{-1/2}\exp(-x^2/2)$, and $\Phi(x) = \int_{-\infty}^{x}\phi(t)dt$.

This distribution has standard normal marginals and is readily generated by the algorithm:

1. Generate (U_1, U_2) having Morgenstern's bivariate uniform distribution with dependence parameter α (Equation (7)).
2. Generate Y having a $\chi^2_{(3)}$ distribution.
3. Set

$$X_1 = Y^{1/2}(2U_1-1)$$
$$X_2 = Y^{1/2}(2U_2-1).$$

Other Multivariate Distributions can be generated by transformations of (easy-to-generate) variates. The Wishart distribution has received some attention (Gleser (1976), Johnson and Hegemann (1974), Odell and Feiveson (1966)), although its use is really limited to normal theory settings. Johnson and Tenenbein (1981) developed some distributions based on linear transformations of independent exponential, Laplace and uniform variates. Multivariate gamma distributions have been studied by number of authors. Schmeiser and Lal (1982) discuss much of the previous work and present a new approach. Schmeiser and Lal (1980) also give a survey of multivariate modeling in simulation with special reference to the field of quality control. Multivariate beta and Dirichlet distributions can be generated by appropriate transformations of independent gamma variates. There seems to be no limit to the types of distributions that can be constructed or generated. An important consideration and one which is frequently overlooked is the appropriateness of particular distributions in simulation studies. The topic of selecting multivariate distributions for inclusion in a simulation study is examined in Section 4.

Comparisons in the Normal Marginals Case. Eight of the bivariate forms given above are compared in the setting in which they have standard normal marginal distributions. In general, this is accomplished by considering a bivariate distribution having density $f(x_1,x_2)$ and component distribution functions F_1 and F_2, which are non-normal. Starting with (X_1,X_2) distributed according to f, the pair (Y_1,Y_2) defined by

$$Y_1 = \Phi^{-1}(F_1(X_1))$$
$$Y_2 = \Phi^{-1}(F_2(X_2))$$

has standard normal marginals, where

$$\Phi(t) = \int_{-\infty}^{t} \frac{1}{\sqrt{2\pi}} \exp\,(-x^2/2)\, dx.$$

The densities of several such (Y_1,Y_2) variates were derived where the starting distributions were taken from Section 3. These distributions and their abbreviations include the bivariate normal (BVN), Burr-Pareto-logistic (B-P-L), Ali-Mikhail-Haq (A-M-H), Khintchine (Хинчин), Morgenstern, Plackett, Gumbel and Cauchy. Figure 1 provides contours for these densities, some for more than one parameter value. The contours in Figure 1 are not labeled but correspond to .03 increments in f. Obviously, a diverse set of shapes were obtained and some interesting interrelationships were revealed. The cases BVN, Morgenstern, Plackett and Gumbel all look roughly the same, although among these, Gumbel's contours demonstrate some slight asymmetry. The B-P-L and A-M-H cases are similar in general and identical for $\alpha = 1$. Other than that parameter value, the distributions are however different. The Khintchine case is unique in that it reveals a sharp edge along the positive diagonal for $\alpha = 1$ or .5 and along both diagonals for $\alpha = 0$. In fact, for the $\alpha = 0$ case, the components are uncorrelated but not independent. Also, in the Cauchy example, the standard normal components are also uncorrelated but not independent. Figure 1 provides an unusual albeit limited first look at comparison plots. Other intriguing comparison plots, and a more detailed discussion of distributional properties, can be found in Johnson (1986).

4. DESIGN OF SIMULATION EXPERIMENTS.

The purpose of this paper has been to provide generation algorithms for a variety of multivariate distributions for possible use in statistical Monte Carlo studies. We must emphasize the word "possible" since the thoroughness of an investigation should not be measured by the number of distributions included, but rather by the extent to which the original motivating questions have been addressed. Thus, selection of distributions is critical in the initial stages of a study if the final analysis is to avoid being a hodge podge of tabled values. This section

Figure 1. Constant-Density Contours of Various Bivariate Distributions for which Each Marginal Distribution is Standard Normal.

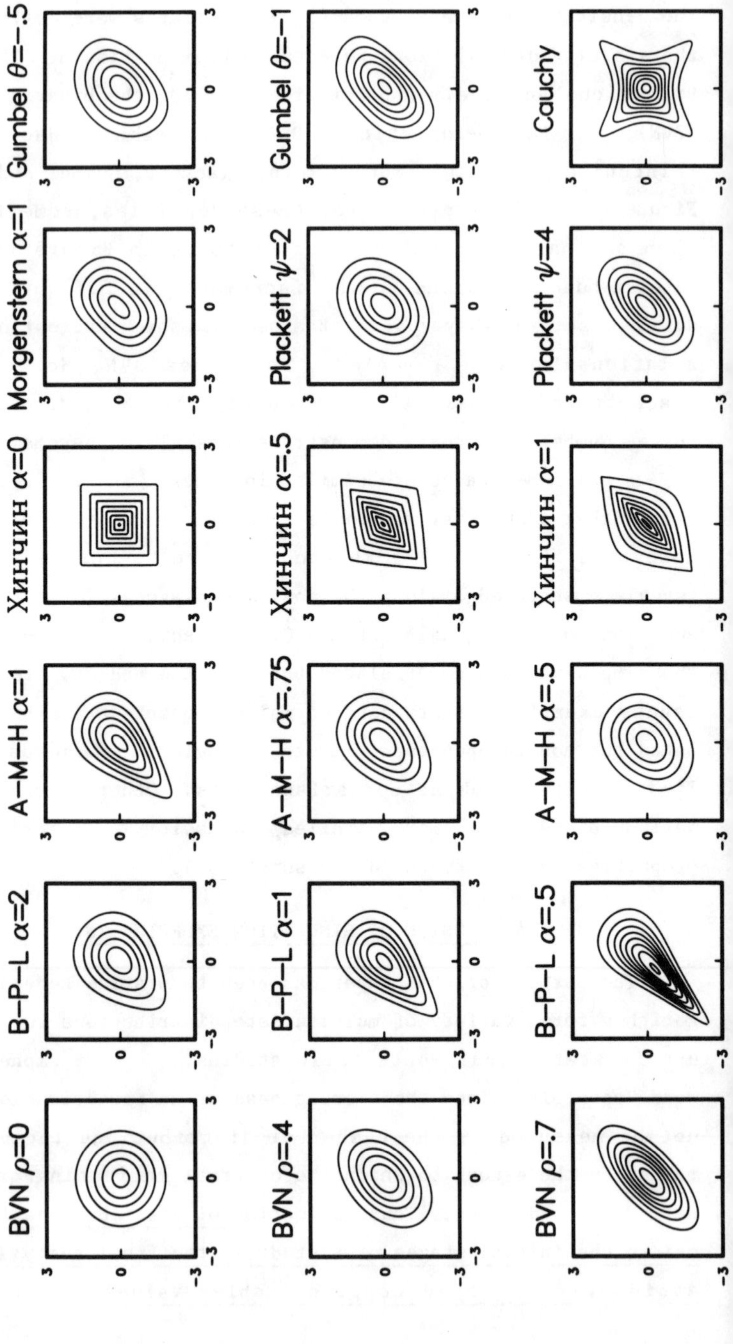

presents a number of issues which must be considered to avoid the many pitfalls inherent in conducting a multivariate Monte Carlo study.

The first step in selecting distributions involves the new (statistical or other) procedure itself. Are there important factors besides distribution which if overlooked or ignored, could become potential confounders? Typically these factors will include sample size, dimension, location (mean vectors) and scale (covariance structure). Sample size is certainly a relevant concern if the new procedure is valid only asymptotically. If multiple groups are involved then effects due to imbalance and individual group sample size may also need to be evaluated. Covariance structure across these groups has been a troublesome concern in discriminant analysis studies. Johnson, Ramberg and Wang (1982) noted several earlier simulation studies of discriminant analysis methods which confounded the effects of non-normality and unequal covariance matrices. Another problem with these studies is that the dimensions considered were large (4 and 10), although the results in two dimensions were not thoroughly understood.

Having identified other relevant factors, an investigator can now return to distribution selection. Two typical motivating questions are the following:

1. How well does the proposed procedure work locally -- for small departures from the assumed model?
2. How well does the proposed procedure work generally -- over a broad set of circumstances?

In many investigations, the assumed model is the multivariate normal distribution. Addressing these questions in this context is facilitated by the distributions in section 3. For question 1, some of the elliptically symmetric distributions can be employed, as well as the Burr-Pareto-logistic distribution with normal marginals. For more extreme departures, the Johnson translation system can be helpful, with covariance structures specified if necessary. A study related to question 2 was reported by Beckman and Johnson (1981), who examined a ranking procedure in discriminant analysis. They included bivariate normal, lognormal and Pearson VII (m = 5/2) distributions and examined the effects of sample size, mean location and covariance structure.

It is certainly difficult to give more than broad guidelines for distribution selection. Serious scrutiny of a proposed method is required to determine the appropriate cases. However, this effort can be rewarded in the long run. A carefully designed and implemented multivariate Monte Carlo study offers the following advantages:

1. Attention can be focused on the results of the study and not its methodology.
2. Confounding is avoided.
3. A framework for comparison with future methods is established.
4. The original questions that motivated the study are addressed.

ACKNOWLEDGMENTS.

We are grateful to the referee for comments leading specifically to fine tuning of the Morgenstern and Ali-Mikhail-Haq algorithms and generally to improvements in the presentation. This paper was written while Dr. Johnson was on sabbatical leave from the Statistics Group, Los Alamos National Laboratory, Los Alamos, New Mexico. Dr. Wang's present affiliation is Department of Management, California State University, Sacremento, California.

REFERENCES

Ali, M. M., Mikhail, N. N. and Haq, M. S. (1978). A class of bivariate distributions including the bivariate logistic. Journal of Multivariate Analysis, 8, 405-412.

Beckman, R. J. and Johnson, M. E. (1981). A ranking procedure for partial discriminant analysis. Journal of the American Statistical Association, 76, 671-675.

Box, G. E. P. and Muller, M. E. (1958). A note on the generation of random normal deviates. The Annals of Mathematical Statistics, 29, 610-611.

Bryson, M. C. and Johnson, M. E. (1982). Constructing and simulating multivariate distributions using Khintchine's theorem. Journal of Statistical Computation and Simulation, 16, 129-137.

Burr, I. W. (1942). Cumulative frequency functions. Annals of Mathematical Statistics, 13, 215-232.

Cambanis, S. (1977). Some properties and generalizations of multivariate Eyraud-Gumbel-Morgenstern distributions. Journal of Multivariate Analysis, 7, 551-559.

Cambanis, S., Huang, S. and Simons, G. (1981). On the theory of elliptically contoured distributions. Journal of Multivariate Analysis, 11, 368-385.

Chmielewski, M. A. (1981a). A re-appraisal of tests for normality. Communications in Statistics -- Theory and Methods tMultivariate Analysis, 10, 343-350.

Chmielewski, M. A. (1981b). A re-appraisal of tests for normality. Communications in Statistics -- Theory and Methods, 10, 2005-2014.

Chmielewski, M. A. (1981b). Elliptically symmetric distributions: a bibliography and review. International Statistical Review, 49, 67-74.

Cook, R. D. and Johnson, M. E. (1981). A family of distributions for modelling non-elliptically symmetric multivariate data. Journal of the Royal Statistical Society, Series B, 43, 210-218.

Dongarra, J. J., Moler, C. B., Bunch, J. R., Stewart, G. W. (1979). LINPACK User's Guide, SIAM, Philadelphia, Pennsylvania.

Dudewicz, E. J. and Ralley, T. G. (1981). The Handbook of Random Number Generation and Testing with TESTRAND Computer Code. American Sciences Press, Inc., Box 21161, Columbus, Ohio 43221.

Eyraud, H. (1936). Les principes de la mesure des correlations. Annales Universite Lyons, Series A, Sciences Mathematiques et Astronomie, 1, 30-47.

Gleser, L. J. (1976). A canonical representation for the noncentral Wishart distribution useful for simulation. Journal of the American Statistical Association, 71, 690-695.

Gumbel, E. J. (1960). Bivariate exponential distributions. Journal of the American Statistical Association, 55, 698-707.

Hawkins, D. M. (1981). A new test for multivariate normality and homoscedasticity. Technometrics, 23, 105-110.

Hogg, R. V. and Craig, A. T. (1978). Introduction to Mathematical Statistics, Fourth Edition, MacMillian Publishing Co., Inc. New York.

Johnson, D. E. and Hegemann, V. (1974). Procedures to generate random matrices with noncentral distributions. Communications in Statistics, 3, 691-699.

Johnson, M. E. (1982). Computer generation of the generalized Eyraud distribution. Journal of Statistical Computation and Simulation, 15, 333-335.

Johnson, M. E. (1986). Multivariate Statistical Simulation. In preparation.

Johnson, M. E. and Ramberg, J. S. (1977). Elliptically symmetric distributions: characterizations and random variate generation. Statistical Computing Section Proceedings of the American Statistical Association, 262-265.

Johnson, M. E., Ramberg, J. S., and Wang, C. (1982). The Johnson translation system in Monte Carlo studies. Communications in Statistics -- Simulation and Computation, 11, 521-525.

Johnson, M. E. and Tenenbein, A. (1981). A bivariate distribution family with specified marginals. Journal of the American Statistical Association, 76, 198-201.

Johnson, N. L. (1949). Bivariate distributions based on simple translation systems. Biometrika, 36, 297-304.

Johnson, N. L. and Kotz, S. (1972). Distributions in Statistics: Continuous Multivariate Distributions. John Wiley & Sons, Inc., New York.

Kennedy, W. J. Jr., and Gentle, J. E. (1980). Statistical Computing. Marcel Dekker, Inc., New York.

Khintchine, A. Y. (1938). On unimodal distributions. Tomsk. Universitet. Nauchno-issledovatel´skii institut matematiki i mekhaniki IZVESTIIA, 2, 1-7.

Kinderman, A. J., Monahan, J. F. and J. G. Ramage (1977). Computer methods for sampling from Student´s t distribution. Mathematics of Computation, 31, 1009-1018.

Malkovich, J. F. and Afifi, A. A. (1973). On tests for multivariate normality. Journal of the American Statistical Association, 68, 176-179.

Mardia, K. V. (1967). Some contributions to contingency-type distributions. Biometrika, 54, 235-249. (Corrections: 1968, 55, 597.)

Mardia, K. V. (1970). Families of Bivariate Distributions. Hafner Publishing Company, Darien, Conneticut.

Marsaglia, G. and Bray, T. A. (1964). A convenient method for generating normal variables. SIAM Review, 6, 101-102.

Mihram, G. A. and Hultquist, R. A. (1967). A bivariate warning-time/failure-time distribution. Journal of the American Statistical Association, 62, 589-599.

Muller, M. E. (1959). A note on a method for generating points uniformly on n-dimensional spheres. Communications of the ACM, 2, 19-20.

Odell, P. L. and Feiveson, A. H. (1966). A numerical procedure to generate a sample covariance matrix. Journal of the American Statistical Association, 61, 199-203.

Plackett, R. L. (1965). A class of bivariate distributions. Journal of the American Statistical Association, 60, 516-522.

Rosenblatt, M. (1952). Remarks on a multivariate transformation. Annals of Mathematical Statistics, 23, 470-472.

Scheuer, E. M. and Stoller, D. S. (1962). On the generation of normal random vectors. Technometrics, 4, 278-281.

Schmeiser, B. and Lal, R. (1980). Multivariate modeling in simulation: a survey. ASQC Technical Conference Transactions, 252-261.

Schmeiser, B. and Lal, R. (1982). Bivariate gamma random vectors. Operations Research, 30, 358-374.

Schoenberg, I. J. (1938). Metric spaces and completely monotone functions. Annals of Mathematics, 39, 811-841.

Stacy, E. W. (1962). A generalization of the gamma distribution. The Annals of Mathematical Statistics, 33, 1187-1192.

Tadikamalla, P. R. and Johnson, M. E. (1981). A complete guide to gamma variate generation. American Journal of Mathematical and Management Sciences, 1, 213-236.

Takahasi. K. (1965). Note on the multivariate Burr's distribution. Annals of the Institute of Statistical Mathematics, 17, 257-260.

Tashiro, Y. (1977). On methods for generating uniform points on the surface of a sphere. Annals of the Institute of Statistical Mathematics, 29, 295-300.

Wahrendorf, J. (1980). Inference in contingency tables with ordered categories using Plackett's coefficient of association for bivariate distributions. Biometrika, 67, 15-21.

Received 2/14/83; Revised 7/25/84.

AMERICAN JOURNAL OF MATHEMATICAL AND MANAGEMENT SCIENCES

DESIGN OF EXPERIMENTS IN SIMULATION

Dennis E. Smith and Carl A. Mauro
Desmatics, Inc.
P.O. Box 618
State College, Pennsylvania 16804

SYNOPTIC ABSTRACT

Many simulation studies may be viewed as experimental situations in which a number of factors (independent variables) are to be investigated. There are, however, a number of special characteristics that distinguish simulation experiments from statistical experiments in general. In this paper we discuss four topics which are of particular interest and relevance in the simulation context: (1) Identification of the important factors (i.e., input variables); (2) Investigation of the statistical relationship between the output and input variables; (3) Determination of the combination of factor levels for which the response (i.e., output variable) is optimized; and (4) The use of variance reduction techniques.

Key Words and Phrases: experimental design; computer simulation; factor screening; optimization of simulation outputs; investigating statistical relationships; variance reduction.

1984, VOL. 4, NOS. 3 & 4, 249-275
0196-6324/84/030249-27 $8.40

1. INTRODUCTION

Computer simulation is a very useful and powerful technique for studying the behavior of complex real-world systems. There are a number of important steps to a successful simulation study (see, for instance, Gordon (1978), Kleijnen (1974), and Law and Kelton (1982)). The two most critical steps are (1) model validation, and (2) the design and analysis of the simulation experiments. Careful attention to both is necessary for a meaningful and sound simulation study. For instance, if a simulation model is not sufficiently representative of the system under study (i.e., valid), the output data may be misleading and result in erroneous conclusions about the system. On the other hand, even if the model satisfactorily mimics the system, an optimal experimental design is still needed in order to derive maximum benefit from the time and cost incurred.

As in any experimental investigation, a simulation study requires careful planning, data collection, output data analysis, and proper interpretation of the experimental data. The problem of design is to ensure that data relevant to the proposed study is both adequate and obtained in as efficient a manner as possible. In this paper we are primarily concerned with the problem of experimental design; we will assume that the simulation model is an adequate representation of the system under consideration. (General discussions of simulation validation are given by Gass (1977), Law and Kelton (1982), Naylor and Burdick (1975), Schellenberger (1974), and Van Horn (1971).) We will also assume that the computer program (code) used to execute the simulation model has been properly debugged so that the system model functions as intended.

There are a number of special characteristics that distinguish simulation experimentation from statistical experimentation in general. First, in simulation we have much more control over the experimental conditions than we do in the real world. This often allows us to use the simulation model to examine a number of "what if" questions about which little or no data currently exists. For example, using a simulation model of a nuclear power plant, we may wish to determine what would happen in the event of a loss-of-coolant accident. Second, we can control much of the underlying randomness in a simulation by controlling the streams of pseudorandom numbers that drive and determine the stochastic events that occur in a simulation. This capability often allows us to use variance-reduction techniques to obtain estimators having greater statistical precision. Moreover, there is generally no need for randomization of experimental conditions and run order to guard against the inadvertent introduction of systematic biases and variation. Such protection is usually provided by the random-number generators already present in the simulation model. We caution, however, that it is possible for a random-number generator to be adequate in one application but noticeably biased in another. In cases where there is doubt about the "randomness" of the random-number generator, we recommend that the generator be suitably tested (see, for example, Dudewicz and Ralley (1981) or Knuth (1981)).

A third characteristic is that simulations often take into account a number of detailed aspects of the system under investigation, and as a result many simulation studies involve an exceptionally large number of input variables. Lastly, the problems of missing data and outliers which can handicap and reduce the effectiveness of any experimental investigation are generally of no concern in simulation studies. Outliers (in the form of contaminant observations) cannot arise because a simulation model is essentially a "closed" system. Missing output data can occur only if the time and/or funds allocated for experimentation are insufficient.

It is beyond the scope of this paper to consider all the many facets of experimental design; the current literature in this subject area is vast. Instead we discuss the salient aspects of four selected topics which are of particular interest and relevance in the simulation context: (1) Identification of the important factors (i.e., input variables); (2) Investigation of the statistical relationship between the output and input variables; (3) Determination of the combination of factor levels for which the response (i.e., output variable) is optimized; and (4) The use of variance reduction techniques. We address these topics in the ensuing sections.

Throughout our discussions we assume that there is but a single response variable, and we restrict ourselves to the situation in which all the factors are quantitative. For a discussion of the multiple response problem we refer to Kleijnen (1974), Montgomery and Bettencourt (1977) and Schruben (1981).

2. FACTOR SCREENING

As noted previously, simulation models often involve a great many factors. Because of their size, such models can require a prohibitively large and costly experimental program to study their behavior. Therefore we may want to concentrate our analysis on the set of "most important" factors. Factor screening methods (see, for instance, Kleijnen (1975), Montgomery (1979), and Smith and Mauro (1982)) attempt to determine the set of most important factors in an efficient and economical manner. Once the most important factors have been identified, subsequent simulation experimentation can concentrate more intensively on these particular factors, thereby eliminating experimentation with relatively unimportant factors which can needlessly consume resources. Screening experiments, then, are not usually an end in themselves but are performed as a preliminary step in the experimentation process.

In general, in screening experiments we want (a) to detect as many important factors as possible, (b) to declare important as few unimportant factors as possible, and (c) to expend as few runs as possible. Thus, one must generally consider both how many runs a screening strategy requires and how accurately it identifies factors. Although one may wish to obtain finer factor groupings than simply "important" or "unimportant", to effectively accomplish this would most certainly require more screening runs than are normally reasonable or affordable. In any event, the greater (lesser) the degree of importance a factor has, the larger (smaller) should be the probability of classifying that factor as important.

In screening designs a relatively small number of factor levels is generally employed; in fact, most screening experiments are two-level experiments. There are two reasons for this. First, two levels of each factor are usually sufficient to detect which factors have major effects. Second, two-level designs maximize the number of factors that can be examined in a given number of runs because the number of factor level combinations is minimized when each factor has only two levels.

The full statistical model for a two-level complete factorial experiment for k factors contains 2^k terms: a mean effect, k main effects, $\binom{k}{2}$ two-factor interaction effects, $\binom{k}{3}$ three-factor interaction effects, ..., and a k-factor interaction effect. To estimate every effect in the full model, one must run the complete factorial experiment consisting of $N = 2^k$ runs. This many runs, however, is rarely practical in simulation experimentation; for even a moderate number of factors the implications in terms of money invested and overall run time can be quite overwhelming. However, if we can reasonably assume that certain higher order interactions are negligible, we can make a less than complete investigation by running only a fraction of the 2^k treatment combinations.

In this section, we will consider two basic situations: (1) the unsaturated/saturated case, and (2) the supersaturated case. In the first case, one can afford to invest more runs than there are factors, but still considerably less than 2^k; in the second case, the number of runs available for screening is less than or equal to the number of factors to be screened. In the remainder of this section we present and discuss experimental plans which are particularly well suited for screening in these two cases. Before proceeding with the main discussion, however, we digress to review a few fundamental terms and concepts in design theory.

2.1. Orthogonality, Confounding, and Resolution. The levels to be run in a two-level screening experiment can be conveniently displayed in a design matrix such as is given in Table 1. We have arbitrarily coded the two levels of each factor as +1 (high) and -1 (low). In run #1, for example, all factors except x_4 are held at their high level.

TABLE 1: A Two-Level Design for a Five-Factor Experiment in Four Runs

Run	x_1	x_2	x_3	x_4	x_5
1	+1	+1	+1	-1	+1
2	+1	-1	-1	-1	+1
3	+1	+1	+1	-1	-1
4	-1	-1	+1	+1	-1

When ±1 coding is used, we call two design columns orthogonal if the sum of their cross products is zero. Equivalently, two columns are orthogonal if their factor levels are balanced, i.e., are different just as often as they are the same. Orthogonality is a desirable design property because estimates of the (main) effects of orthogonal factors are independent. In other words, if one of two orthogonal factors has an effect, it cannot cause the other, perhaps erroneously, to appear to have an effect. For the design matrix in Table 1, x_1 and x_3, x_2 and x_5, and x_3 and x_4 are orthogonal.

If two design columns are not orthogonal, we call the corresponding factors confounded. When two factors are confounded, it is impossible to statistically separate their effects. In the extreme case, two factors are completely confounded if their design columns are identical or are reflections of one another. For example, in Table 1, x_1 and x_4 are completely confounded. Factors x_1 and x_2, on the other hand, although not completely confounded, are not orthogonal either. In this case, we say that they are partially confounded.

The extent of confounding that a design possesses is known as its resolution. In a design of resolution R, a p-factor interaction is unconfounded with any other effect containing less than R-p factors. For example, in a resolution III design, main effects are not confounded with other main effects; in a resolution IV design, main effects are not confounded with other main effects or two-factor interactions. The principal implication of a resolution R design is that p-factor interactions ($p < R/2$) are estimable under the assumption that all interactions of order R-p or more are negligible.

The resolution of a design is often restricted by the number of runs that can be made. For instance, in order for all columns in a design matrix to be mutually orthogonal, the number of runs must exceed the number of factors. Consequently, we can obtain unconfounded estimates of main effects only in the unsaturated/saturated case. It follows that in the supersaturated case, design resolution must be less than R = III, i.e., we cannot avoid confounding main effects in some manner.

2.2. The Unsaturated/Saturated Case. We now present two types of designs that are especially useful in the unsaturated/saturated case. These are Plackett-Burman (PB) designs and resolution IV foldover designs.

2.2.1. Plackett-Burman Designs. PB designs are specially constructed two-level minimal resolution III designs for studying up to $k = 4m-1$ factors in $N = 4m$ runs. PB designs, therefore, are only available for numbers of runs that are multiples of four. Assuming that all interactions can be ignored, unbiased estimation of the k main effects is possible in a PB design. The arrangements for these designs were derived by Plackett and Burman (1946); see also Raghavarao (1971). It can be noted that when N is a power of two, PB designs are the same as the well-known resolution III 2^{k-p} fractional factorial designs, which are discussed in detail by Box and Hunter (1961).

To analyze PB designs one can use standard analysis of variance methods and conduct formal significance testing. A useful alternative approach is to plot the estimated effects on normal probability paper. In this technique, due to Daniel (1959), negligible effects should fall approximately along a straight line, while large effects should tend to fall far from the line. The latter method of analysis is especially helpful when the design is saturated (i.e., when $N = k-1$ and no degrees of freedom are left to estimate experimental error) or when only a few degrees of freedom are available for estimating experimental error.

2.2.2. Resolution IV Foldover Designs. Resolution IV foldover designs are easily constructed by "folding over" a resolution III design, i.e. the design matrix $\underline{D}$ can be written as

$$\underline{D} = \begin{bmatrix} \underline{D}^* \\ -\underline{D}^* \end{bmatrix}$$

where the matrix $\underline{D}^*$ is a PB design matrix. Such designs have resolution IV and allow us to study up to k factors in $N = 2k$ runs where N is a multiple of eight. In these designs unbiased estimates of main effects can be obtained even if two-factor interactions exist.

2.2.3. Additional Remarks. For screening in the unsaturated/saturated case, resolution III and IV designs usually suffice. A resolution IV design, of course, provides more reliable information than a resolution III design but requires twice as many runs. If the simulation user is willing to invest in more than k but less than 2k runs, he or she may wish to consider other possible main-effects designs, such as "D-optimal" designs. For construction of D-optimal designs we refer the reader to the extensive literature on these designs; see, for instance, Box and Draper (1971), Dykstra (1971), Mitchell (1974), and St. John and Draper (1975). We should remark, however, that PB designs are D-optimal for their number of runs. Another interesting design optimality criterion is that of "tr(L)-optimality" for detecting the presence of two-factor interactions. These designs are studied by Morris and Mitchell (1983).

2.3. The Supersaturated Case. The supersaturated case arises when there is a severe limitation on the number of runs available for screening. Such situations are frequently encountered in simulation studies, especially in the analysis of large-scale models. The design situation of fewer runs than factors has received relatively little attention in the statistical literature, however. In fact, the performance characteristics of the supersaturated methods presently available are largely unknown.

In this subsection we describe four basic types of designs that have been proposed for use in supersaturated situations. These are: random balance (RB) designs, systematic supersaturated (SS) designs, group screening (GS) designs, and RB/PB combination designs. Each of these design strategies is characterized by having an equal number of runs at the high and low levels of each factor. These designs, therefore, are of resolution II. That is, main effects are not confounded with the overall mean effect.

2.3.1. Random Balance Designs. In a two-level RB design, each column of the design matrix consists of N/2 +1's and N/2 -1's where N (an even number) denotes the total number of runs to be made. The +1's and -1's in each column are assigned randomly, making all possible combinations of N/2 +1's and N/2 -1's equally likely, with each column receiving an independent randomization.

The principal advantage to the RB method is its flexibility; the sample size N is fixed by the simulation analyst and can be selected independently of the number of factors, k, to be screened. A second advantage is the ease with which we can prepare RB designs regardless of the magnitudes of N and k.

There are two primary disadvantages to RB sampling. The first of these is that factors are confounded to a random degree. Anscombe (1959; p. 201) has written, "The fact that the degree of nonorthogonality or unbalance is random can be made the basis for an objection to the whole notion of random balance designs. Such designs may work well on the average, but should I trust one to this occasion?" The second disadvantage is that there is no generally accepted method of analysis for RB designs. The simplest approach is to consider each factor separately, ignoring all other factors, and apply some standard analysis technique such as a normal-theory F-test. More sophisticated analysis methods include variable selection procedures such as stagewise and least-squares stepwise regression methods. For a more complete discussion of RB experimentation we refer to Anscombe (1959), Budne (1959), Satterthwaite (1959), and Youden, Kempthorne, Tukey, Box, and Hunter (1959).

2.3.2. Systematic Supersaturated Designs. Because of the random confounding that occurs in RB designs, Booth and Cox (1962) introduced two-level designs which systematically attempt to minimize confounding. Noting that not all design columns can be orthogonal when $N \leq k$, Booth and Cox constructed designs that minimize $\max_{i \neq j} |c_{ij}|$ where c_{ij} is the inner product of design columns i and j. Presumably, SS designs are the best alternative to orthogonal designs, which are, of course, impossible to construct in the supersaturated case.

Booth and Cox tabulated their designs for various values of N and k($k \leq 36$) and outlined, for other combinations of N and k, an iterative computer procedure for generating the required designs. However, the cost of writing and running the program may be prohibitive if k is large.

2.3.3. Group Screening Designs. GS designs have been studied by Li (1962), Patel (1962), and Watson (1961). In a GS design the individual factors are partitioned into groups of suitable sizes. The groups are then tested by considering each as a single factor. Because the number of groups is generally much smaller than the original number of factors, we can usually study the group-factors in a standard orthogonal design such as a PB design. Moreover, we can repeat the grouping and testing process for any number of stages. At a given stage, however, we repartition only those individual factors within significant groups as determined in the preceding stage.

The level of a group-factor is defined by assigning the group level (e.g., +1) to all component factors. This, of course, induces complete confounding of the factors within a group, which is the basic idea. At each stage of screening we can eliminate the individual factors from those groups which appear relatively unimportant.

The main advantage of GS designs is that we can to some extent control the confounding pattern. There are two disadvantages to GS designs. First, the number of runs required by a GS experiment is not fixed but is random (when one progresses beyond the first stage). Mauro and Burns (1984) suggest a modified two-stage GS procedure in which the total number of runs can be predetermined. Second, important effects may cancel within a group. As a simple example, consider two factors which have effects that are negatives or near negatives of each other. If these two factors are the only important factors in a group, their effects will cancel or their combined effect may be masked by experimental error. Mauro (1984), Mauro and Burns (1984), and Mauro and Smith (1982) have examined the cancellation problem. Their results tend to indicate that cancellation does not pose a major problem to the use of GS designs.

2.3.4. RB/PB Combination Designs. An RB/PB screening plan is a two-stage strategy having an RB first-stage experiment followed by the use of a PB second-stage experiment. A factor is included in the second-stage PB design only if it is determined to have a significant effect in the first stage.

As in GS designs, a disadvantage of RB/PB designs is that the total number of runs required is random (since the number of second-stage runs is random). An advantage of these designs is that the use of a PB experiment in the second stage separates any confounding between the factors that are carried over from the RB first-stage experiment.

2.3.5. Further Discussion. Because of the lack of comparative performance data, there are currently no definitive guidelines for the selection and use of supersaturated screening methods. Nevertheless, of the supersaturated screening methods presently available, the GS method has been generally recommended. Mauro (1983) and Mauro and Burns (1984), however, have pointed out certain practical considerations that make group screening less attractive as a technique for factor screening.

The performance characteristics of RB and RB/PB designs have been studied by Mauro and Smith (1984). They determined that RB/PB strategies perform better than RB strategies in those situations where it is important that Type I error (i.e., the chance of classifying unimportant factors as important) be maintained at a low level. In comparing SS with RB designs, Booth and Cox (1962) concluded that unless $k < 2N$, SS designs have little advantage over RB designs.

3. INVESTIGATING THE FUNCTIONAL RELATIONSHIP

In many cases the relationship between a simulation response y and the k factors $x_1,\ldots,x_k$ can be expressed as

$$y=g(x_1,\ldots,x_k) + \varepsilon$$

where g is an unknown function and ε denotes a random error component. We often desire to know what this relationship is. In other words, we wish to determine the functional form of $g(\underline{x})$ where $\underline{x}=(x_1,x_2,\ldots,x_k)$.

Below we assume that both y and the x_i's are not only quantitative, but also continuous. Furthermore, we assume that the error component ε is normally distributed with mean 0 and variance σ^2, where σ^2 is unknown. Thus, the expected value of any observed response y corresponding to $\underline{x}$ is:

$$E(y) = g(\underline{x}).$$

Under these assumptions response surface methodology, or RSM for short, proves valuable. RSM, which is essentially a blending of statistical experimental design and regression analysis, has its foundation in a paper by Box and Wilson (1951). The terminology "response surface" derives from the fact that the mean response lies on a surface in (k+1) -dimensional space.

In industry RSM has often been applied to two general problems associated with the E(y) response surface. These are:

(a) Describing the response surface in some region of interest

and (b) Determining the values of the factors which produce the optimum response.

This section addresses the former topic; Section 4 discusses the latter topic. A detailed description of RSM and its applications is available in Davies (1978) and Myers (1971).

Basic to RSM is the 2^{k-p} fractional factorial, which is an experimental design consisting of a specific fraction ($1/2^p$) of the 2^k possible points which form a full 2^k factorial experiment. In accordance with our previous discussion, we assume that the levels of each factor in the fractional factorial are coded ±1.

Under the assumption that the function g may be expressed in a Taylor series expansion about a point $\underline{x}_0=(x_{10},\ldots,x_{k0})$, its value at a point $\underline{x}=(x_1,\ldots,x_k)$ is given by

$$g(\underline{x})=g(\underline{x}_0)+\sum_1^k(x_i-x_{i0})\left(\frac{\partial g}{\partial x_i}\right)_{\underline{x}_0}+\tfrac{1}{2}\sum_1^k(x_i-x_{i0})^2\left(\frac{\partial^2 g}{\partial x_i^2}\right)_{\underline{x}_0}$$

$$+\tfrac{1}{2}\sum_{i\neq j}^k(x_i-x_{i0})(x_j-x_{j0})\left(\frac{\partial^2 g}{\partial x_i\,\partial x_j}\right)_{\underline{x}_0}+\ldots$$

where the notation $(\cdot)_{\underline{x}_0}$ indicates that the quantity in parentheses is to be evaluated at the point $\underline{x}_0$. It should be noted that by rearranging terms, g may be expressed as a polynomial:

$$g(\underline{x})=\beta_0+\sum_1^k\beta_i x_i+\sum_1^k\sum_1^k\beta_{ij}x_i x_j+\ldots$$

Depending upon the region of interest to the experimenter (i.e., the simulation user), it may be possible that a first-order polynomial provides a good approximation to $g(\underline{x})$ within that region. We can use a 2^{k-p} fractional factorial of at least resolution III to fit a first-order equation. This would, of course, yield the estimate

$$g(\underline{x})=b_0+\sum_1^k b_i x_i$$

where b_i is an estimate of β_i.

The b_i's are obtained by the method of least squares through the use of the equation

$$\underline{b}=(\underline{X}'\underline{X})^{-1}\underline{X}'\underline{y} \tag{1}$$

where $\underline{b}$ is a column vector of the b_i's, $\underline{y}$ is a column vector whose j^{th} entry consists of the value of the response corresponding to the jth run, and $\underline{X}$ is the matrix $\underline{X}=[\underline{1},\underline{D}]$. Here $\underline{1}$ denotes a column vector of +1's and $\underline{D}$ is the design matrix.

The estimates b_i are uncorrelated and, among all unbiased linear estimates, have minimum variance. Although other designs (e.g., the simplex designs studied by Box (1952)) also provide uncorrelated, minimum variance estimates, the 2^{k-p} fractional factorial has the added advantage of being able, by the addition of specific points, to evolve directly to a second-order design which can be used to estimate quadratic effects (the β_{ij}'s). This proves valuable if it is determined that a first-order approximation is not adequate.

Because simulation runs are usually at a premium, it is a good idea to use the smallest possible 2^{k-p} fractional factorial of resolution III. These designs are easily obtained; rules for their generation are given in Box and Hunter (1961), for example. The number of runs, N, required by these designs is, of course, given by $N=2^{k-p}$ where p is the maximum integer selected such that $2^{k-p} > k$.

As a check on how well a first-order approximation fits the true response surface, a lack-of-fit test may be conducted. In order to test lack of fit, a center point of the fractional factorial levels should be run in addition to the N points in the 2^{k-p} fractional factorial. Moreover, to obtain degrees of freedom for testing lack of fit, the center point should be replicated, i.e. run a number of times. If this point is replicated m times, then there will be m-1 degrees of freedom for the appropriate error term for testing lack-of-fit.

It can easily be shown that for a 2^{k-p} fractional factorial augmented with m runs at the center point, the estimated coefficients $b_0,b_1,\ldots,b_k$ are given by

$$b_0 = (\sum_1^N y_j + \sum_1^m y_{0,r})/(N+m) \text{ and } b_i = \sum_1^N y_j x_{ji}/N \quad (i=1,\ldots,k)$$

where y_j denotes the observed response for the $j^{\underline{th}}$ run in the fractional factorial

$y_{0,r}$ denotes the observed response for the $r^{\underline{th}}$ run at the center point, and

x_{ji} denotes the $(j,i)^{\underline{th}}$ entry (either a +1 or a -1) in the design matrix.

The lack of fit statistic can be obtained and tested from an analysis of variance decomposition of the overall variation in the observed simulation runs corresponding to the fractional factorial points and to the center points. The replicated runs at the center point provide the "pure" error sum of squares given by

$$SS_e = \sum_{r=1}^m [y_{0,r} - (\sum_{r=1}^m y_{0,r})/m]/(m-1).$$

The complete partition of the total sum of squares and the N+m degrees of freedom is given in Figure 1.

Source	Degrees of Freedom	Sum of Squares	Mean Square
b_0	1	SS_{b_0}	$MS_{b_0}=SS_{b_0}$
b_1	1	SS_{b_1}	$MS_{b_1}=SS_{b_1}$
.	.	.	.
.	.	.	.
.	.	.	.
b_k	1	SS_{b_k}	$MS_{b_k}=SS_{b_k}$
Lack of Fit			
Pure Quadratic	1	SS_q	$MS_q=SS_q$
Cross Products	N-k-1	SS_c	$MS_c=SS_c/(N-k-1)$
Pure Error	m-1	SS_e	$MS_e=SS_e/(m-1)$
Total	N+m	SS_t	

FIGURE 1: Partition of the Sums of Squares and the Degrees of Freedom in Fractional Factorial and Center Points.

It can be shown that the sum of squares due to b_i, denoted by SS_{b_i}, is given by

$$SS_{b_i} = \begin{cases} (N+m)b_0^2 & i=0 \\ Nb_i^2 & i=1,\ldots,k. \end{cases}$$

The "pure" quadratic sum of squares SS_q (resulting from contributions of terms of the form x_i^2) is given by

$$SS_q = mN(\bar{y}_F-\bar{y}_C)^2/(N+m),$$

where $\bar{y}_F$ denotes the average response over the N points in the fractional factorial and $\bar{y}_C$ denotes the average response over the m runs at the center point. We see from Figure 1 that the cross-products sum of squares SS_c, arising from the terms of the type β_{ij} $(i\neq j)$, is not available when $k=N-1$. If, however, $k<N-1$, this term may be obtained most easily by subtracting all other sums of squares from the total sum of squares, SS_t, where

$$SS_t = \sum_1^N y_j^2 + \sum_1^m y_{0,r}^2.$$

Under the hypothesis that a first-order fit is adequate, each of the two lack-of-fit terms SS_q and SS_c should measure only random error. Therefore, the corresponding mean squares MS_q = SS_q and $MS_c = SS_c/(N-k-1)$ should be approximately the same size as the pure error mean square, $MS_e = SS_e/(m-1)$.

Lack of fit may be judged by the appropriate F-tests involving the ratios MS_q/MS_e and MS_c/MS_e. These ratios may be compared with the upper α points of F-distributions with (1,m-1) and (N-k-1, m-1) degrees of freedom, respectively. The significance level α is, of course, selected by the experimenter, although α=.05 is an old standby.

If no lack of fit is indicated by either F-test, the fitted functional equation may be used, within the factorial region, as a description of the unknown function $g(\underline{x})$. A significant lack of fit, however, indicates that the first-order model does not provide an adequate explanation of the observed data. In this situation our next step would be to take curvature of the response surface into account by fitting a second-order model of the form:

$$y = \beta_0 + \sum_1^k \beta_i x_i + \sum_1^k \sum_1^k \beta_{ij} x_i x_j .$$

This may be accomplished by adding the 2k axial points $(\pm\gamma,0,\ldots,0)$, $(0,\pm\gamma,\ldots,0),\ldots,(0,0,\ldots,\pm\gamma)$ to the existing fractional factorial points and center points, in order to complete what is known as a central composite design (CCD). This design has a number of excellent properties. For a more detailed discussion of the CCD, including how to choose the value of γ, see Myers (1971).

As an aside, it should be noted that the decision to add axial points is not made until after the data resulting from the fractional factorial and center points is analyzed. In many experimental situations this would dictate the necessity for statistical blocking because the two sets of observations are not made under homogeneous conditions. However, in simulation experiments we need not worry about this, because the underlying conditions (except, of course, for any generated random numbers) will not change.

4. OPTIMUM-SEEKING

Often the goal of simulation experimentation is not to describe the response surface in a given region, but instead to obtain an optimum response. In other words, often the objective is to determine the values of $\underline{x} = (x_1,\ldots,x_k)$ that maximize (or minimize) the unknown function $g(\underline{x})$.

In a sense, this type of problem-solving situation is similar to an optimization problem to be solved by mathematical programming techniques. The major difference is that no explicit objective function is stated and, in fact, exists only implicitly in the multitude of computer instructions in the programs comprising the simulation. Thus, the task of finding the best solution cannot rely on those analytical methods which are applicable when an explicit objective function exists. Instead, a search of the relevant factor space must be made.

In many cases the search for the best simulation response is conducted by an analyst who estimates factor values which he/she believes correspond to a reasonably good solution. The analyst then uses these values as input to the simulation and observes the corresponding response. He/she may then postulate new factor values and repeat the process a number of times. Unfortunately, an analyst's search has a tendency to turn into a trial-and-error process involving a large amount of analyst effort and computer time.

As an alternative, a search algorithm may be used for exploring the factor space. Smith (1973) examined seven search algorithms and concluded that an RSM search tended to be the best choice. However, it is not without drawbacks. For example, an RSM-based search may yield a local optimum rather than a global optimum if local optima exist.

Optimum-seeking via RSM may involve up to four phases:

(1) First-order design phase

(2) Steepest ascent phase

(3) Second-order design phase

(4) Ridge analysis phase.

In the first-order design phase we must select the initial interval of values to be considered for each factor. Estimates of the first-order effects within the initial region defined by the specified intervals may be obtained from a 2^{k-p} fractional factorial. Assuming there is no lack-of-fit, the estimated coefficients $(b_1,\ldots,b_k)$ indicate the direction in which maximum improvement in the response is predicted. This direction is known as "the path of steepest ascent."

Simulation runs corresponding to steps out on this path are then made. These runs should be made cautiously since the prediction becomes less reliable as the distance from the initial region increases. (Selection of appropriate step size is more an art than a science. See Davies (1978) for an example.) When the observed responses worsen, the process outlined in the previous paragraph is repeated unless lack-of-fit for the first-order model is noted. In that event, the existing fractional factorial is augmented by axial points to form a CCD. In this second-order design phase the resulting estimated second-order equation may then be used to predict the factor values which yield the best response. If these values fall within the experimental region, a corresponding simulation run should be made. Otherwise, the best direction in which to proceed should be determined, with simulation runs then conducted in that direction. This involves the ridge analysis phase. Ridge analysis (Draper (1963)) is the analogue of the steepest ascent procedure used with the fitted first-order equation.

5. APPLICATION OF RSM

In Sections 3 and 4 we have only briefly outlined how RSM may be used in the simulation situation. The best bet for the simulation user who wises an adequate background in RSM for use either in investigating the functional relationship in a given region (Section 3) or in optimum-seeking (Section 4) would be to read the statistical, rather than the simulation, literature. (The simulation literature reflects inadequate attention to these points.) A thorough study of the pertinent sections of Cochran and Cox (1957), Davies (1978), and Myers (1971) should provide the information necessary for applying RSM techniques. Needless to say, this implies a large investment of time and effort, an investment which most people cannot afford. An excellent alternative is to obtain consulting from a statistician who is versed in the practical and theoretical aspects of experimental design.

As an aside, it should be noted that because of the independence of RSM from the simulation itself, it is feasible to automate RSM application to a large degree. In fact, Smith (1976) has developed a modular computer FORTRAN program, based on RSM, for optimum-seeking in the simulation situation. This program, which may be used for constrained as well as unconstrained optimum-seeking, is designed to function as an executive program which may be interfaced with an existing FORTRAN-based simulation. Application of the automated RSM program requires only minor modification of any simulation with which it is to be used. Although not a panacea, this program might prove useful.

6. VARIANCE REDUCTION TECHNIQUES

In Section 1 we mentioned that simulation users can, to a certain degree, control the random number streams used in simulation experiments. The basic idea of variance reduction techniques (VRT's) is to exploit this control in order to increase the precision of the simulation results. The following two simple examples illustrate the potentially beneficial effects of such techniques.

Example 1 Let X_1 and X_2 denote the outputs of two different system variants in the same simulation model. The statistic $W=X_1-X_2$ is an unbiased estimator of the difference between the two mean responses, and has variance given by $\mathrm{Var}(W) = \mathrm{Var}(X_1)+\mathrm{Var}(X_2)-2\mathrm{Cov}(X_1,X_2)$. If we use independent streams of random numbers in the two different simulations, we expect $\mathrm{Cov}(X_1,X_2)=0$. If, however, we deliberately use the same stream of random numbers in the two situations, we expect $\mathrm{Cov}(X_1,X_2)>0$, in which case W would have a smaller variance than would occur with independent streams.

Example 2 Let Y_1 and Y_2 denote two outputs of the same system variant in a simulation model. The statistic $Z=(Y_1+Y_2)/2$ is an unbiased estimator of the common response mean and has variance given by $Var(Z) = Var(Y_1)/4+Var(Y_2)/4+Cov(Y_1,Y_2)/2$. If we deliberately use random input streams that are negatively correlated, we expect $Cov(Y_1,Y_2)<0$, in which case Z would have a smaller variance than would occur with independent streams.

The two variance reduction strategies illustrated in Examples 1 and 2 are known as common random numbers and antithetic variates, respectively. These methods are the two simplest, most straightforward, and most widely applied VRT's. For an excellent discussion of these two techniques we refer the reader to Schruben (1979) and Schruben and Margolin (1978). As noted by Schruben (1979), variances are not reduced uniformly by the use of these techniques but are merely shifted from more important estimators to less important estimators. For instance, in Example 1, although $Var(X_1-X_2)$ is decreased, $Var(X_1+X_2)$ is increased by a corresponding amount.

In addition to common random numbers and antithetic variates, other principal VRT's include importance sampling, conditional expectations, stratified sampling, selective sampling, and control variates (or regression sampling). Detailed discussions of these techniques are presented in Kleijnen (1974) and Law and Kelton (1982) (also see Wilson (1983)). These techniques vary in their complexity and applicability. In general, the use of these VRT's involves replacing or modifying the original sampling procedure, or using the same sampling process but employing a more sophisticated estimator.

It has been demonstrated in the literature that VRT's (in particular, common random numbers and antithetic variates) can, when appropriately applied, significantly increase the statistical efficiency of simulation results. For example, with a judicious selection of random number streams the variances of an analyst-specified subset of b_i's, the estimates of the β_i's obtained by least squares via equation (1), can show a marked decrease compared to variances resulting from using independent input streams.

The use of VRT's is, however, not without its drawbacks. First, it is not always clear if the use of a VRT will result in a variance reduction; in fact, a variance augmentation may actually result. (See, for instance, Kleijnen (1974) and Ramsay and Wright (1979).) Second, analysis of the output data is generally complicated by the use of these techniques. Third, VRT's often result in increased computing costs and analyst effort, which may offset any potential gains in efficiency.

In summary, we find ourselves somewhat ambivalent about the practical value of VRT's in simulation. Nonetheless, we would not discourage a potential user from exploring these techniques. We would, however, emphasize that he/she should not only be aware of their potential advantages and disadvantages, but also intimately acquainted with both the simulation and the VRT's under consideration.

7. ACKNOWLEDGMENTS

The research on which this paper is based was supported by the Office of Naval Research under Contract No. N00014-79-C-0650.

8. REFERENCES

Anscombe, F. J. (1959). Quick analysis methods for random balance screening experiments. Technometrics, 1, 195-209.

Booth, K. H. V. and Cox, D. R. (1962). Some systematic supersaturated designs. Technometrics, 4, 489-495.

Box, G. E. P. (1952). Multi-factor designs of first order. Biometrika, 39, 49-57.

Box, G. E. P. and Hunter, J. S. (1961). The 2^{k-p} fractional factorial designs, part I and part II. Technometrics, 3, 311-351 and 449-458.

Box, G. E. P. and Wilson, K. B. (1951). On the experimental attainment of optimum conditions. Journal of the Royal Statistical Society, (Series B), 13, 1-38.

Box, M. J. and Draper, N. R. (1971). Factorial designs, the $|\underline{X}'\underline{X}|$ criterion, and some related matters. Technometrics, 13, 731-742.

Budne, T. A. (1959). The application of random balance designs. Technometrics, 1, 139-155.

Cochran, W. G. and Cox, G. M. (1957). Experimental Designs (Second Edition). John Wiley & Sons, Inc., New York.

Daniel, C. (1959). Use of half-normal plots in interpreting factorial two-level experiments. Technometrics, 1, 311-341.

Davies, O. L., editor (1978). The Design and Analysis of Industrial Experiments (Second Edition). Longman, Inc., New York.

Draper, N. R. (1963). Ridge analysis of response surfaces. Technometrics, 5, 469-479.

Dudewicz, E. J. and Ralley, T. G. (1981). The Handbook of Random Number Generation and Testing with TESTRAND Computer Code. American Science Press, Columbus, Ohio.

Dykstra, O. (1971). The augmentation of experimental data to maximize $|\underline{X}'\underline{X}|$. Technometrics, 13, 682-688.

Gass, S. I. (1977). Evaluation of complex models. Computers and Operations Research, 4, 25-37.

Gordon, G. (1978). System Simulation (Second Edition). Prentice-Hall, Englewood Cliffs, New Jersey.

Kleijnen, J. P. C. (1974). Statistical Techniques in Simulation (in two parts). Marcel Dekker, Inc., New York.

Kleijnen, J. P. C. (1975). Screening designs for poly-factor experimentation. Technometrics, 17, 487-493.

Knuth, D. E. (1981). The Art of Computer Programming, Vol. 2, (Second Edition). Addison-Wesley, Reading, MA.

Law, A. V. and Kelton, W. D. (1982). Simulation Modeling and Analysis. McGraw-Hill, New York.

Li, C. H. (1962). A sequential method for screening experimental variables. Journal of the American Statistical Association, 57, 455-477.

Mauro, C. A. (1983). A comparison of random balance and two-stage group screening designs - part I. Desmatics, Inc. Technical Report No. 113-12. (AD-A136487)

Mauro, C. A. (1984). On the performance of two-stage group screening. Technometrics, 26, to appear.

Mauro, C. A. and Burns, K. C. (1984). A comparison of random balance and two-stage group screening designs - part II. Desmatics, Inc. Technical Report No. 113-14. (AD-A137994)

Mauro, C. A. and Smith, D. E. (1982). The performance of two-stage group screening in factor screening experiments. Technometrics, 24, 325-330.

Mauro, C. A. and Smith, D. E. (1984). Factor screening in simulation: evaluation of two strategies based on random balance sampling. Management Science, 30, 209-221.

Mitchell, T. J. (1974). An algorithm for the construction of "D-optimal" experimental designs. Technometrics, 16, 203-210.

Montgomery, D. C. (1979). Methods for factor screening in computer simulation experiments. Final Report (AD-A073449), Georgia Institute of Technology, Atlanta, Georgia.

Montgomery, D. C. and Bettencourt, V. M. (1977). Multiple response surface methods in computer simulation. Simulation, 29, 113-121.

Morris, M. D. and Mitchell, T. J. (1983). Two-level multifactor designs for detecting the presence of interactions. Technometrics, 25, 345-355.

Myers, R. H. (1971). Response Surface Methodology. Allyn and Bacon, Inc., Boston.

Naylor, T. H. and Burdick, D. G. (1975). The interface between simulation experiments and real world experiments. In A Survey of Statistical Designs and Linear Models (J. N. Srivastava, Editor), 427-442, North Holland, Amsterdam.

Patel, M. S. (1962). Group screening with more than two stages. Technometrics, 4, 209-217.

Plackett, R. L. and Burman, J. P. (1946). The design of optimum multifactor experiments. Biometrika, 33, 305-325.

Raghavarao, D. (1971). Constructions and Combinatorial Problems in Design of Experiments. John Wiley & Sons, Inc., New York.

Ramsay, T. E. and Wright, R. D. (1979). Variance reduction techniques: some limitations and efficiency limits. Modeling and Simulation, 10, 2083-2090.

Satterthwaite, F. E. (1959). Random balance experimentation. Technometrics, 1, 111-137.

Schellenberger, R. E. (1974). Criteria for assessing model validity for managerial purposes. Decision Sciences, 5, 644-653.

Schruben, L. W. (1979). Designing correlation induction strategies for simulation experiments. In Current Issues in Computer Simulation, (N.R. Adam and A. Dogramaci, editors), Academic Press, Inc., New York.

Schruben, L. W. (1981). Control of initialization bias in multivariate simulation response. Communications of the Association for Computing Machinery, 24, 246-252.

Schruben, L. W. and Margolin, B. H. (1978). Pseudorandom number assignment in statistically designed simulation and distribution sampling experiments. Journal of the American Statistical Association, 73, 504-520.

Smith, D. E. (1973). An empirical investigation of optimum-seeking in the computer simulation situation. Operations Research, 21, 475-497.

Smith, D. E. (1976). Automatic optimum-seeking program for digital simulation. Simulation, 27, 27-31.

Smith, D. E. and Mauro, C. A. (1982). Factor screening in computer simulation. Simulation, 38, 49-54.

St. John, R. C. and Draper, N. R. (1975). D-optimality for regression designs: a review. Technometrics, 17, 15-23.

Van Horn, R. L. (1971). Validation of simulation results. Management Science, 17, 247-258.

Watson, G. S. (1961). A study of the group screening method. Technometrics, 3, 371-388.

Wilson, J. R. (1983). Variance reduction: the current state. Mathematics and Computers in Simulation, 25, 55-59.

Youden, W. J., Kempthorne, O., Tukey, J. W., Box, G. E. P., and Hunter, J. S. (1959). Discussions of the papers of Messrs. Satterthwaite and Budne. Technometrics, 1, 157-193.

Received 7/28/83; Revised 4/3/84.

AMERICAN JOURNAL OF MATHEMATICAL AND MANAGEMENT SCIENCES

VARIANCE REDUCTION TECHNIQUES FOR DIGITAL SIMULATION

James R. Wilson
Purdue University
West Lafayette, Indiana 47907, U.S.A.

SYNOPTIC ABSTRACT

In the design and analysis of large-scale simulation experiments, it is generally difficult to estimate model performance parameters with adequate precision at an acceptable sampling cost. This paper provides a state-of-the-art survey of the principal variance reduction techniques that can improve the efficiency of such experiments.

Key Words and Phrases: antithetic variates; common random numbers; conditional Monte Carlo; control variates; importance sampling; Monte Carlo methods; simulation; stratified sampling; systematic sampling; variance reduction techniques.

1984, VOL. 4, NOS. 3 & 4, 277-312
0196-6324/84/030277-36 $10.20

1. INTRODUCTION

Large-scale systems analysis frequently involves extensive experimentation with a digital simulation model. **The main disadvantage of simulated experimentation is the computing cost** arising from direct simulation of a complex stochastic system. In particular, excessive sample sizes may be required to yield acceptable precision in simulation-based estimators of relevant system parameters. **This paper surveys recent research on each of the "variance reduction" techniques that have been developed for or adapted to digital simulation.** Current unresolved problems and directions for future research are also discussed.

To achieve a unified exposition, we represent the basic simulation model as a **response function** $\psi(\cdot)$ whose **input** process $\{U_i : i \geq 1\}$ consists of independent random numbers. Following Hammersley and Handscomb (1964), we reserve the term **random number** to refer to a variate that is uniformly distributed on the unit interval (0, 1). For simplicity, we also assume that there is a finite upper bound m on the number of input variates sampled during one run of the model; thus the set of arguments for $\psi(\cdot)$ can be represented by an $m \times 1$ random vector $\mathbf{U} = [U_1, ..., U_m]'$ that is uniformly distributed over the m-dimensional unit cube

$$I^m \equiv \prod_{j=1}^{m} (0, 1)$$

with probability density function

$$f_0(\mathbf{u}) = \begin{cases} 1, \mathbf{u} \in I^m \\ 0, \mathbf{u} \in R^m - I^m \end{cases} . \tag{1}$$

In terms of the random variable $Y = \psi(\mathbf{U})$, the estimand of interest is

$$\theta = E(Y) = \int_{R^m} \psi(\mathbf{u}) f_0(\mathbf{u})\, d\mathbf{u} = \int_{I^m} \psi(\mathbf{u})\, d\mathbf{u} . \tag{2}$$

1.1. The Variance Reduction Problem. **"Direct simulation"** consists of computing the sample mean response $\overline{Y}_n$ over n independent replications of the basic model; this yields an unbiased estimator of θ with $\mathrm{Var}(\overline{Y}_n) = \mathrm{Var}(Y)/n$. For a fixed sample size n, the problem is to apply an appropriate variance reduction technique (**VRT**) to the basic model to obtain an alternative estimator $\hat{\theta}_n$ with

$$E(\hat{\theta}_n) = \theta \quad \text{and} \quad Var(\hat{\theta}_n) < Var(\overline{Y}_n) . \tag{3}$$

Now different VRTs usually require different amounts of computing time to complete one replication; and some VRTs inherently require a random replication count (see Subsection 3.1.2 on dynamic importance sampling) or a random run length (see Subsection 3.4.2 on dynamic systematic sampling). To take these phenomena into account, a more comprehensive formulation of the variance reduction problem is required.

In general let $\hat{\theta}$ denote an estimator for θ that is based on a VRT with total computing time $C^{\dagger}(\hat{\theta})$. Relative to the direct simulation estimator $\overline{Y}_n$ with total computing time $C^{\dagger}(\overline{Y}_n)$, the **efficiency** of $\hat{\theta}$ is

$$\eta(\hat{\theta}: \overline{Y}_n) \equiv Var(\overline{Y}_n)E[C^{\dagger}(\overline{Y}_n)]/\{Var(\hat{\theta})E[C^{\dagger}(\hat{\theta})]\} \tag{4}$$

(see Hammersley and Handscomb (1964), Section 5.1). **The general variance reduction problem** is to construct $\hat{\theta}$ so as to maximize the efficiency $\eta(\hat{\theta}: \overline{Y}_n)$ subject to the constraints

$$E(\hat{\theta}) = \theta \quad \text{and} \quad \eta(\hat{\theta}: \overline{Y}_n) \geq 1 . \tag{5}$$

Although $\eta(\hat{\theta}: \overline{Y}_n)$ is the classical figure of merit for a VRT, it is only one of many possible efficiency measures. Let $A^{\dagger}(\hat{\theta})$ denote the analyst's total time to implement the estimator $\hat{\theta}$. The fundamental performance criteria for $\hat{\theta}$ are the analyst's time $A^{\dagger}(\hat{\theta})$, the computer time $C^{\dagger}(\hat{\theta})$ and the estimation error $(\hat{\theta}-\theta)$. Within the framework of statistical decision theory, we may define an appropriate loss function $\ell(\theta, \hat{\theta}) = \ell[\theta, (\hat{\theta}-\theta), C^{\dagger}(\hat{\theta}), A^{\dagger}(\hat{\theta})]$ and then use the risk function $R(\theta, \hat{\theta}) \equiv E[\ell(\theta, \hat{\theta})]$ to derive an alternative efficiency measure for $\hat{\theta}$ (see Berger (1980)). The formulation of the variance reduction problem given in (4) and (5) ignores $A^{\dagger}(\hat{\theta})$, which is often the factor of overriding practical importance. To avoid prohibitive setup time in the application of a VRT, practitioners frequently implement a crude version of the VRT with disappointing results. The formulation of (4) and (5) also ignores another practical aspect of the variance reduction problem. It is sometimes advantageous to use a VRT yielding a biased estimator $\hat{\theta}$; but (4) does not take the bias of $\hat{\theta}$ into account, and (5) actually excludes all biased estimators from consideration. In spite of these drawbacks, $\eta(\hat{\theta}: \overline{Y}_n)$ continues to be one of the most widely reported measures of efficiency in the literature. Moreover, relations (4) and (5) define an appropriate context for a systematic discussion of the current status of the principal VRTs used in digital simulation.

1.2. A Taxonomy of Variance Reduction Techniques. As a means of organizing the subsequent discussion, **we classify all VRTs into two major categories -- correlation methods and importance methods.** (This is essentially the same classification used by Kohlas (1982).)

The **correlation methods** include three techniques that take advantage of linear correlation among simulation responses to yield an efficiency increase. The techniques of **common random numbers** and **antithetic variates** respectively require the experimenter to induce positive and negative response correlations within blocks of simulation runs by forcing an appropriate functional or stochastic dependence among the input vectors $\{\mathbf{U}_j\colon 1 \leq j \leq n\}$ used on those runs. In contrast to this approach, the **control variates** technique uses regression methods to exploit any inherent correlation between the output Y and a selected concomitant random vector **X** with known mean μ_X that is observed on each run.

The **importance methods** include four techniques that achieve improved efficiency by ultimately concentrating the sampling effort in those subregions of the input domain I^m that make the greatest contribution to the integral (2). Among the variants of the technique called **importance sampling, Russian roulette** and **splitting** are most easily adapted to discrete-event simulation because they are applied dynamically as the simulation progresses through time. The technique of **conditional Monte Carlo** achieves an efficiency increase by converting an estimation problem expressed as a conditional expectation (respectively, as an unconditional expectation) into another problem expressed as an unconditional expectation (respectively, a conditional expectation). Whereas the control variates technique is effective when there is a strong linear association between the response Y and some auxiliary random vector **X** with known mean, **stratified sampling** exploits prior knowledge of the entire distribution of **X** to yield an efficiency increase whatever the (possibly nonlinear) relationship between Y and **X**. As an alternative means of ensuring that the importance regions of I^m (or the time domain) are adequately represented, **systematic sampling** forces uniform sampling throughout the domain of interest by partitioning that domain into directly congruent strata so that a single point randomly sampled in one stratum automatically identifies a corresponding sample point in each stratum.

A fundamentally new framework for the analysis of VRTs was recently developed by Nelson and Schmeiser (1983; 1984a, b, c). This is discussed in Section 4 below.

2. CORRELATION METHODS

2.1. Induced Correlation Methods

2.1.1. General Principles. If $Y_1 = \psi_1(\mathbf{U}_1)$ and $Y_2 = \psi_2(\mathbf{U}_2)$ are the responses of a pair of simulation runs for which the difference $E(Y_1)-E(Y_2)$ is to be estimated, then the technique of **common random numbers** is used to reduce the variance of $Y^o = Y_1-Y_2$

$$\mathrm{Var}(Y_1-Y_2) = \mathrm{Var}(Y_1) + \mathrm{Var}(Y_2) - 2\mathrm{Cov}(Y_1, Y_2)$$

by inducing $\mathrm{Cov}(Y_1, Y_2) > 0$. If instead $E(Y_1)$ is to be estimated and Y_1, Y_2 represent replicates so that $\psi_1 = \psi_2$, then the method of **antithetic variates** is used to reduce the variance of $Y^o = \frac{1}{2}(Y_1+Y_2)$

$$\begin{aligned}\mathrm{Var}[\frac{1}{2}(Y_1+Y_2)] &= \frac{1}{4}\mathrm{Var}(Y_1) + \frac{1}{4}\mathrm{Var}(Y_2) + \frac{1}{2}\mathrm{Cov}(Y_1, Y_2)\\ &= \frac{1}{2}\mathrm{Var}(Y_1) + \frac{1}{2}\mathrm{Cov}(Y_1, Y_2)\end{aligned}$$

by inducing $\mathrm{Cov}(Y_1, Y_2) < 0$. In each case, the direct-simulation approach would be simply to execute two independent runs to obtain a single observation of Y^o. For both of the induced correlation techniques, the final estimator $\hat{\theta}_n$ is the average $\overline{Y}^o_{n/2}$ of a random sample of n/2 observations of the associated variate Y^o.

To induce $\mathrm{Cov}(Y_1, Y_2) > 0$, the technique of common random numbers consists of taking

$$\mathbf{U}_2 = \mathbf{U}_1 \ . \tag{6}$$

Similarly, to induce $\mathrm{Cov}(Y_1, Y_2) < 0$, the simplest version of the method of antithetic variates uses the relation

$$\mathbf{U}_2 = \underset{\sim}{1}_m - \mathbf{U}_1 \ , \quad \text{where} \ \ \underset{\sim}{1}_m \equiv [1, ..., 1]' \ \text{ is } m\times 1 \ . \tag{7}$$

Although statements frequently appear in the literature to the effect that (6) and (7) are not guaranteed to produce the desired correlations in complex simulations, efficiency gains are ensured in the important special case that the response functions ψ_1 and ψ_2 are **concordant** for each of the random numbers constituting their input sequences. This means that with respect to each input coordinate, the functions ψ_1 and ψ_2 are monotone in the same direction; however, both functions may be monotone nondecreasing in one coordinate and monotone nonincreasing in another coordinate. Bratley, Fox and Schrage (1983) gave a definitive treatment of the methods of common random numbers and antithetic variates based on these considerations. Rubinstein and his collaborators carried out an extensive investigation of the conditions under which (6) and (7) yield optimal variance reductions (see Gal, Rubinstein and Ziv (1981); Rubinstein and Samorodnitsky (1982); and Rubinstein, Samorodnitsky and Shaked (1985)).

To compare and estimate response parameters for more than two configurations of the basic simulation, we let $\mathbf{d}_j \equiv [d_{j1}, ..., d_{jr}]$ denote the values for r selected independent variables at the jth design point of an experiment consisting of n runs. We seek to estimate the parameters $\underset{\sim}{\theta} \equiv [\theta_1, \ldots, \theta_r]$ in the **general linear model**

$$Y_j \equiv \psi_j(\mathbf{U}_j) = \sum_{\ell=1}^{r} d_{j\ell}\,\theta_\ell + e_j\,, \qquad 1 \leq j \leq n\,. \tag{8}$$

Schruben and Margolin (1978) considered the problem of respectively assigning the common input $\mathbf{U}$ and the antithetic input $\underset{\sim}{1}_m - \mathbf{U}$ to some of the design points in the experiment so as to yield a decomposition of the error term e_j into a **random block effect** b_j and residual e_j° with the following dependence on the assigned input for $1 \leq i, j \leq n$:

$$\left.\begin{array}{l} e_j(\mathbf{U}) = b_j(\mathbf{U}) + e_j^\circ(\mathbf{U});\ \ E[b_j(\mathbf{U})] = E[e_j^\circ(\mathbf{U})] = 0; \\ \mathrm{Var}(Y_j) = \mathrm{Var}[\psi_j(\mathbf{U})] = \sigma_Y^2\,; \\ \mathrm{Cov}[b_i(\mathbf{U}),\, b_j(\mathbf{U})] = \rho_+ \geq 0;\ \ \mathrm{Var}[e_i^\circ(\mathbf{U})] = \sigma_Y^2 - \rho_+\,; \\ \mathrm{Cov}[b_i(\mathbf{U}),\, b_j(\underset{\sim}{1}_m - \mathbf{U})] = -\rho_- \leq 0\ \ (\rho_- \leq \rho_+)\,; \\ \mathrm{Cov}[b_i(\mathbf{U}),\, e_j^\circ(\mathbf{U})] = \mathrm{Cov}[b_i(\mathbf{U}),\, e_j^\circ(\underset{\sim}{1}_m - \mathbf{U})] = 0; \text{ and} \\ i \neq j \Rightarrow \mathrm{Cov}[e_i^\circ(\mathbf{U}),\, e_j^\circ(\mathbf{U})] = \mathrm{Cov}[e_i^\circ(\mathbf{U}),\, e_j^\circ(\underset{\sim}{1}_m - \mathbf{U})] = 0 \end{array}\right\} . \qquad (9)$$

Assuming that (9) is a valid description of the induced correlation structure at all pairs of design points where common random numbers or antithetic random numbers are assigned, Schruben and Margolin proposed the following experimental "**Assignment Rule**": If the n-point experimental design admits orthogonal blocking into two blocks of size n_1 and n_2 respectively (preferably with $n_1 \approx n_2$), then for all n_1 design points in the first block, use the common input $\mathbf{U}$; and for all n_2 design points in the second block, use the antithetic input $\underset{\sim}{1}_m - \mathbf{U}$.

Now suppose that each $\mathbf{d}_j$ is a known function of k factors each with two levels and that we seek to estimate $\underset{\sim}{\theta}$ using $n = 2^{k-p}$ design points, where $1 \leq p < k$, $r < n$ and $\rho_+ = \rho_-$. Schruben and Margolin proved that over the class of all 2^{k-p} fractional factorial designs for this situation, the assignment rule minimizes the determinant of the covariance matrix for the ordinary least squares (OLS) estimator $\hat{\underset{\sim}{\theta}}_{OLS}$ and for the weighted least squares (WLS) estimator $\hat{\underset{\sim}{\theta}}_{WLS}$. (Actually the assignment rule satisfies a wide variety of design optimality criteria for this class of designs; see Schruben (1979).)

The dependencies $b_j = b_j(\mathbf{U})$ and $e_j^\circ = e_j^\circ(\mathbf{U})$ postulated in (9) are somewhat controversial. In particular, if a deterministic random number generator is used to sample the input vector $\mathbf{U}$, then the selection of a seed (that is, a starting value for the generator) is the **only** potential source of random variation in the associated simulation experiment. Thus if the same seed is used for all n_1 design points in the first block of the experiment, then the same input $\mathbf{U}$ is generated for the first n_1 runs as prescribed by the assignment rule; and in this case the corresponding residuals $\{e_j^o : 1 \leq j \leq n_1\}$ cannot properly be attributed to any independent source of random variation. (See Mihram (1974) for an elaboration of this point.) Moreover, some authors question the representation of common random numbers as a block effect (Kleijnen (1975), p. 355). The fundamental problem underlying these objections is that classical techniques for the analysis of statistically designed simulation experiments (Kleijnen (1975), Chapter IV) may not always be suitable for the designs proposed by Schruben and Margolin. Recently Nozari, Arnold and Pegden (1984b) derived statistical-estimation and hypothesis-testing procedures that are appropriate for these designs. However, a prerequisite for the practical application of these procedures is the development of validation tests for the proposed linear model (8) and the assumed dependency structure (9).

2.1.2. Antithetic-Variates Methods. Cheng (1981, 1982, 1983, 1984) developed a comprehensive antithetic-variates methodology for estimating selected parameters of the target response Y; this includes the mean and variance as well as selected quantiles and percentages of the associated output distribution $F_Y(\cdot)$. For simplicity we only discuss the estimation of the mean $\theta = E(Y)$ using the average $\hat{\theta} = \frac{1}{2}(Y_1+Y_2)$ of two antithetic replicates. As a preliminary step in Cheng's procedure, we must identify an **intermediary variable** $X = \beta(\mathbf{U})$ with the following properties:

(i) the distribution $F_X(x) \equiv \Pr\{X \leq x\}, -\infty < x < \infty$, is known;

(ii) there is a strong linear correlation Corr(Y, X) between Y and X on each run; and

(iii) a conditional input-generation algorithm is available such that for any given $X = x_0$, the input vector $\mathbf{U}$ can be sampled according to the conditional density $f_0(\mathbf{u} \mid \beta(\mathbf{u}) = x_0)$.

To induce a negative correlation between the responses Y_1 and Y_2 on two antithetic runs, the basic idea is to arrange a negative correlation between the corresponding intermediary variables X_1 and X_2 whose sampling can be completely controlled. (Although Cheng calls X_1 and X_2 "antithetic control variables," this is really a misnomer; as discussed in Section 2.2 below, the usual requirements for a control variable are much less stringent than properties (i), (ii) and (iii) above. The term "intermediary variable" seems more appropriate.) The steps of Cheng's procedure are:

(a) generate $\mathbf{U}_1 \sim f_0(\cdot)$ and compute the response $Y_1 = \psi(\mathbf{U}_1)$ and the intermediary $X_1 = \beta(\mathbf{U}_1)$;

(b) compute the antithetic intermediary $X_2 = F_X^{-1}[1 - F_X(X_1)]$;

(c) generate the antithetic input $\mathbf{U}_2$ from the conditional input density given the antithetic intermediary X_2: $\mathbf{U}_2 \sim f_0(\cdot \mid X_2)$; and

(d) compute the antithetic response $Y_2 = \psi(\mathbf{U}_2)$ and the overall antithetic estimator $\hat{\theta} = \frac{1}{2}(Y_1+Y_2)$.

Cheng has adapted this estimation procedure to a wide variety of functional forms for Y as well as X, and his experimental results show that large efficiency increases can be realized with this approach. Note, however, that merely inducing a negative correlation between the intermediaries X_1 and X_2 is not generally sufficient to yield a negative correlation between the responses Y_1 and Y_2. Consider the following quadrivariate normal counterexample:

$$\begin{bmatrix} Y_1 \\ X_1 \\ Y_2 \\ X_2 \end{bmatrix} \sim N_4 \left(\begin{bmatrix} \theta \\ 0 \\ \theta \\ 0 \end{bmatrix}, \begin{bmatrix} 1 & \rho & \rho & 0 \\ \rho & 1 & 0 & -\rho \\ \rho & 0 & 1 & \rho \\ 0 & -\rho & \rho & 1 \end{bmatrix} \right) \quad \text{with } \rho > 0 .$$

Now the matrix given above is positive definite (and hence a valid covariance matrix) if and only if its leading principal minors are all positive (Hadley (1973), p. 260); and this condition is equivalent to requiring that $|\rho| < 1/\sqrt{2}$. Thus when $0 < \rho < 1/\sqrt{2}$, we have the seemingly counterintuitive result

$$\left.\begin{array}{ll} \mathrm{Corr}(Y_1, X_1) = \mathrm{Corr}(Y_2, X_2) = \rho > 0 \text{ and} & \\ \mathrm{Corr}(X_1, X_2) = -\rho < 0 & \text{while } \mathrm{Corr}(Y_1, Y_2) = \rho > 0 \end{array}\right\} .$$

Moreover, as ρ increases in the interval $(0, 1/\sqrt{2})$, the negative correlation between the intermediaries X_1 and X_2 is strengthened while at the same time the positive correlation between the responses Y_1 and Y_2 is also strengthened! This apparent paradox can be resolved by considering the geometric interpretation of the correlation coefficient (Anderson (1958), p. 49). This counterexample shows that intuition is not always a reliable guide for the development of correlation induction strategies.

In its most general formulation, the method of antithetic variates is used to estimate a scalar θ by means of an unbiased statistic of the form

$$\hat{\theta}_n = \sum_{j=1}^{n} \psi_j(\mathbf{U}_j) .$$

To reduce $\mathrm{Var}(\hat{\theta}_n)$ while keeping $\hat{\theta}_n$ unbiased, we week to induce appropriate dependencies among the input vectors $\{\mathbf{U}_j\}$ while preserving their marginal distributions given by (1). Wilson (1983) showed that the greatest lower bound of $\mathrm{Var}(\hat{\theta}_n)$ over all joint input distributions with the fixed marginals (1) can be approached by selecting an appropriate set of input transformations $\{\underset{\sim}{\tau}_j : 1 \leq j \leq n\}$ from the class $\mathfrak{T}$ described below; then by generating a **single** input vector $\mathbf{U}_0 \sim f_0(\cdot)$ and setting $\mathbf{U}_j = \underset{\sim}{\tau}_j(\mathbf{U}_0)$ for $1 \leq j \leq n$, we obtain the required dependencies among the components of $\hat{\theta}_n$ such that $\mathrm{Var}(\hat{\theta}_n)$ is arbitrarily close to its greatest lower bound. The search for optimal antithetic transformations can be confined to the class $\mathfrak{T}$ of mappings $\underset{\sim}{\tau} : I^m \to I^m$ that possess the following properties: (a) there is an open set $B \subset I^m$ such that $\Pr\{\mathbf{U}_0 \in B\} = 1$ and the restriction $\underset{\sim}{\tau} : B \to \underset{\sim}{\tau}(B)$ is one-to-one and continuously differentiable; and (b) the Jacobian $J_{\tau}(\mathbf{u})$ of $\underset{\sim}{\tau}$ evaluated at every point $\mathbf{u} \in B$ has absolute value one. Rubinstein and Samorodnitsky (1983) formulated conditions under which the greatest lower bound for $\mathrm{Var}(\hat{\theta}_n)$ can actually be achieved.

It is hoped that these recent extensions of the antithetic-variates theorem (Hammersley and Handscomb (1964), pp. 61-62) will aid in the discovery of feasible methods for constructing optimal antithetic input transformations. This point is elaborated in Section 5 of Wilson (1983). Much fundamental research remains to be done in this area before the general antithetic-variates technique can be applied to practical problems. As a first step in this direction, it may be advantageous to look for optimal antithetic input transformations in the context of special applications -- for example, network reliability problems and stochastic activity networks.

2.2. Control Variates

2.2.1. General Principles. In this section we assume that the simulation response is a p-dimensional column vector: $\mathbf{Y} = [Y_1, \ldots, Y_p]'$. To construct an estimator for $\underset{\sim}{\theta} = E(\mathbf{Y})$ using control variates, we must identify a q-dimensional column vector of concomitant random variables $\mathbf{X} = [X_1, \ldots, X_q]'$ having both a known expectation $\underset{\sim}{\mu}_X$ and a strong linear association with $\mathbf{Y}$. In essence, we try to predict and counteract the unknown deviation $\mathbf{Y}-\underset{\sim}{\theta}$ by subtracting from $\mathbf{Y}$ an appropriate linear transformation of the known deviation $\mathbf{X}-\underset{\sim}{\mu}_X$:

$$\mathbf{Y}(\mathbf{b}) = \mathbf{Y} - \mathbf{b}(\mathbf{X}-\underset{\sim}{\mu}_X)\,. \tag{10}$$

The controlled response $\mathbf{Y}(\mathbf{b})$ is unbiased for any fixed $p\times q$ control coefficient matrix $\mathbf{b}$. Let $\underset{\sim}{\Sigma}_Y$ and $\underset{\sim}{\Sigma}_X$ denote the covariance matrices of $\mathbf{Y}$ and $\mathbf{X}$ respectively, and let $\underset{\sim}{\Sigma}_{YX}$ denote the covariance matrix between $\mathbf{Y}$ and $\mathbf{X}$. Rubinstein and Markus (1981) showed that the covariance matrix of $\mathbf{Y}(\mathbf{b})$ is given by

$$\underset{\sim}{\Sigma}_{Y(b)} \equiv \mathrm{Cov}[\mathbf{Y}(\mathbf{b})] = \underset{\sim}{\Sigma}_Y - \mathbf{b}\underset{\sim}{\Sigma}'_{YX} - \underset{\sim}{\Sigma}_{YX}\mathbf{b}' + \mathbf{b}\underset{\sim}{\Sigma}_X\,\mathbf{b}'\,, \tag{11}$$

and the **generalized variance** of $\mathbf{Y}(\mathbf{b})$ (that is, $\det[\underset{\sim}{\Sigma}_{Y(b)}]$) is minimized by the optimal control coefficient matrix

$$\underset{\sim}{\beta} = \underset{\sim}{\Sigma}_{YX}\,\underset{\sim}{\Sigma}_X^{-1}\,. \tag{12}$$

The resulting minimum generalized variance is

$$\det[\underset{\sim}{\Sigma}_{Y(\beta)}] = \det(\underset{\sim}{\Sigma}_Y)\det(\mathbf{I}_p - \underset{\sim}{\Sigma}_{YX}\,\underset{\sim}{\Sigma}_X^{-1}\,\underset{\sim}{\Sigma}'_{YX}\,\underset{\sim}{\Sigma}_Y^{-1}) \tag{13}$$

$$= \det(\underset{\sim}{\Sigma}_Y)[\prod_{i=1}^{s}(1-\rho_i^2)]\,,$$

where $s = \mathrm{rank}(\underset{\sim}{\Sigma}_{YX})$ and $\{\rho_i : 1 \leq i \leq s\}$ are the **canonical correlations** between $\mathbf{Y}$ and $\mathbf{X}$.

In practice $\underset{\sim}{\Sigma}_{YX}$ and $\underset{\sim}{\Sigma}_X$ are usually unknown and hence $\underset{\sim}{\beta}$ must be estimated. Let $\{(\mathbf{Y}_j, \mathbf{X}_j) : 1 \leq j \leq n\}$ denote the results observed on n independent replications of the simulation. In terms of the statistics

$$\overline{\mathbf{Y}} = n^{-1} \sum_{j=1}^{n} \mathbf{Y}_j\,, \quad \mathbf{S}_Y = (n-1)^{-1} \sum_{j=1}^{n} (\mathbf{Y}_j - \overline{\mathbf{Y}})(\mathbf{Y}_j - \overline{\mathbf{Y}})'\,, \tag{14}$$

$$\overline{\mathbf{X}} = n^{-1} \sum_{j=1}^{n} \mathbf{X}_j\,, \quad \mathbf{S}_X = (n-1)^{-1} \sum_{j=1}^{n} (\mathbf{X}_j - \overline{\mathbf{X}})(\mathbf{X}_j - \overline{\mathbf{X}})'\,, \text{ and} \tag{15}$$

$$\mathbf{S}_{YX} = (n-1)^{-1} \sum_{j=1}^{n} (\mathbf{Y}_j - \overline{\mathbf{Y}})(\mathbf{X}_j - \overline{\mathbf{X}})'\,, \tag{16}$$

the sample analogue of (12) is

$$\hat{\underset{\sim}{\beta}} = \mathbf{S}_{YX}\mathbf{S}_X^{-1}\,. \tag{17}$$

Thus a point estimator for $\underset{\sim}{\theta}$ is

$$\hat{\underset{\sim}{\theta}} \equiv \overline{\mathbf{Y}}(\hat{\underset{\sim}{\beta}}) = \overline{\mathbf{Y}} - \hat{\underset{\sim}{\beta}}(\overline{\mathbf{X}} - \underset{\sim}{\mu}_X)\,. \tag{18}$$

To provide a meaningful assessment of the accuracy of $\hat{\underset{\sim}{\theta}}$, we require a corresponding confidence-region estimator for $\underset{\sim}{\theta}$. In the following subsections we present two methods for constructing confidence regions in the context of independent replications of the simulation model. The first method assumes that the outputs $\mathbf{Y}$ and $\mathbf{X}$ jointly have a multivariate normal distribution. The second method employs jackknifing and is applicable to a wide variety of nonnormal simulation outputs.

2.2.2. Analysis Techniques for Normal Outputs. Under the assumption that $\mathbf{Y}$ and $\mathbf{X}$ have a joint normal distribution

$$\begin{bmatrix} \mathbf{Y} \\ \mathbf{X} \end{bmatrix} \sim N_{p+q}\left(\begin{bmatrix} \underset{\sim}{\theta} \\ \underset{\sim}{\mu}_X \end{bmatrix}, \begin{bmatrix} \underset{\sim}{\Sigma}_Y & \underset{\sim}{\Sigma}_{YX} \\ \underset{\sim}{\Sigma}'_{YX} & \underset{\sim}{\Sigma}_X \end{bmatrix} \right), \tag{19}$$

Rubinstein and Markus (1981) derived the following exact $100(1-\gamma)\%$ confidence region for $\underset{\sim}{\theta}$:

$$\left\{ \mathbf{t} \in R^p : [\overline{\mathbf{Y}}(\hat{\underset{\sim}{\beta}}) - \mathbf{t}]'\, \hat{\underset{\sim}{\Sigma}}_{Y\cdot X}^{-1} [\overline{\mathbf{Y}}(\hat{\underset{\sim}{\beta}}) - \mathbf{t}] \le \delta \frac{(n-q-1)p}{(n-q-p)} F_{1-\gamma}(p, n-q-p) \right\} \tag{20}$$

where

$$\hat{\underset{\sim}{\Sigma}}_{Y\cdot X} \equiv (n-q-1)^{-1}(n-1)(\mathbf{S}_Y - \mathbf{S}_{YX}\mathbf{S}_X^{-1}\mathbf{S}'_{YX})\,, \tag{21}$$

$$\delta \equiv n^{-1} + (n-1)^{-1}(\overline{\mathbf{X}} - \underset{\sim}{\mu}_X)'\, \mathbf{S}_X^{-1}(\overline{\mathbf{X}} - \underset{\sim}{\mu}_X)\,, \tag{22}$$

and $F_{1-\gamma}(p, n-q-p)$ denotes the $(1-\gamma)^{th}$ quantile of an F-distribution with p and (n-q-p) degrees of freedom.

Now the use of $\hat{\beta}$ rather than β means that the minimum generalized variance $\det[\Sigma_{Y(\beta)}]$ is not achieved. To measure the efficiency loss arising from estimation of the optimal control coefficients in the case of a univariate response (that is, when p = 1), Lavenberg, Moeller and Welch (1982) derived the **loss factor**

$$\mathrm{Var}[\overline{Y}(\hat{\beta})]/\mathrm{Var}[\overline{Y}(\beta)] = (n-2)/(n-q-2)\,. \tag{23}$$

For the case of a multivariate response (that is, for $p \geq 1$), Venkatraman (1983) showed that

$$\det\{\mathrm{Cov}[\overline{\mathbf{Y}}(\hat{\beta})]\}/\det\{\mathrm{Cov}[\overline{\mathbf{Y}}(\beta)]\} = [(n-2)/(n-q-2)]^{p}\,. \tag{24}$$

Rubinstein and Markus (1981) developed another extension of (23), which is substantially more complicated than (24).

Nozari, Arnold and Pegden (1984a) carried out a development similar to (10) through (23) above for the case of a univariate response (p = 1) and multiple controls ($q \geq 1$) where the objective is to estimate a linear model (8) with $r \geq 1$ terms. To complete this line of inquiry, Porta Nova (1985) performed a comparable analysis for the application of multiple controls ($q \geq 1$) to the estimation of a multivariate general linear model ($p \geq 1$, $r \geq 1$).

As a means of validating the use of the estimation procedures described in this subsection, the extended Shapiro-Wilk statistics (Shapiro (1980), Royston (1982a, b; 1983a, b)) provide excellent omnibus tests for univariate and multivariate normality. For multivariate normality, see also Siotani, Hayakawa and Fujikoshi (1985), which includes the required computer software.

2.2.3. Analysis Techniques for Nonnormal Outputs. If **Y** and **X** do not jointly possess a multivariate normal distribution, then the point estimator $\hat{\theta} = \overline{\mathbf{Y}} - \hat{\beta}(\overline{\mathbf{X}}-\mu_X)$ is generally biased because $\hat{\beta}$ and $\overline{\mathbf{X}}$ are not independent. To reduce the bias of $\hat{\theta}$ and to construct an asymptotically valid confidence region for θ, we use the **jackknife statistic** (Kleijnen (1974), pp. 158-159; Bratley, Fox and Schrage (1983), Section 2.7). Let

$\hat{\underset{\sim}{\theta}}_{(k)}$ denote the estimator computed from (14) through (18) when the kth observation $(\mathbf{Y}_k, \mathbf{X}_k)$ has been deleted from the original data set $\{(\mathbf{Y}_j, \mathbf{X}_j) : 1 \leq j \leq n\}$. Using the "pseudovalues" $\mathbf{J}_k \equiv n\hat{\underset{\sim}{\theta}} - (n-1)\hat{\underset{\sim}{\theta}}_{(k)}$, $1 \leq k \leq n$, we calculate the jackknife statistic

$$\bar{\mathbf{J}} \equiv n^{-1} \sum_{k=1}^{n} \mathbf{J}_k$$

and the associated sample covariance matrix

$$\mathbf{S}_J = (n-1)^{-1} \sum_{k=1}^{n} (\mathbf{J}_k - \bar{\mathbf{J}})(\mathbf{J}_k - \bar{\mathbf{J}})' .$$

When the joint distribution of $\mathbf{Y}$ and $\mathbf{X}$ satisfies certain mild regularity conditions, the jackknifed point estimator of $\underset{\sim}{\theta}$ has reduced bias: $E(\bar{\mathbf{J}}) = \underset{\sim}{\theta} + O(n^{-2})$; and an asymptotically exact $100(1-\gamma)\%$ confidence region for $\underset{\sim}{\theta}$ is given by

$$\left\{ \mathbf{t} \in R^p : (\bar{\mathbf{J}} - \mathbf{t})' \, \mathbf{S}_J^{-1} \, (\bar{\mathbf{J}} - \mathbf{t}) \leq \frac{(n-1)p}{(n-p)n} F_{1-\gamma}(p, n-p) \right\} ,$$

where $F_{1-\gamma}(p, n-p)$ denotes the $(1-\gamma)^{th}$ quantile of an F-distribution with p and (n-p) degrees of freedom (Efron (1982), Section 3.8).

2.2.4. Applications of Control Variates. The control variates technique is easy to apply and has demonstrated potential for improving the efficiency of a wide variety of digital simulation experiments. In each specific application, the user can exploit his knowledge of the operation of the simulation model and of the joint behavior of relevant simulation outputs to construct appropriate controls. Some examples are discussed below.

Distribution-sampling experiments are particularly well-suited to the use of control variates. To estimate the power of a statistical test based on a nonparametric measure of intraclass correlation in some one-way models with normally distributed effects, Rothery (1982) used as a control the F-statistic for the corresponding one-way analysis of variance. Rothery obtained efficiencies in the range $1.32 \leq \eta(\hat{\theta}: \bar{Y}_n) \leq 5.98$ with this approach. In the context of nonlinear regression problems, Swain and Schmeiser (1984a, b) sought to estimate the sampling distribution of the nonlinear parameter estimators. Using as controls the linear approximators to the regression solution, Swain and Schmeiser achieved large efficiency increases (typically $\eta(\underset{\sim}{\hat{\theta}}: \overline{\mathbf{Y}}_n) > 10^6$) when estimating the moments of the nonlinear parameter estimators. See also Swain (1984).

Several types of control variates have also been proposed recently for different classes of discrete-event simulations. Wilson and Pritsker (1984a, b) developed a set of asymptotically stable **"standardized service-time controls"** for use in queueing network simulations; see also Cheng and Feast (1980). Grant and Solberg (1983) and Venkatraman (1983) devised effective controls for stochastic activity networks.

In all of the foregoing discussion of control variates, the output analysis was based on the method of independent replications. For the case of a univariate response, Lavenberg and Welch (1981) also discussed the application of control variates in conjunction with the method of batch means and the regenerative method of simulation analysis.

3. IMPORTANCE METHODS

3.1. Importance Sampling

3.1.1. Static Importance Sampling. This technique requires the input vector $\mathbf{U}$ to be sampled from an alternative density $f(\cdot)$ instead of the uniform density $f_0(\cdot)$. To compensate for this distortion of the input so as to achieve condition (3), the original response $Y = \psi(\mathbf{U})$ is replaced by the variate $Y^o = \psi(\mathbf{U})/f(\mathbf{U})$. The importance estimator $\hat{\theta}_n$ is then taken to be the sample mean $\overline{Y}^o_n$ computed over n replications of the new response Y^o. When the importance density $f(\cdot)$ closely mimics $\psi(\cdot)$, the ratio $\psi(\mathbf{U})/f(\mathbf{U})$ is nearly constant, and a substantial variance reduction is achieved. Sampling from the optimal importance density

$$f^*(\mathbf{u}) = |\psi(\mathbf{u})| \Big/ \int_{I^m} |\psi(\mathbf{w})| \, d\mathbf{w}\,, \qquad \mathbf{u} \in I^m\,,$$

minimizes $\mathrm{Var}(\hat{\theta}_n)$ (Kleijnen (1974)). This technique has been successfully applied to many distribution sampling experiments. In such situations, there is no notion of a stochastic process evolving over time; and thus the general behavior of $\psi(\cdot)$ is relatively easy to explore. However, in complex discrete-event simulations exhibiting dynamic behavior over (simulated) time, it is almost impossible to arrange even a general similarity between

$\psi(\cdot)$ and $f(\cdot)$. Note that this technique is not guaranteed to yield a variance reduction: with poorly chosen importance density $f(\cdot)$, large variance increases can occur (Bratley, Fox and Schrage (1983)).

3.1.2. Dynamic Importance Sampling. Kioussis and Miller (1983) successfully applied a variant of importance sampling to estimate the probability of system failure in a fault-tolerant computer system. In such systems, failure is a rare event; typically its probability of occurrence is 0.0001 or less. Clearly an effective variance reduction technique is essential to the feasibility of simulation-based reliability analyses of this type. Although the basic idea of importance sampling is relevant to the estimation of rare-event probabilities, the complexity of the response function $\psi(\cdot)$ precludes the approach outlined in Subsection 3.1.1. Using the techniques of Russian roulette and splitting, Kioussis and Miller gave a general formulation of dynamic importance sampling for transient simulations.

Let $\{\mathbf{M}(t) : 0 \leq t \leq t^{\dagger}\}$ be a stochastic process with state space S such that $\mathbf{M}(t)$ denotes the status of the simulation model at time t, and $t^{\dagger}$ is the simulation ending time. Let $\{B_i : 1 \leq i \leq b\}$ denote disjoint subsets of S that are "bad" in the following sense: if $\mathbf{M}(t)$ hits a state in B_i at time t, a degradation in system status occurs; and the system failure event F is more likely to occur in the remaining time interval $(t, t^{\dagger}]$. We also have disjoint subsets $\{G_i : 1 \leq i \leq g\}$ of S that are "good" in the opposite sense: if $\mathbf{M}(t)$ hits a state in G_i at time t, the event F is less likely to occur in the remaining time interval $(t, t^{\dagger}]$.

The **Russian roulette technique** is applied when the sample path of the process $\{\mathbf{M}(t)\}$ hits a "good" subset G_i at time t: (a) The path is continued with probability $p_i(t)$, and it is terminated with probability $1-p_i(t)$ (so that the associated simulation outputs are discarded); (b) If the path is continued, its weight is increased by the factor $1/p_i(t)$ (so that the indicator function I_F for the event F is replaced by $I_F/p_i(t)$). The **splitting technique** is applied when the sample path of $\{\mathbf{M}(t)\}$ hits a "bad" subset B_i at time t: (a) The path is split into $s_i(t)$ separate paths, each of which continues in time independently of the others (conditional on the common history up to time t); (b) The weight of each path is decreased by the factor $1/s_i(t)$ (so that I_F is replaced by $I_F/s_i(t)$). Independent replications of this entire procedure can be used to construct point and interval estimators of the failure probability $\theta = \Pr\{F\}$. Using a fixed path-splitting scheme with every splitting factor $s_i(t) \equiv 5$, Kioussis and Miller obtained efficiencies in the range $1.67 \leq \eta(\hat{\theta}: \overline{Y}_n) \leq 2.50$ for a fault-tolerant computer system with four parallel processors.

Suppose that the time interval $[0, t^{\dagger}]$ for simulating the Markov process $\{\mathbf{M}(t)\}$ includes a (possibly random) peak-load period $[T_1, T_2]$ with response $Y_1 = \psi_1\{\mathbf{M}(t) : t \in [T_1, T_2]\}$ and complementary off-peak periods with response $Y_2 = \psi_2\{\mathbf{M}(t) : t \in [0, T_1) \cup (T_2, t^{\dagger}]\}$. Frequently the overall response $Y = Y_1 + Y_2$ is dominated by a "**rush-hour**" effect in the sense that Y_1 has larger mean and variance than Y_2. Thus the peak-load period makes the major contribution not only to the parameter $\theta = E(Y) = E(Y_1) + E(Y_2)$ but also to the distribution of any estimator for θ. To exploit this effect on each run, Fox and Glynn (1985a) applied splitting and Russian roulette respectively at the start and end of the peak-load period. Specifically each run consists of: (a) a single sample path over the subinterval $[0, T_1]$; (b) s paths over the peak-load period $[T_1, T_2]$ that are conditionally independent given the state $\mathbf{M}(T_1)$ reached at the end of the first subinterval; and (c) a single path continued beyond time T_2 to complete the final subinterval $[T_2, t^{\dagger}]$. To maximize the asymptotic efficiency of this procedure as the number of runs tends to infinity, Fox and Glynn developed an adaptive scheme for estimating the optimal splitting factor s^*.

In the context of steady-state simulation, Bayes (1972) applied dynamic importance sampling to estimate the probability of overloading in a teleprocessing computer system. Using a path-splitting scheme with optimized steady-state splitting factors $\{s_i(t) = s_i^* : \text{all } i, t\}$, Bayes obtained $\eta(\hat{\theta}: \overline{Y}_n) = 69.59$. Similarly, Hopmans and Kleijnen (1979) applied dynamic importance sampling in conjunction with regenerative analysis to estimate the proportion θ of calls coming into a telephone exchange that encounter a busy signal and thus are blocked (lost). Using an optimized path-splitting scheme, Hopmans and Kleijnen reported results in the range $0.859 \leq \eta(\hat{\theta}: \overline{Y}_n) \leq 1.06$; thus in some instances the net efficiency increase required by (5) was not achieved.

3.2. Conditional Monte Carlo

3.2.1. Classical Unconditioning, General Formulation. The conditional Monte Carlo technique was originally developed to estimate the conditional expectation of the response $Y = \psi(\mathbf{U})$ given a fixed value $\mathbf{x}_0$ for some auxiliary random vector $\mathbf{X} = \underset{\sim}{\beta}(\mathbf{U})$. When $\mathbf{X}$ is continuous, we have $\Pr\{\mathbf{X} = \mathbf{x}_0\} = 0$; and in this case direct simulation cannot be applied to the estimation of

$$\theta = E(Y \mid \mathbf{X} = \mathbf{x}_0) = \int_{I^m} \psi(\mathbf{u}) f_0(\mathbf{u} \mid \underset{\sim}{\beta}(\mathbf{u}) = \mathbf{x}_0)\, d\mathbf{u}\,. \tag{25}$$

To reformulate the estimand θ as an unconditional expectation taken with respect to the original input density $f_0(\cdot)$, the key step of conditional Monte Carlo consists of finding suitable spaces A, B together with an open set $C \subset I^m$ and a one-to-one, continuously differentiable map

$$\underset{\sim}{\omega} : \mathbf{u} \in C \rightarrow [\underset{\sim}{\alpha}(\mathbf{u}), \underset{\sim}{\beta}(\mathbf{u})] \in A \times B$$

such that: (a) the input vector $\mathbf{U} \sim f_0(\cdot)$ falls in C with probability one; and (b) the inverse map $\underset{\sim}{\tau} \equiv \underset{\sim}{\omega}^{-1} : \underset{\sim}{\omega}(C) \rightarrow C$ is also continuously differentiable. Now if we generate a random sample $\{\mathbf{U}_j : 1 \leq j \leq n\}$ from $f_0(\cdot)$ and apply the input transformation

$$\mathbf{T} : \mathbf{u} \in C \rightarrow \underset{\sim}{\tau}[\underset{\sim}{\alpha}(\mathbf{u}), \mathbf{x}_0] \in \underset{\sim}{\beta}^{-1}(\mathbf{x}_0)\,, \tag{26}$$

then the conditional Monte Carlo estimator of (25) is given by

$$\hat{\theta}_n = n^{-1} \sum_{j=1}^{n} \psi[\mathbf{T}(\mathbf{U}_j)] W(\mathbf{U}_j)\,,$$

where the weight function $W(\cdot)$ is chosen to satisfy (3). Note that the integrand in (25) vanishes outside the **importance region** $\underset{\sim}{\beta}^{-1}(\mathbf{x}_0) \equiv \{\mathbf{u} \in I^m : \underset{\sim}{\beta}(\mathbf{u}) = \mathbf{x}_0\}$. The transformation $\mathbf{T}(\cdot)$ essentially concentrates the sampling effort in this region, and the weight function $W(\cdot)$ compensates for the resulting distortion of the input distribution to yield an unbiased estimator for θ. Let $J_\tau(\mathbf{v}, \mathbf{x})$ denote the Jacobian of $\underset{\sim}{\tau}$ evaluated at the point $(\mathbf{v}, \mathbf{x}) \in A \times B$. Moreover, let $f_V(\mathbf{v})$ and $f_X(\mathbf{x})$ respectively denote the marginal densities of the random vectors $\mathbf{V} = \underset{\sim}{\alpha}(\mathbf{U})$ and $\mathbf{X} = \underset{\sim}{\beta}(\mathbf{U})$ when $\mathbf{U}$ is sampled from $f_0(\cdot)$. Granovsky (1981) showed that the variance of $\hat{\theta}_n$ is minimized by the optimal weight function

$$W^*(\mathbf{u}) = \frac{|\, J_\tau[\, \underset{\sim}{\alpha}(\mathbf{u}), \mathbf{x}_0] \,|}{f_V[\, \underset{\sim}{\alpha}(\mathbf{u})] f_X(\mathbf{x}_0)}, \qquad \mathbf{u} \in C\,. \tag{27}$$

Example. To clarify the essential features of this latest version of conditional Monte Carlo, we update the normal distribution-sampling application that prompted the development of the original conditional Monte Carlo method (Hammersley and Handscomb (1964), Section 6.4). Let $\mathbf{Z} = \{Z_i : 1 \le i \le m\}$ denote a random sample of size m from the standard normal distribution with the sample range $X \equiv \max_i\{Z_i\} - \min_i\{Z_i\}$. For a target event G defined by certain configurations of the sample $\mathbf{Z}$, let $I_G(\cdot)$ denote the corresponding indicator function

$$I_G(\mathbf{z}) = \begin{cases} 1 & \text{if the components } \{z_i\} \text{ yield event G} \\ 0 & \text{otherwise} \end{cases} .$$

Given a fixed value x_0 for the range, we seek to estimate the conditional probability of G. Thus the desired estimand may be expressed as $\theta = \Pr\{G \mid X{=}x_0\} = E[I_G(\mathbf{Z}) \mid X{=}x_0]$. A direct simulation estimator of θ would require generating standard normal samples of size m, rejecting each sample not having range x_0, and computing the percentage of unrejected samples that yield event G. Since rejection is certain for every sample, direct simulation is infeasible. To avoid the problems associated with a rejection method, conditional Monte Carlo seeks to transform every sample into one with the prespecified range x_0. Now the observed range X is a measure of scale; and the simplest appropriate transformation of the sample merely rescales each observation by the multiplier x_0/X. To obtain a statistic from the transformed sample that is a minimum variance unbiased estimator of θ, conditional Monte Carlo multiplies an appropriate weight function by the indicator function I_G for the transformed sample. In the rest of this subsection, we develop explicitly the rescaling transformation and the corresponding optimal weight function. The details of this development may be skipped on first reading without loss of continuity.

Let $\phi(z) \equiv (2\pi)^{\frac{1}{2}} \exp(-\frac{1}{2} z^2)$ and $\Phi(z) \equiv \int_{-\infty}^{z} \phi(t)dt$, $-\infty < z < \infty$, respectively denote the probability density function and cumulative distribution function of the standard normal distribution. If we use the inverse transform method to sample from this distribution, then we have

$$\mathbf{Z} = \underset{\sim}{\varsigma}(\mathbf{U}) \equiv [\Phi^{-1}(U_1), \ldots, \Phi^{-1}(U_m)] \quad \text{with } \mathbf{U} \sim f_0(\cdot) .$$

(The specific method for generating $\mathbf{Z}$ is irrelevant to the application; we chose the inverse transform method merely for the sake of simplicity and concreteness.) Within the current framework for conditional Monte Carlo, $Y = \psi(\mathbf{U}) = I_G[\underset{\sim}{\varsigma}(\mathbf{U})]$ represents the simulation response as an explicit function of its input; and the auxiliary variate has the form $X = \beta(\mathbf{U}) = \max_i\{\Phi^{-1}(U_i)\} - \min_i\{\Phi^{-1}(U_i)\}$.

The obvious choice for B is the space of X: $B \equiv \{x \in R^1 : x > 0\}$. (We exclude the origin for reasons that will become immediately apparent.) Now the scale-invariant properties of the random sample $\mathbf{Z}$ are preserved in the "standardized" sample $\mathbf{Z}/X$; and this suggests using the map $\underset{\sim}{\alpha}(\mathbf{u}) = \underset{\sim}{\varsigma}(\mathbf{u})/\beta(\mathbf{u})$ from I^m into the (m-1)-dimensional space

$$A \equiv \{\mathbf{v} = [v_1, \ldots, v_m] \in R^m : \max_i(v_i) - \min_i(v_i) = 1\} .$$

Thus the map

$$\underset{\sim}{\omega} : \mathbf{u} \in I^m - \beta^{-1}(0) \rightarrow [\underset{\sim}{\varsigma}(\mathbf{u})/\beta(\mathbf{u}), \beta(\mathbf{u})] \in A \times B$$

has inverse

$$\underset{\sim}{\tau} : (\mathbf{v}, x) \in A \times B \rightarrow [\Phi(v_1 x), \ldots, \Phi(v_m x)] \in I^m - \beta^{-1}(0) .$$

In seeking an appropriate open set $C \subset I^m$, we observe that the definition of $\underset{\sim}{\omega}$ requires C to be a subset of $I^m - \beta^{-1}(0) = \{\mathbf{u} \in I^m : u_i \neq u_j$ for **some** $i \neq j\}$. To complete the specification of C, we look for relevant restrictions on the inverse mapping $\underset{\sim}{\tau}$. In particular, to avoid difficulties in the computation given below for the Jacobian $J_\tau(\mathbf{v}, x)$ of $\underset{\sim}{\tau}$ at the point $(\mathbf{v}, x) \in A \times B$, we must exclude points at which two or more of the components of $\mathbf{v}$ are equal; and it follows that we should take $C \equiv \{\mathbf{u} \in I^m : u_i \neq u_j$ for **all** $i \neq j\}$. Clearly C is an open subset of I^m with $\Pr\{\mathbf{U} \in C\} = 1$. Moreover, the restriction $\underset{\sim}{\omega} : C \rightarrow \underset{\sim}{\omega}(C)$ is one-to-one and continuously differentiable with continuously differentiable inverse. Therefore the input transformation $\mathbf{T}(\cdot)$ defined by (26) has the form

$$\mathbf{T}(\mathbf{u}) = \left[\Phi\left\{\frac{x_0}{\beta(\mathbf{u})}\Phi^{-1}(u_1)\right\}, \ldots, \Phi\left\{\frac{x_0}{\beta(\mathbf{u})}\Phi^{-1}(u_m)\right\}\right], \quad \mathbf{u} \in C, \tag{28}$$

and the associated simulation response is

$$\psi[\mathbf{T}(\mathbf{u})] = I_G\left[\frac{x_0}{\beta(\mathbf{u})}\Phi^{-1}(u_1), \ldots, \frac{x_0}{\beta(\mathbf{u})}\Phi^{-1}(u_m)\right], \quad \mathbf{u} \in C .$$

To determine the corresponding optimal weight $W^*(\mathbf{u})$, we must first compute the Jacobian $J_\tau(\mathbf{v}, x)$ for all $(\mathbf{v}, x) \in \underset{\sim}{\omega}(C)$ and then find the marginal densities of $\mathbf{V} = \underset{\sim}{\varsigma}(\mathbf{U})/\beta(\mathbf{U})$ and $X = \beta(\mathbf{U})$.

Given $(\mathbf{v}, x) \in \underset{\sim}{\omega}(C)$, we know that all of the components $\{v_i\}$ are different. For the sake of definiteness, we suppose that $v_1 < v_2 < \cdots < v_{m-1} < v_m$ so the constraint $v_m = v_1 + 1$ applies. In this case, there is a neighborhood $N^o(\mathbf{v}, x)$ of $(\mathbf{v}, x)$ in the space $A \times B$ where the components of each point have the same relative rankings and satisfy the same constraint as for $(\mathbf{v}, x)$; thus when $(\mathbf{a}, b) = ([a_1, \ldots, a_m], b) \in N^o(\mathbf{v}, x)$, we have $a_1 < \cdots < a_{m-1} < a_m$ and $a_m = a_1 + 1$. In this neighborhood we may therefore take $[a_1, \ldots, a_{m-1}, b]$ as the free arguments of the transformation $\underset{\sim}{\tau}$:

$$\underset{\sim}{\tau}(\mathbf{a}, b) = [\Phi(a_1 b), \ldots, \Phi(a_{m-1} b), \Phi\{(a_1+1)b\}] \quad \text{for all } (\mathbf{a}, b) \in N^o(\mathbf{v}, x) .$$

It follows that the Jacobian of $\underset{\sim}{\tau}$ evaluated at the point $(\mathbf{v}, x)$ is

$$J_\tau(\mathbf{v}, x) = \det \begin{bmatrix} x\phi(v_1 x) & 0 & \cdots & 0 & v_1\phi(v_1 x) \\ 0 & x\phi(v_2 x) & \cdots & 0 & v_2\phi(v_2 x) \\ \cdot & \cdot & & \cdot & \cdot \\ \cdot & & \cdot & \cdot & \cdot \\ \cdot & & \cdot & \cdot & \cdot \\ 0 & 0 & \cdots & x\phi(v_{m-1}x) & \\ x\phi(v_m x) & 0 & \cdots & 0 & v_m\phi(v_m x) \end{bmatrix}$$

$$= (2\pi)^{-m/2} x^{m-1} \exp\left(-\frac{1}{2}\sum_{i=1}^{m} v_i^2 x^2\right), \quad (\mathbf{v}, x) \in \underset{\sim}{\omega}(C) . \tag{29}$$

Note that if $(\mathbf{v}, x) \in A \times B - \underset{\sim}{\omega}(C)$, then $v_j = v_k$ for some $j \neq k$ $(1 \leq j, k \leq m)$; and in this case there is no clear-cut definition for the corresponding partial derivatives $\partial\tau_i/\partial v_j$ and $\partial\tau_i/\partial v_k$. We avoid such anomalies by our choice of C. The same expression (29) is obtained at every point $(\mathbf{v}, x) \in \underset{\sim}{\omega}(C)$, regardless of the relative rankings of the components of $\mathbf{v}$.

By the change of variables formula (Bickel and Doksum (1977), equation 1.2.3), $\mathbf{V}$ and X have the joint density

$$f_{VX}(\mathbf{v}, x) = f_0[\underset{\sim}{\tau}(\mathbf{v}, x)] \mid J_\tau(\mathbf{v}, x) \mid$$

$$= (2\pi)^{-m/2} x^{m-1} \exp\left(-\frac{1}{2} \sum_{i=1}^{m} v_i^2 x^2 \right), \qquad (\mathbf{v}, x) \in A \times B .$$

(We can extend the domain of f_{VX} from $\underset{\sim}{\omega}(C)$ to all of $A \times B$ since the integral of f_{VX} over the "bad" set $A \times B - \underset{\sim}{\omega}(C)$ is zero.) Thus the marginal density of $\mathbf{V}$ is given by

$$f_V(\mathbf{v}) = \int_B f_{VX}(\mathbf{v}, x)\, dx = \frac{1}{2} \Gamma(m/2) \left(\pi \sum_{i=1}^{n} v_i^2 \right)^{-m/2}, \qquad \mathbf{v} \in A . \quad (30)$$

The marginal density of the sample range X has the asymptotic expansion

$$f_X(x) \sim \frac{m(m-1)\pi^{\frac{1}{2}} \phi^2(x)[2\Phi(x)-1]^{m-\frac{3}{2}}}{[2\Phi(x) - 1 + (m-2)x\phi(x)]^{\frac{1}{2}}}, \qquad x \in B \quad (31)$$

(David (1981), equation (9.4.6)). Inserting (28), (29), (30) and (31) into (27), we see that the optimal weight is given by

$$W^*(\mathbf{u}) = \frac{2\left[\dfrac{x_0}{\beta(\mathbf{u})} \right]^m \exp\left\{ -\dfrac{1}{2} \displaystyle\sum_{i=1}^{m} \left[\dfrac{x_0}{\beta(\mathbf{u})} \Phi^{-1}(u_i) \right]^2 \right\}}{\Gamma(m/2) x_0 \left\{ \dfrac{1}{2} \displaystyle\sum_{i=1}^{m} [\Phi^{-1}(u_i)]^2 \right\}^{-m/2} f_X(x_0)}, \qquad \mathbf{u} \in C .$$

Recapitulation. Our discussion of classical conditional Monte Carlo conforms to Granovsky's (1981) formulation, which is not only more accessible but also more efficient than previous approaches. This technique is crucial to the success of many distribution-sampling studies, and thus there is a need for clear-cut guidelines regarding the application of the method. Although our example is offered as a first step in this direction, it is not comprehensive in scope. Perhaps a set of prototype problems can be assembled to illustrate the relevant principles governing the use of classical conditional Monte Carlo. Moreover, further theoretical development of this technique is a challenging research problem. As in the case of the antithetic-variates technique, no methods are currently available for constructing optimal transformations of the input random vector $\mathbf{U} \sim f_0(\cdot)$. Granovsky's analysis yields the optimal weight function $W^*(\cdot)$ corresponding to a particular (usually nonoptimal) input transformation $\mathbf{T}(\cdot)$ of the form (26); perhaps his approach can be extended to yield an optimal transformation $\mathbf{T}^*(\cdot)$ that minimizes $\mathrm{Var}\{\psi[\mathbf{T}(\mathbf{U})]W^*(\mathbf{U})\}$ over all $\mathbf{T}(\cdot)$ satisfying the following constraints: (a) $\not{\beta}[\mathbf{T}(\mathbf{U})] = \mathbf{x}_0$ with probability one; and (b) $E\{\psi[\mathbf{T}(\mathbf{U})]W^*(\mathbf{U})\} = \theta$ as prescribed by (25).

3.2.2. Conditional Expectations. In recent years the terms **conditional Monte Carlo** and **method of conditional expectations** have been used to refer to a class of specialized techniques for which we obtain a more precise estimator of an unconditional expectation $\theta = E(Y)$ by conditioning on an appropriate auxiliary variate $\mathbf{X} = \not{\beta}(\mathbf{U})$ at some stage in the estimation procedure; see Bratley, Fox and Schrage (1983). The double expectation theorem (Bickel and Doksum (1977)) ensures that the new response

$$Y^{\circ} \equiv E(Y \mid \mathbf{X}) \equiv \psi^{\circ}(\mathbf{U}) \equiv E[Y \mid \not{\beta}(\mathbf{U})]$$

is unbiased. Moreover, the variance decomposition

$$\mathrm{Var}(Y) = \mathrm{Var}[\, E(Y \mid \mathbf{X}) \,] + E[\, \mathrm{Var}(Y \mid \mathbf{X}) \,]$$

reveals that $\mathrm{Var}(Y^{\circ}) < \mathrm{Var}(Y)$ unless Y has a strict functional dependence on $\mathbf{X}$ (that is, unless $\mathrm{Var}(Y \mid \mathbf{X}) = 0$ with probability one). Thus with n independent replications of the pair $(Y, \mathbf{X})$, the corresponding conditional Monte Carlo estimator $\hat{\theta}_n = \overline{Y}^{\circ}_n$ is more precise than the direct simulation estimator $\overline{Y}_n$:

$$\mathrm{Var}(\hat{\theta}_n) = \mathrm{Var}(Y^{\circ})/n < \mathrm{Var}(\overline{Y}_n) \,. \tag{32}$$

However, when the pairs $\{(Y_j, \mathbf{X}_j) : 1 \leq j \leq n\}$ are not independent, the left-hand equality in relation (32) breaks down and variance increases can occur.

Conditional expectations can be used effectively in simulating Markov and semi-Markov processes. To estimate the first-passage distribution for a Markov process, Ross and Schechner (1985) proposed conditioning on the history of the process in order to compute the **observed hazards.** Although such conditioning must be taken with respect to correlated variates, Ross and Schechner proved that this approach yields a variance reduction. For a continuous-time, uniformizable Markov chain $\{\mathbf{M}(t) : t \geq 0\}$, Fox and Glynn (1985b) sought to estimate the expectation of a general time integral over a finite horizon $t^\dagger$:

$$\theta = E(Y) \text{ and } Y = \int_0^{t^\dagger} \psi[\mathbf{M}(t)]\, dG(t) .$$

To replace the direct-simulation estimator Y, Fox and Glynn subordinated $\{\mathbf{M}(t) : 0 \leq t \leq t^\dagger\}$ to a Poisson process $\{N(t) : 0 \leq t \leq t^\dagger\}$ and then derived the conditional expectation of Y given both the sequence of states visited and the number of transitions $N(t^\dagger)$ in the embedded chain with null transitions. For a positive recurrent semi-Markov process $\{\mathbf{M}(t) : t \geq 0\}$, Fox and Glynn (1985c) sought to estimate the long-run time average

$$\theta = \lim_{t\to\infty} t^{-1} E\left\{ \int_0^t \psi[\mathbf{M}(w)]\, dw \right\}$$

with the regenerative method of simulation analysis. By conditioning on the sequence of states visited in the embedded Markov chain, Fox and Glynn converted the estimation problem to discrete time and simultaneously reduced the variance of the regenerative estimator for θ.

Although the method of conditional expectations has been successfully applied in many distribution-sampling studies (Simon (1976)), it can be difficult to implement in complex discrete-event simulations. In particular, it is generally difficult to identify an auxiliary variable $\mathbf{X}$ on which to condition so that $E(Y|\mathbf{X})$ can be evaluated analytically or numerically. Even when it is feasible to evaluate $E(Y|\mathbf{X})$, the associated computing overhead can be relatively large (Carter and Ignall (1975)). Finally, no general techniques are currently available for ensuring a variance reduction when conditioning on a correlated process. As a result of these problems, the method of conditional expectations may yield unacceptably low efficiency (4) when it is applied to a discrete-event simulation.

3.3. Stratified Sampling

3.3.1. Prestratification. In some instances the effective use of an auxiliary variate $\mathbf{X} = \mathcal{B}(\mathbf{U})$ to estimate $\theta = E(Y)$ may require partitioning the space of $\mathbf{X}$ into, say, L strata $\{S_h : 1 \leq h \leq L\}$ with **known** weights

$$\pi_h \equiv \Pr\{\mathbf{X} \in S_h\} = \int_{\mathcal{B}^{-1}(S_h)} f_0(\mathbf{u})\, d\mathbf{u}, \quad 1 \leq h \leq L .$$

If in stratum h we randomly sample n_h pairs $\{(Y_{hj}, \mathbf{X}_{hj}) : 1 \leq j \leq n_h\}$ (where n_h is fixed in advance) and calculate the associated mean response

$$\overline{Y}_h = n_h^{-1} \sum_{j=1}^{n_h} Y_{hj} \qquad \text{for } 1 \leq h \leq L ,$$

then the prestratified estimator of θ is given by

$$\hat{\theta}_n = \sum_{h=1}^{L} \pi_h \overline{Y}_h .$$

In effect we are forcing a random sample of n_h inputs $\{\mathbf{U}_j\}$ to fall in the subregion $\mathcal{B}^{-1}(S_h)$ of I^m. Let

$$\mu_{Yh} \equiv E(Y \mid \mathbf{X} \in S_h) \quad \text{and} \quad \sigma_{Yh}^2 \equiv E(Y^2 \mid \mathbf{X} \in S_h) - \mu_{Yh}^2$$

respectively denote the mean and variance of the response Y within the hth stratum, and let

$$\overline{\sigma}_Y \equiv \sum_{h=1}^{L} \pi_h \sigma_{Yh} .$$

With the **optimal allocation** $n_h^* = n\pi_h\sigma_{Yh}/\overline{\sigma}_Y$ for $1 \leq h \leq L$, the variance of the corresponding prestratified estimator $\hat{\theta}_n^*$ is minimized:

$$\mathrm{Var}(\hat{\theta}_n^*) = n^{-1} \left\{ \mathrm{Var}(Y) - \sum_{h=1}^{L} \pi_h \left[(\mu_{Yh} - \theta)^2 + (\sigma_{Yh} - \overline{\sigma}_Y)^2 \right] \right\} .$$

Unfortunately the within-stratum variances $\{\sigma_{Yh}^2 : 1 \leq h \leq L\}$ are usually unknown so that the optimal allocation cannot be used. With the **proportional allocation** $n_h^\circ \equiv n\pi_h$ for $1 \leq h \leq L$, the variance of the corresponding prestratified estimator $\hat{\theta}_n^\circ$ is

$$\mathrm{Var}(\hat{\theta}_n^o) = n^{-1}\left[\mathrm{Var}(Y) - \sum_{h=1}^{L} \pi_h(\mu_{Yh} - \theta)^2 \right]. \tag{33}$$

See Cochran (1977) for a comprehensive treatment of prestratification. Fox and Glynn (1985b) recently developed methods for prestratified generation of a Poisson process.

3.3.2. Poststratification. Prestratification is sometimes awkward to implement in discrete-event simulation. By contrast, poststratification merely requires the experimenter to make n independent replications of his original simulation model in order to generate a random sample $\{(Y_j, \mathbf{X}_j) : 1 \le j \le n\}$ of size n. **After** the jth replication, the observed auxiliary variate $\mathbf{X}_j$ is used to classify the corresponding response Y_j into its appropriate stratum. Let $\{Y_{hj} : 1 \le j \le N_h\}$ denote the subsample of random size N_h falling in stratum h, $1 \le h \le L$. Subject to the condition that all strata are nonempty (that is, $N_h > 0$ for $1 \le h \le L$), the poststratified estimator for θ

$$\hat{\theta}_n = \sum_{h=1}^{L} \pi_h \left(N_h^{-1} \sum_{j=1}^{N_h} Y_{hj} \right)$$

is unbiased with variance

$$\mathrm{Var}(\hat{\theta}_n) = n^{-1} \sum_{h=1}^{L} [\pi_h + (1-\pi_h)/n]\sigma_{Yh}^2 \quad + \quad o(n^{-2}) \tag{34}$$

(see Section 5A.9 of Cochran (1977)). After some manipulation of (33) and (34), we see that the efficiency of poststratification is asymptotically equivalent to that of prestratification with proportional allocation. Wilson and Pritsker (1984a, b) developed poststratified point and interval estimators for the regenerative method of simulation analysis as well as for the method of independent replications.

3.4. Systematic Sampling

3.4.1. Static Systematic Sampling. Based on a partition of the input domain I^m into n directly congruent strata $\{S_j\}$, systematic sampling requires the selection of a single observation from each stratum. Although this technique appears to resemble stratified sampling, it does not involve a separate randomization within each stratum. Once the first sample point $\mathbf{U}_1 \in S_1$ is determined, all of the other points $\{\mathbf{U}_j \in S_j : 2 \leq j \leq n\}$ are chosen to occupy the same relative position within their respective strata. The systematic sampling estimator of θ is

$$\hat{\theta}_n = n^{-1} \sum_{j=1}^{n} \psi(\mathbf{U}_j) .$$

This technique is attractive because it is both simpler and easier to implement than the other importance methods.

In the context of a distribution sampling experiment with univariate input (that is, with m = 1), Fishman and Huang (1983) performed a comprehensive analysis of a variant of systematic sampling that they called **"rotation sampling."** For a fixed replication count n, this technique involves the following steps:

(a) choose a set of rotation angles $\{\omega_j : 1 \leq j \leq n\}$ satisfying $0 \leq \omega_j \leq \omega_{j+1} \leq 1$ for $1 \leq j \leq n-1$;

(b) generate a single random number U;

(c) take the translation modulo 1 of U by ω_j to obtain the jth input variate:

$$U_j \equiv U \oplus \omega_j \equiv \begin{cases} U + \omega_j & \text{if } U + \omega_j \leq 1 \\ U + \omega_j - 1 & \text{if } U + \omega_j > 1 \end{cases} \quad 1 \leq j \leq n; \quad \text{and}$$

(d) average the corresponding outputs to obtain the rotation sampling estimator for θ:

$$\hat{\theta}_n = n^{-1} \sum_{j=1}^{n} \psi(U_j) = n^{-1} \sum_{j=1}^{n} \psi(U \oplus \omega_j) . \tag{35}$$

Using the regularly spaced angles of rotation

$$\omega_j^o \equiv (j-1)/n \qquad \text{for } 1 \leq j \leq n , \tag{36}$$

Fishman and Huang showed that the corresponding rotation sampling estimator $\hat{\theta}_n^o$ has the following properties in a wide variety of distribution sampling applications:

$$\text{Var}(\hat{\theta}_n^o) = O(n^{-2}) \tag{37}$$

$$E[C^{\dagger}(\hat{\theta}_n^o)] = O(n) \tag{38}$$

$$\Rightarrow 1/\eta(\hat{\theta}_n^o : \overline{Y}_n) = O(n^{-1}) . \tag{39}$$

Although rotation sampling in its most general form (35) can properly be regarded as a special case of antithetic variates, the sampling scheme prescribed by (36) clearly employs the principle of systematic selection and thus possesses the characteristics typical of systematic sampling plans (Cochran (1977)).

3.4.2. Dynamic Systematic Sampling. In the simulation of an ergodic Markov chain with rewards, Fishman (1983a, b) applied systematic sampling at each time step to estimate the mean reward accumulated during the first passage between two specified states. To generate n parallel correlated replications of a given chain, Fishman proposed that all of the state transitions starting from state s at time i should be simulated with a single independent random number U_{si}. If K_{si} denotes the number of replications of the chain that reside in state s at time i, then the next transition of the jth such replication is sampled using the random number input $U_{sij} = U_{si} \oplus [(j-1)/K_{si}]$ for $1 \leq j \leq K_{si}$. In a broad class of infinite-state Markov chains, Fishman established the following properties of the resulting rotation sampling estimator $\hat{\theta}_n^{\circ}$ and its associated computing time $C^{\dagger}(\hat{\theta}_n^{\circ})$:

$$\mathrm{Var}(\hat{\theta}_n^{\circ}) = O\{[\ln(n)]^4/n^2\} \tag{40}$$

$$E[C^{\dagger}(\hat{\theta}_n^{\circ})] = O\{[\ln(n)]^2\} \tag{41}$$

$$\Rightarrow 1/\eta(\hat{\theta}_n^{\circ}: \overline{Y}_n) = O\{[\ln(n)]^6/n^2\} = o(n^{-1}) \,. \tag{42}$$

Relations (37) through (39) and (40) through (42) are remarkable results. Clearly systematic sampling merits further attention from researchers and practitioners alike.

4. A NEW ANALYTICAL FRAMEWORK FOR VARIANCE REDUCTION

To identify a set of elemental concepts from which all variance reduction techniques are composed, Nelson and Schmeiser (1983; 1984a, b, c) began with a model of any simulation experiment as a triple of probability spaces related by (measurable) mappings that represent the simulation processing logic for converting inputs to outputs and for converting outputs to a final vector of system performance estimators. We assume that a p-dimensional vector $\underset{\sim}{\theta} = [\theta_1, \ldots, \theta_p]$ of system performance parameters is to be estimated using a simulation model that is driven by k scalar input processes and that generates ℓ scalar output processes. In contrast to the setup used in previous sections of this paper, the input processes used by Nelson and Schmeiser are not merely composed of independent random numbers; moreover, these input processes are not generally of finite length.

The Probability Space of Inputs. Let X_{ij} denote the ith variate sampled from the jth input process ($i \geq 1$, $1 \leq j \leq k$), and let $\mathbf{X}_i \equiv [X_{i1}, ..., X_{ik}]$. Then the family of random vectors $\mathbf{X} \equiv \{\mathbf{X}_i : i \geq 1\}$ determines a probability measure $P_X(\cdot)$ on (the Borel field $\mathfrak{B}^{\infty}$ of Borel sets of) infinite-dimensional Euclidean space R^{∞}. A suitable method is assumed to be available for generating $\mathbf{X}$ according to the probability law P_X. The triple $(R^{\infty}, \mathfrak{B}^{\infty}, P_X)$ is the probability space for the inputs to the simulation experiment.

The Probability Space of Outputs. Let Y_{ij} denote the ith variate generated by the jth output process ($i \geq 1$, $1 \leq j \leq \ell$), and let $\mathbf{Y}_i \equiv [Y_{i1}, ..., Y_{i\ell}]$. If we take $\mathbf{Y} \equiv \{\mathbf{Y}_i : i \geq 1\}$, then the mechanism by which the simulation generates outputs from its inputs can be represented as follows:

$$\mathbf{Y} = \underset{\sim}{\psi}(\mathbf{X}) \quad \text{and} \quad \mathbf{n}^{\dagger} = [n_1^{\dagger}, ..., n_{\ell}^{\dagger}] = \underset{\sim}{\nu}(\mathbf{X}),$$

where $n_j^{\dagger} = \nu_j(\mathbf{X})$ denotes the simulation **stopping time** for the jth output process, $1 \leq j \leq \ell$. Let N denote the set of positive integers and let $\mathfrak{B}^{o}$ denote the Borel field of Borel sets of the Cartesian product $R^{\infty} \times N^{\ell}$. Then the pair $(\mathbf{Y}, \mathbf{n}^{\dagger})$ determines a probability measure $P^{o}(\cdot)$ (on $\mathfrak{B}^{o}$). The probability space for the outputs of the simulation experiment is represented by the triple $(R^{\infty} \times N^{\ell}, \mathfrak{B}^{o}, P^{o})$.

The Probability Space of Performance Statistics. As an estimator for $\underset{\sim}{\theta}$, the vector $\mathbf{Z} = [Z_1, ..., Z_p]$ is computed from a set of arguments $\mathbf{Y}^{o}$ constituting a subset of the final outputs:

$$\mathbf{Y}^{o} \subset \{Y_{ij} : 1 \leq j \leq \ell, \ 1 \leq i \leq n_j^{\dagger}\} \ \text{and} \ \mathbf{Z} = \mathbf{h}(\mathbf{Y}^{o}).$$

Thus $\mathbf{Z}$ induces a probability measure $P_Z(\cdot)$ on (the Borel field $\mathfrak{B}^{p}$ of Borel sets of) R^p. The triple $(R^p, \mathfrak{B}^p, P_Z)$ is the probability space of system performance statistics for the simulation experiment.

The overall probabilistic model for the simulation experiment $S(\underset{\sim}{\theta})$ with target estimand $\underset{\sim}{\theta}$ may be summarized by the following diagram:

$$S(\underset{\sim}{\theta}) : (R^{\infty}, \mathfrak{B}^{\infty}, P_X) \xrightarrow{(\underset{\sim}{\psi}, \underset{\sim}{\nu})} (R^{\infty} \times N^{\ell}, \mathfrak{B}^{o}, P^{o}) \xrightarrow{h} (R^p, \mathfrak{B}^p, P_Z).$$

The Basic Transformations of Variance Reduction. Within the framework established by Nelson and Schmeiser, effective variance reduction amounts to finding a transformation T from the original experiment $S(\underset{\sim}{\theta})$ to a new experiment $S^{\#}(\underset{\sim}{\theta})$ such that the associated statistic $\mathbf{Z}^{\#}$ is a more efficient estimator of $\underset{\sim}{\theta}$ than the original statistic **Z**. Nelson and Schmeiser showed that any such transformation $T : S(\underset{\sim}{\theta}) \rightarrow S^{\#}(\underset{\sim}{\theta})$ is a composition of elemental transformations from the following mutually exclusive and exhaustive classes:

I. **Transformations of the input space** $(R^{\infty}, \mathfrak{B}^{\infty}, P_X)$.

   A. **Distribution replacement (DR):** Redefine univariate marginal distributions of P_X without altering any statistical dependencies.

   B. **Dependence induction (DI):** Redefine statistical dependencies without altering any univariate marginals of P_X.

II. **Transformations of the output space** $(R^{\infty} \times N^{\ell}, \mathfrak{B}^{o}, P^{o})$.

   A. **Equivalent allocation (EA):** Redefine the outputs $\mathbf{Y} = \underset{\sim}{\psi}(\mathbf{X})$ without redefining the stopping times $\mathbf{n}^{\dagger} = \underset{\sim}{\nu}(\mathbf{X})$.

   B. **Sample allocation (SA):** Redefine the stopping times $\mathbf{n}^{\dagger} = \underset{\sim}{\nu}(\mathbf{X})$ without redefining the outputs $\mathbf{Y} = \underset{\sim}{\psi}(\mathbf{X})$.

III. **Transformations of the statistics space** $(R^p, \mathfrak{B}^p, P_Z)$.

   A. **Auxiliary information (AI):** Redefine the argument set $\mathbf{Y}^{o}$ of the statistic $\mathbf{Z} = \mathbf{h}(\mathbf{Y}^{o})$ without altering its functional form.

   B. **Equivalent information (EI):** Redefine the functional form $\mathbf{h}(\cdot)$ of the statistic $\mathbf{Z} = \mathbf{h}(\mathbf{Y}^{o})$ without altering its argument set $\mathbf{Y}^{o}$.

It is hoped that the use of this framework will stimulate the synthesis of new VRTs in situations where conventional approaches cannot be used effectively.

5. SUMMARY AND CONCLUSIONS

Several directions for future research have been outlined in this paper. Because it has the greatest potential impact on actual practice, research should continue on correlation induction strategies for large-scale simulation experiments using common random numbers and antithetic variates. In particular, we need new statistical techniques for experimental design and analysis that are based on less restrictive assumptions than either classical analysis of variance or the Schruben-Margolin approach; moreover, we require a means to validate the assumptions underlying the new analysis techniques. For both the general method of antithetic variates and classical conditional Monte Carlo, we need computationally feasible procedures to construct optimal (or improved) input transformations. Researchers working on the method of conditional expectations should formulate general test criteria sufficient to ensure that conditioning taken with respect to a correlated process will yield a variance reduction. Finally, the ramifications of the variance-reduction framework outlined in Section 4 should be thoroughly investigated with the following dual objectives: (a) the composition of fundamentally new techniques for improving the efficiency of simulated experimentation; and (b) the development of simulation software that facilitates the effective application of appropriate variance reduction techniques in practical problems.

ACKNOWLEDGMENT

The author has benefited from the suggestions of Edward Dudewicz, Pandu Tadikamalla and the referees as well as from discussions with George Fishman, Bennett Fox, Jack Kleijnen, Barry Nelson, Ardavan Nozari, Acacio Porta Nova, Bruce Schmeiser, Lee Schruben, Jeff Tew and Sekhar Venkatraman.

REFERENCES

Anderson, T.W. (1958). *An Introduction to Multivariate Statistical Analysis.* John Wiley & Sons, New York.

Bayes, A.J. (1972). A minimum variance sampling technique for simulation models. *Journal of the Association for Computing Machinery, 19,* 734-741.

Berger, J.O. (1980). *Statistical Decision Theory: Foundations, Concepts, and Methods.* Springer-Verlag, New York.

Bickel, P.J. and Doksum, K.A. (1977). *Mathematical Statistics: Basic Ideas and Selected Topics.* Holden-Day, Inc., San Francisco, California.

Bratley, P., Fox, B.L. and Schrage, L.E. (1983). *A Guide to Simulation.* Springer-Verlag, New York.

Carter, G. and Ignall, E.J. (1975). Virtual measures: a variance reduction technique for simulation. *Management Science, 21,* 607-616.

Cheng, R.C.H. (1981). The use of antithetic control variates in computer simulations. *Proceedings of the 1981 Winter Simulation Conference.* Institute of Electrical and Electronic Engineers, Atlanta, Georgia, 313-318.

Cheng, R.C.H. (1982). The use of antithetic variates in computer simulations. *Journal of the Operational Research Society, 33,* 229-237.

Cheng, R.C.H. (1983). Random samples with known sample statistics: with application to variance reduction. *Proceedings of the 1983 Winter Simulation Conference.* Institute of Electrical and Electronic Engineers, Washington, D.C., 395-400.

Cheng, R.C.H. (1984). Antithetic variate methods for simulation of processes with peaks and troughs. *European Journal of Operational Research, 15,* 227-236.

Cheng, R.C.H. and Feast, G.M. (1980). Control variables with known mean and variance. *Journal of the Operational Research Society, 31,* 51-56.

Cochran, W.G. (1977). *Sampling Techniques,* Third Edition. John Wiley & Sons, New York.

David, H.A. (1981). *Order Statistics,* Second Edition. John Wiley & Sons, New York.

Efron, B. (1982). *The Jackknife, the Bootstrap and Other Resampling*

Plans. Society for Industrial and Applied Mathematics, Philadelphia, Pennsylvania.

Fishman, G.S. (1983a). Accelerated accuracy in the simulation of Markov chains. *Operations Research, 31,* 466-487.

Fishman, G.S. (1983b). Accelerated convergence in the simulation of countably infinite state Markov chains. *Operations Research, 31,* 1074-1089.

Fishman, G.S. and Huang, B.D. (1983). Antithetic variates revisited. *Communications of the ACM, 26,* 964-971.

Fox, B.L. and Glynn, P.W. (1985a). Efficient rush-hour simulation. *Technical Report,* Departement d'informatique et de recherche operationelle, Universite de Montreal, Montreal, Canada.

Fox, B.L. and Glynn, P.W. (1985b). Discrete-time conversion for finite-horizon Markov processes. *Technical Report,* Departement d'informatique et de recherche operationelle, Universite de Montreal, Montreal, Canada.

Fox, B.L. and Glynn, P.W. (1985c). Discrete-time conversion for simulating semi-Markov processes. *Technical Report,* Departement d'informatique et de recherche operationelle, Universite de Montreal, Montreal, Canada.

Gal, S., Rubinstein, R.Y. and Ziv, A. (1981). On the optimality and efficiency of common random numbers. *Technical Report,* IBM Israel Scientific Center, Haifa, Israel.

Granovsky, B.L. (1981). Optimal formulae of the conditional Monte Carlo. *SIAM Journal on Algebraic and Discrete Methods, 2,* 289-294.

Grant, F.H. and Solberg, J.J. (1983). Variance reduction techniques in stochastic shortest route analysis: application procedures and results. *Mathematics and Computers in Simulation, XXV,* 366-375.

Hadley, G. (1973). *Linear Algebra.* Addison-Wesley Publishing Company, Reading, Massachusetts.

Hammersley, J.M. and Handscomb, D.C. (1964). *Monte Carlo Methods.* Methuen & Co. Ltd., London.

Hopmans, A.C.M. and Kleijnen, J.P.C. (1979). Importance sampling in systems simulation: a practical failure? *Mathematics and Computers in Simulation, XXI,* 209-220.

Kioussis, L.C. and Miller, D.R. (1983). An importance sampling scheme for simulating the degradation and failure of complex systems during finite missions. *Proceedings of the 1983 Winter Simulation Conference.*

Institute of Electrical and Electronic Engineers, Washington, D.C., 631-639.

Kleijnen, J.P.C. (1974). *Statistical Techniques in Simulation, Part I.* Marcel Dekker, New York.

Kleijnen, J.P.C. (1975). *Statistical Techniques in Simulation, Part II.* Marcel Dekker, New York.

Kohlas, J. (1982). *Stochastic Methods of Operations Research.* Cambridge University Press, Cambridge.

Lavenberg, S.S. and Welch, P.D. (1981). A perspective on the use of control variables to increase the efficiency of Monte Carlo simulations. *Management Science, 27,* 322-335.

Lavenberg, S.S., Moeller, T.L. and Welch, P.D. (1982). Statistical results on control variables with application to queueing network simulation. *Operations Research, 30,* 182-202.

Mihram, G.A. (1974). Blocking in simular experimental designs. *Journal of Statistical Computation and Simulation, 3,* 29-32.

Nelson, B.L. and Schmeiser, B.W. (1983). Variance reduction: basic transformations. *Proceedings of the 1983 Winter Simulation Conference.* Institute of Electrical and Electronic Engineers, Washington, D.C., 255-258.

Nelson, B.L. and Schmeiser, B.W. (1984a). A mathematical-statistical framework for variance reduction, part I: simulation experiments. *Research Memorandum 84-4,* School of Industrial Engineering, Purdue University, West Lafayette, Indiana.

Nelson, B.L. and Schmeiser, B.W. (1984b). A mathematical-statistical framework for variance reduction, part II: classes of transformations. *Research Memorandum 84-5,* School of Industrial Engineering, Purdue University, West Lafayette, Indiana.

Nelson, B.L. and Schmeiser, B.W. (1984c). Decomposition of some well-known variance reduction techniques. *Research Memorandum 84-6,* School of Industrial Engineering, Purdue University, West Lafayette, Indiana.

Nozari, A., Arnold, S.F. and Pegden, C.D. (1984a). Control variates for multipopulation simulation experiments. *IIE Transactions, 16,* 159-169.

Nozari, A., Arnold, S.F. and Pegden, C.D. (1984b). Statistical analysis under Schruben and Margolin correlation induction strategy. *Technical Report,* School of Industrial Engineering, University of Oklahoma, Norman, Oklahoma.

Porta Nova, A. (1985). A generalized approach to variance reduction in discrete-event simulation using control variables. *Unpublished Ph.D. Dissertation,* Mechanical Engineering Department, University of Texas, Austin, Texas.

Ross, S.M. and Schechner, Z. (1985). Using simulation to estimate first passage distribution. *Management Science, 31,* 224-234.

Rothery, P. (1982). The use of control variates in Monte Carlo estimation of power. *Applied Statistics, 31,* 125-129.

Royston, J.P. (1982a). An extension of Shapiro and Wilk's *W* test for normality to large samples. *Applied Statistics, 31,* 115-124.

Royston, J.P. (1982b). Algorithm AS 181. The *W* test for normality. *Applied Statistics, 31,* 176-180.

Royston, J.P. (1983a). Some techniques for assessing multivariate normality based on the Shapiro-Wilk *W*. *Applied Statistics, 32,* 121-133.

Royston, J.P. (1983b). Correction to algorithm AS 181. *Applied Statistics, 32,* 244.

Rubinstein, R.Y. and Markus, R. (1981). Efficiency of multivariate control variates in Monte Carlo simulation. *Technical Report No. I 339,* National Research Institute for Mathematical Sciences, Pretoria, South Africa; to appear in *Operations Research.*

Rubinstein, R.Y. and Samorodnitsky, G. (1982). Antithetic and common random numbers in simulation of stochastic systems. *Mimeograph Series No. 308,* Technion, Haifa, Israel.

Rubinstein, R.Y. and Samorodnitsky, G. (1983). A modified version of the antithetic variates theorem. *Mimeograph Series No. 346,* Technion, Haifa, Israel.

Rubinstein, R.Y., Samorodnitsky, G. and Shaked, M. (1985). Antithetic variates, multivariate dependence and simulation of complex stochastic systems. *Management Science, 31,* 66-77.

Schruben, L.W. and Margolin, B.H. (1978). Pseudorandom number assignment in statistically designed simulation and distribution sampling experiments. *Journal of the American Statistical Association, 73,* 504-520.

Schruben, L.W. (1979). Designing correlation induction strategies for simulation experiments. In *Current Issues in Computer Simulation* (edited by N.R. Adam and A. Dogramaci), pp. 235-256. Academic Press, New York.

Shapiro, S.S. (1980). *How To Test Normality and Other Distributional*

Assumptions. Volume 3 in The ASQC Basic References in Qualit Control: Statistical Techniques (edited by E.J. Dudewicz). America Society for Quality Control, Milwaukee, Wisconsin.

Simon, G. (1976). Computer simulation swindles, with applications t estimates of location and dispersion. *Applied Statistics, 25,* 266-274.

Siotani, M., Hayakawa, T., and Fujikoshi, Y. (1985). *Modern Multivariat Statistical Analysis: A Graduate Course and Handbook.* America Sciences Press, Inc., Columbus, Ohio.

Swain, J.J. and Schmeiser, B.W. (1984a). Monte Carlo analysis o nonlinear statistical models, I: theory. *Technical Report J-84-11,* School o Industrial and Systems Engineering, Georgia Institute of Technology Atlanta, Georgia.

Swain, J.J. and Schmeiser, B.W. (1984b). Monte Carlo analysis o nonlinear statistical models, II: moments and variances. *Technical Repor J-84-12,* School of Industrial and Systems Engineering, Georgia Institute o Technology, Atlanta, Georgia.

Swain, J.J. (1984). Monte Carlo analysis of nonlinear statistical models III: efficiency, nonlinearity, and parameter transformations. *Technica Report J-84-13,* School of Industrial and Systems Engineering, Georgi Institute of Technology, Atlanta, Georgia.

Venkatraman, S. (1983). Application of the control variate technique t multiple simulation output analysis. *Unpublished M.S. Thesis,* Mechanica Engineering Department, University of Texas, Austin, Texas.

Wilson, J.R. (1983). Antithetic sampling with multivariate inputs *American Journal of Mathematical and Management Sciences, 3,* 121-144.

Wilson, J.R. and Pritsker, A.A.B. (1984a). Variance reduction in queuein simulation using generalized concomitant variables. *Journal of Statistica Computation and Simulation, 19,* 129-153.

Wilson, J.R. and Pritsker, A.A.B. (1984b). Experimental evaluation o variance reduction techniques for queueing simulations using generalize concomitant variables. *Management Science, 30,* 1459-1472.

Received 1983; Revised 4/16/85.

AMERICAN JOURNAL OF MATHEMATICAL AND MANAGEMENT SCIENCES

MULTIVARIATE SIMULATION OUTPUT ANALYSIS

Andrew F. Seila
University of Georgia

SYNOPTIC ABSTRACT

Procedures are discussed for estimating multiple means in simulations with multivariate outputs. These techniques include classical procedures (applicable to independent and identically distributed observations), procedures for regenerative processes, multivariate batch-means, and a new batch-ratio method. Conditions under which each method can be applied are discussed, as well as implementation.

Key Words and Phrases: Discrete event simulation; multivariate estimation; stationary processes; regenerative processes.

1984, VOL. 4, NOS. 3 & 4, 313-334
0196-6324/84/030313-22 $7.40

1. INTRODUCTION.

Most research on analysis of output data from discrete event simulations has been concerned with (statistical) inference for a single parameter using data from one or more simulation runs. In practice, however, the information one seeks from a simulation usually cannot be summarized in a single system parameter. Rather, it is frequently the case that the output process is multivariate, and the means of two (or more) components must be estimated simultaneously. In this case, multivariate inference procedures must be applied (to compute simultaneous confidence intervals, or joint confidence regions, or to test hypotheses concerning these values). Relatively little research has been devoted to multivariate estimation problems in discrete event simulation. In this article we summarize inference procedures that are available for the analysis of multivariate simulation data, and focus attention on problems in this area where additional research appears promising.

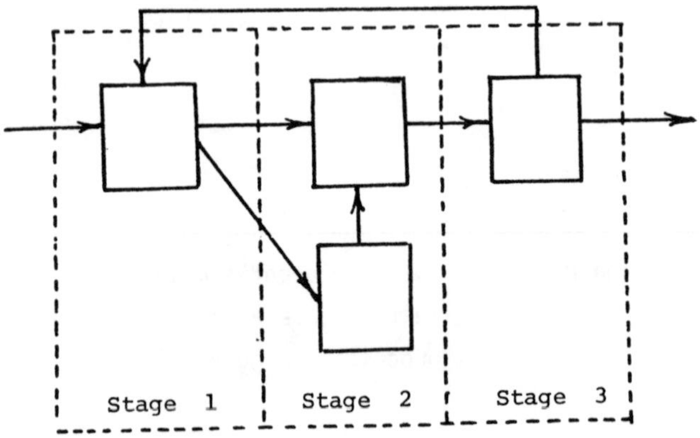

Figure 1: A Production System.

For example, consider a production system that can be represented as a network of queues. Such a system is shown in Figure 1. The operations have been grouped into three stages. Let μ_i be the mean delay in stage i, and suppose that design criteria require that μ_i not differ by more than δ_0 from a specified value, β_i, i = 1, 2, 3. If, for example, this system represents the production of a food product, $\mu_i > \beta_i$ would indicate an increased probability of spoilage while $\mu_i < \beta_i$ would indicate unused production capacity. Even if the estimators for μ_1, μ_2, and μ_3 were independent, it would be incorrect to compute 100(1 - α)-percent univariate confidence intervals for each parameter and state that they have simultaneous confidence coefficient 100(1 - α).

In some cases, classical multivariate procedures can be applied. Section 2 briefly reviews these methods (which assume that observations are independent and identially distributed with a multivariate normal distribution). Since the estimators in other procedures are asymptotically normal, this section also serves as a foundation for those methods. When classical methods cannot be applied, as for example, when estimating stationary parameters, other inference procedures are needed that apply to the specific type of output data generated by the simulation. In Section 3, the use of Bonferroni's inequality is discussed for computing a lower bound to a simultaneous confidence coefficient for a set of univariate confidence intervals. Section 4 discusses multivariate inference procedures for stationary parameters in systems whose output processes are regenerative. The methodology in Section 5 concerns inference procedures which do not require output processes to be regenerative. Finally, the discussion and commentary in Section 6 provide perspective on the methods discussed and problems encountered in applying these methods in practice.

2. MULTIVARIATE INFERENCE WITH INDEPENDENT OBSERVATIONS

There is a large body of literature on multivariate statistical inference when the vectors of observations are independent and identically distributed and have a multivariate normal distribution; see Anderson (1958), Morrison (1976), and Siotani, Hayakawa and Fujikoshi (1985) and their references. Let $\underline{X}_1, \underline{X}_2, \ldots, \underline{X}_n$ be a sample of n independent and identically distributed random vectors having h components each, so that $\underline{X}_i = (\underline{X}_{i1}, \underline{X}_{i2}, \ldots, \underline{X}_{ih})' \in \mathbf{R}^h$, where $\mathbf{R}^h$ denotes h-dimensional Euclidean space. (The notation $\underline{X}'$ denotes the transpose of $\underline{X}$.) Let $\underline{\mu} = E(\underline{X}_i) \in \mathbf{R}^h$ denote the vector of means and $\underline{\Sigma} = E[(\underline{X}_i - \underline{\mu})(\underline{X}_i - \underline{\mu})']$ denote the covariance matrix for the components of each observation, with $(j,k)^{th}$ element $\sigma_{jk} = E[(X_{ik} - \mu_k)(X_{ij} - \mu_j)]$ for each i. The usual point estimator for $\underline{\mu}$ is the multivariate sample mean $\hat{\underline{\mu}} = \bar{\underline{X}}_n = n^{-1} \sum_{i=1}^{n} \underline{X}_i$, where the sum is applied to each component. It is well-known (Billingsley (1979), Theorem 29.5) that if $0 < \sigma_{jj} < \infty$, $j = 1, 2, \ldots, h$, then $\lim_{n\,\infty} \sqrt{n}(\bar{\underline{X}}_n - \underline{\mu}) \sim \mathbf{N}(\underline{0},\underline{\Sigma})$, where $\mathbf{N}(\underline{0},\underline{\Sigma})$ denotes the multivariate normal distribution with mean $\underline{0}$ and covariance matrix $\underline{\Sigma}$. Therefore, if n is sufficiently large, one can approximate the distribution of $\bar{\underline{X}}_n$ by the multivariate normal distribution with mean $\underline{\mu}$ and covariance matrix $n^{-1}\underline{\Sigma}$.

Let $\underline{S}$ be the usual estimator for $\underline{\Sigma}$, given by

$$\underline{S} = \frac{1}{n-1} \sum_{i=1}^{n} (\underline{X}_i - \bar{\underline{X}}_n)(\underline{X}_i - \bar{\underline{X}}_n)' \,, \tag{1}$$

and define

$$T^2 = n(\bar{\underline{X}}_n - \underline{\mu})' \, \underline{S}^{-1}(\bar{\underline{X}}_n - \underline{\mu}) \,. \tag{2}$$

If $\underline{X}_1, \underline{X}_2, \ldots, \underline{X}_n$ are multivariate normal with mean $\underline{\mu}$ then $[T^2/(n-1)][(n-h)/h]$ has an F-distribution with h and n-h degrees of freedom (Anderson (1958), Corollary 5.2.1). A 100(1 - α)-percent confidence region, R, for a vector $\underline{\mu} \in \mathbf{R}^h$ is a (random) subset of $\mathbf{R}^h$ such that $P(\mu \in R) \equiv 1 - \alpha$. Such a confidence region for $\underline{\mu}$ is given by all vectors $\underline{\delta}$ for which

$$n(\bar{\underline{X}}_n - \underline{\delta})' \, \underline{S}^{-1} (\bar{\underline{X}}_n - \underline{\delta}) \le \frac{(n-1)h}{n-h} F_{\alpha;h,n-h} \tag{3}$$

where $F_{\alpha;h,n-h}$ is the 100(1 - α)-percentage point of the F-distribution with h and n-h degrees of freedom in the numerator and denominator, respectively. See Morrison (1976), chapter 4, for a derivation and further discussion. One can show, moreover, that the hypothesis H_0: $\underline{\mu} = \underline{\mu}_0$ would be rejected at significance level α if and only if the point μ_0 is outside the 100(1 - α)-percent confidence region.

Let $\underline{\pi}_1, \underline{\pi}_2, \ldots, \underline{\pi}_p$ be a p h-dimensional non-null vectors of constants, and consider the p linear combinations of $\underline{\mu}$:

$$\Phi_r = \underline{\pi}_r' \underline{\mu} = \sum_{j=1}^{h} \pi_{rj} \mu_j, \quad r = 1, 2, \ldots, p, \tag{4}$$

where π_{rj} is the jth component of $\underline{\pi}_r$. The minimum variance unbiased estimator for Φ_r is $\hat{\Phi}_r = \underline{\pi}_r' \bar{\underline{X}}_n$, r = 1, 2, ..., p. IF $\bar{X}_n$ has a multivariate normal distribution with mean $\underline{\mu}$ and covariance matrix $\underline{\Sigma}/n$, then $\hat{\underline{\Phi}} = (\hat{\Phi}_1 \ \hat{\Phi}_2, \ldots, \hat{\Phi}_p)$ has a multivariate normal distribution with mean $\underline{\Phi} = (\Phi_1, \Phi_2, \ldots, \Phi_p) \in \mathbf{R}^p$ and covariance matrix $\boldsymbol{\pi}'\boldsymbol{\Sigma}\boldsymbol{\pi}$, where $\boldsymbol{\pi}$ is a p-by-h matrix whose r^{th} row is $\underline{\pi}_r$. If $p \le h$ and the vectors $\underline{\pi}_1, \underline{\pi}_2, \ldots, \underline{\pi}_p$ are linearly independent, then a 100(1 - α)-percent joint confidence region for $\underline{\Phi}$ is given by all values $\underline{\delta} = (\delta_1, \delta_2, \ldots, \delta_p)$ for which

$$n(\hat{\underline{\Phi}} - \underline{\delta})'[\underline{\pi}'\underline{S}\,\underline{\pi}]^{-1}(\hat{\underline{\Phi}} - \underline{\delta}) \leq \frac{(n-1)p}{n-p} F_{\alpha;p,n-p} . \quad (5)$$

In particular, the marginal distribution of $\hat{\Phi}_r$ is univariate normal with mean Φ_r and variance

$$\sigma^2(\hat{\Phi}_r) = \sum_{j=1}^{p} \sum_{k=1}^{p} \pi_{rj}\sigma_{jk}\pi_{rk}/n . \quad (6)$$

A 100(1 - α)-percent univariate confidence interval for Φ_r is given by

$$\hat{\Phi}_r \pm t_{\alpha/2;n-1} s(\hat{\Phi}_r) \quad (7)$$

where

$$s^2(\hat{\Phi}_r) = \frac{1}{n} \sum_{j=1}^{h} \sum_{k=1}^{h} \pi_{rj} S_{jk} \pi_{rk}, = \frac{1}{n} \underline{\pi}_r' \underline{S}\, \underline{\pi}_r , \quad (8)$$

S_{jk} is the $(j,k)^{th}$ element of the sample covariance matrix given by (1) and $t_{\alpha/2;n-1}$ is the $100(1 - \alpha/2)^{th}$ percentage point of the Student's-t distribution with n-1 degrees of freedom.

A set $(I_1, I_2, \ldots, I_p)$ of univariate intervals is said to be a 100(1 - α)-percent set of simultaneous confidence intervals for $\underline{\Phi} = (\Phi_1, \Phi_2, \ldots, \Phi_p)$ if $P(\Phi_1, \in I_1, \Phi_2 \in I_2, \ldots, \Phi_p \in I_p) = 1 - \alpha$. There are two primary approaches to constructing simultaneous confidence intervals. A method which uses Bonferroni's inequality will be discussed in Section 3. Another method, which was apparently developed both by Roy and Bose (1953) and Scheffe (1953) (for linear contrasts), uses Hotelling's T^2 distribution. If $\underline{\bar{X}}_n$ has a multivariate normal distribution then the intervals

$$\hat{\Phi}_r \pm T_{\alpha;h,n-h} s(\hat{\Phi}_r), \; r = 1, 2, \ldots, p , \quad (9)$$

where $T^2_{\alpha;h,n-h}$ is the 100(1 - α)-percentage point of Hotelling's T^2 distribution with h and n-h degrees of freedom in the numerator and denominator, respectively, form simultaneous confidence intervals for $\underset{\sim}{\Phi}$ with confidence coefficient at least 100(1 - α). This analysis is true for any p = 1, 2, ... and any non-null vectors $\underset{\sim}{\pi}$. If there are h vectors $\underset{\sim}{\pi}_1$, $\underset{\sim}{\pi}_2$, ..., $\underset{\sim}{\pi}_h$ and $\underset{\sim}{\pi}_r$ has a 1 in component r and 0's in all other components, then $\Phi_r = \mu_r$, $\hat{\Phi}_r = \hat{\mu}_r$, $\underset{\sim}{\pi}$ is the identity matrix, and the intervals in (9) give a set of 100(1 - α)-percent simultaneous confidence intervals for $\underset{\sim}{\mu}$.

The procedures just discussed may be applied if the observations are independent and identically distributed multivariate normal random variables. The critical consideration is how close the distribution of the observations is to multivariate normal. (If the distribution is close, then these procedures will give valid results.) In some cases where the normality of observations is suspect, a nonparametric approach such as the one by Nath and Duran (1983) may be preferable. One situation in which one may justify applying classical procedures is when independently seeded replications are being run for a stationary multivariate output process for which a central limit theorem applies. In this case, each observation would be the vector of sample means from a large sample of observations taken from the stationary portion of the output process. Another situation in which these conditions may be met is what has been called a "terminating simulation" (Law (1980)). Suppose, for example, that one wishes to estimate the mean queue length for each queue in the production system in Figure 1 after ten hours of operation, starting from a fixed system state. In this type of situation, one would perform n independently seeded replications, each starting from the same initial conditions and running for 10 simulated hours. At the end of each replication, a vector of observations would be generated by recording the queue lengths at each of the queues. Since the replications are independently seeded, the queue length observations are independent. Then, queue length averages will be approximately normally distributed by the central limit theorem.

3. SIMULTANEOUS CONFIDENCE INTERVALS USING BONFERRONI'S INEQUALITY.

Let $E_1, E_2, \ldots, E_h$ be h events defined on a sample space. Bonferroni's inequality (Feller (1968)) states that $P(E_1 \cap E_2 \cap \ldots \cap E_h) \geq 1 - \sum_{j=1}^{h}(1 - P(E_j))$. Let I_j be a 100(1 - α)-percent (univariate) confidence interval for μ_j, and let E_j be the event that I_j covers μ_j, j = 1, 2, ..., h. Then, $P(E_j) = 1 - \alpha_j$, and using $1 - \alpha = P(E_1 \cap E_2 \cap \ldots \cap E_h)$ to denote the confidence coefficient for the set of simultaneous confidence intervals $I_1, I_2, \ldots, I_h$, Bonferroni's inequality gives $1 - \alpha \geq 1 - \sum_{j=1}^{h} \alpha_j$. For example, suppose that h = 5 and I_j is a 98-percent confidence interval for μ_j, j = 1, 2, 3, 4, 5. Then, the confidence coefficient for the simultaneous confidence intervals (I_1, I_2, I_3, I_4, I_5) is no smaller than 100(1 - 5(.02)) = 90-percent.

No conditions on the events $E_1, E_2, \ldots, E_h$ are required for Bonferroni's inequality to hold. Therefore, univariate confidence intervals can be computed in any manner, as long as the confidence coefficient, 100(1 - α_j), is correct. In particular, the regenerative method (Crane and Iglehart (1975); Crane and Lemoine (1977); Fishman (1973)), batch-means method (Fishman (1978), Law and Kelton (1984), or any other univariate interval estimation method can be used. (See (Law (1983) for a survey of univariate output analysis methods.)

If classical multivariate procedures can be applied, one has the choice of using Roy-Bose simultaneous confidence intervals, which were discussed in Section 2, or using univariate confidence intervals and Bonferroni's inequality. Neither approach is exact because both give lower bounds for the confidence coefficient, and in general the choice between Bonferroni intervals and Roy-Bose intervals is not a simple one; this is discussed further in Section 6.

4. MULTIVARIATE INFERENCE FOR REGENERATIVE SYSTEMS.

Regenerative processes have received extensive attention in the literature (Feller (1971), Smith (1955)), and methods for estimating the mean of stationary regenerative processes are well-known (Crane and Lemoine (1977), Fishman (1979), Law and Kelton (1982), Rubenstein (1981)). Let $\{Y(t), t \geq 0\}$ be a stochastic process in discrete or continuous time. $\{Y(t), t \geq 0\}$ is said to be regenerative if there is an increasing sequence of points $0 = t_0 < t_1 < t_2 < \ldots$ such that for each $i = 2, 3, \ldots$, the process $\{Y(t), t > t_i\}$ is independent of the process $\{Y(t), 0 \leq t < t_i\}$ and probabilistically identical to the process $\{Y(t), t \geq t_1\}$. Thus, $\{Y(t), t \geq t_1\}$ can be divided into a sequence of independent and identically distributed cycles $\{Y(t), t_{i-1} \leq t < t_i\}$, of length $t_i - t_{i-1}$, $i = 2, 3, \ldots$, such that all properties of the process are contained in a single cycle. If the process is stationary and $|E[Y]| < \infty$, then one can show (Crane and Iglehart (1975), Smith (1955)) that $E(Y) = E(X)/E(N)$, where X is the integral (or sum) of the process over a single cycle and N is the length of the cycle. An example of multivariate inference in regenerative processes, in which passage times for two classes of customers in a closed network of queues are estimated, is given by Iglehart and Shedler (1980). Seila (1982) gives a more general discussion. Let $\underline{\mu} = (\mu_1, \mu_2, \ldots, \mu_h)'$ be a vector of means for h stationary processes, and assume that these processes have a common set of regeneration times.

Normally, a regeneration time will be a point in time when the state vector of the system leaves a particular state or set of states such as the empty and idle state. Usually, a system's output process is shown to be regenerative by showing that the state vector of the system possesses regeneration points. See Iglehart and Shedler (1980), (1983). If this is the case, then all output processes which do not "mix" cycles will be regenerative. Thus, the requirement that the output processes have a common set of regeneration points is in many cases no more restrictive than requiring a single output process to be regenerative. For example, if the system is a nonpreemptive priority queue for which the empty and idle state is a regeneration state, then for each priority class the sequence of queueing times for customers in that class will be a regenerative process, and all of these processes will have a common set of regeneration points.

Represent the output data for a simulation run of n cycles by $\{(\underline{X}_1, \underline{N}_1), (\underline{X}_2, \underline{N}_2), \ldots, (\underline{X}_n, \underline{N}_n)\}$, where $\underline{X}_i = (X_{i1}, X_{i2}, \ldots, X_{ih})'$ and $\underline{N}_i = (N_{i1}, N_{i2}, \ldots, N_{ih})'$. If time is measured in continuous units in the jth output process, then X_{ij} is the integral of the process over the ith cycle and N_{ij} is the length of the ith cycle; if time is measured in discrete units in the jth output process, then X_{ij} is the sum of the observations in the ith cycle and N_{ij} is the number of observations in the ith cycle.

Since the processes are regenerative, $\mu_i = E(X_{ij})/E(N_{ij})$, and the regenerative estimator for μ_j is $\hat{\mu}_j = \bar{X}_j/\bar{N}_j$, where $\bar{X}_j = \frac{1}{n}\sum_{i=1}^{n} X_{ij}$ and $\bar{N}_j = \frac{1}{n}\sum_{i=1}^{n} N_{ij}$, $j = 1, 2, \ldots, h$. Let $\underline{\mu} = (\mu_1, \mu_2, \ldots, \mu_h)'$, $\underline{\bar{N}}_D$ be a diagonal matrix having $\bar{N}$ as the jth diagonal element, and $\underline{\Omega}_D = E[\underline{\bar{N}}_D]$. Then, $\hat{\underline{\mu}} = \underline{\bar{N}}_D^{-1}\underline{\bar{X}}$, where $\underline{\bar{X}} = (\bar{X}_1, \bar{X}_2, \ldots, \bar{X}_h)$. Define $Z_{ij} = X_{ij} - \mu_j N_{ij}$, $j = 1, 2, \ldots, h$, and let $\underline{Z}_i = (Z_{i1}, Z_{i2}, \ldots, Z_{ih})'$,

$i = 1, 2, \ldots, n$. The vectors $\underline{Z}_1, \underline{Z}_2, \ldots, \underline{Z}_n$ are independent and identically distributed with mean $\underline{0}$. Let $\underline{\Sigma}$ denote the covariance matrix of $\underline{Z}_i$. It has been shown (Seila (1982)) that as $n \to \infty$, $\sqrt{n}(\hat{\underline{\mu}} - \underline{\mu})$ converges to a multivariate normal random variable with mean $\underline{0}$ and covariance matrix $\underline{\Omega}_D^{-1}\underline{\Sigma}\ \underline{\Omega}_D^{-1}$.

To compute a confidence region for $\underline{\mu}$, first let $\underline{S} = \frac{1}{n}\sum_{i=1}^{n}\underline{Z}_i\underline{Z}_i'$, where $Z_{ij} = X_{ij} - \mu_j N_{ij}$, $j = 1, 2, \ldots, h$; $i = 1, 2, \ldots, n$. Then $\underline{S}$ is an estimator of $\underline{\Sigma}$, and one can show that $F = \frac{n-h+1}{nh} T^2(\underline{\mu})$, where $T^2(\underline{\mu}) = n(\hat{\underline{\mu}} - \underline{\mu})'\underline{\bar{N}}_D\underline{S}^{-1}\underline{\bar{N}}_D(\hat{\underline{\mu}} - \underline{\mu})$, can be approximated by an F-distribution with h and n-h+1 degrees of freedom. Then an approximate 100(1 - α)-percent confidence region for $\underline{\mu}$ is given by all vectors $\underline{\delta}$ for which $T^2(\underline{\delta}) \leq (nh/(n-h+1))F_{\alpha;h,n-h+1}$. Indeed, one would reject the hypothesis H_0: $\underline{\mu} = \underline{\mu}_o$ at significance level α if $T^2(\mu\ ) > (nh/(n-h+1))F_{\alpha;h,n-h+1}$.

Roy-Bose simultaneous confidence intervals for p linear combinations of $\underline{\mu}$, $\Phi_r = \underline{\pi}_r'\underline{\mu}$, $r = 1, 2, \ldots, p$, with confidence coefficient 100(1 - α), are given by $\hat{\Phi}_r \pm T_{\alpha;h,n-h+1}\ s(\hat{\Phi}_r)$, where $\hat{\Phi}_r = \underline{\pi}_r'\hat{\underline{\mu}}$ and $s^2(\hat{\Phi}_r) = \underline{\pi}_r'\underline{\bar{N}}^{-1}\underline{S}\ \underline{\bar{N}}^{-1}\ \underline{\pi}_r/n$. A set of 100(1 - α)-percent Bonferroni confidence intervals is given by $\hat{\Phi}_r \pm t_{\alpha_r/2;n-1}s(\hat{\Phi}_r)$, $r = 1, 2, \ldots, p$, where $t_{\alpha_r/2;n-1}$ is 100(1 - $\alpha_{r/2}$)-percentage point of the Student's-t distribution with n-1 degrees of freedom, and $\sum_{r=1}^{p}\alpha_r = \alpha$.

Since the regenerative method was first introduced, arguments concerning it usefulness have abounded. The argument has been offered that most systems are not regenerative, or, if they are, regenerations may occur so infrequently that excessive run lengths are required in order to obtain the desired number of cycles. The counter-argument has been that for most systems, one doesn't know whether regenerative states exist, and, if cycles are long, this indicates that the dependence among observations is so strong that very large samples are needed, regardless of the estimation method used. At present there is a concensus that regenerative methods are useful in simple systems, but need more research to be of use in complex simulations.

5. MULTIVARIATE INFERENCE FOR STATIONARY SYSTEMS.

When the regenerative method cannot be applied, other methods are available to estimate stationary mean parameters. There is a large body of literature on multivariate time series analysis (Hannan (1970)); however, for two reasons these inferential procedures are seldom used to analyze multivariate simulation output: (i) the computational techniques are quite complex and software packages for multivariate time series analysis are not generally available; and (ii) the objective of most such procedures is to ascertain the covariance structure of the time series rather than to compute confidence intervals (or regions) for the vector of stationary means. These techniques will not be discussed further except to note that they exist and could theoretically be applied. Another approach would be to use univariate time series methods (Box and Jenkins (1970), Fishman (1979), Heidelberger and Welch (1981)) and Bonferroni's inequality to compute simultaneous confidence intervals.

The batch-means method (Fishman (1978), Law and Kelton (1979)) is commonly used to estimate the mean of a stationary output process. This method, which is easy to apply and has been shown to produce reliable confidence intervals when sufficiently large batches are used, works as follows with univariate data: For a simulation run consisting of $n = mk$

observations, divide the data into k batches with m observations in each batch. Compute the batch means $\bar{X}_1, \bar{X}_2, \ldots, \bar{X}_k$ for the k batches. If the batch size, m, is sufficiently large, and $\sum_{j=-\infty}^{\infty} \mathrm{Cov}(X_i, X_{i+j}) < \infty$, then batch means $\bar{X}_j$ and $\bar{X}_r$ in distinct batches ($j \neq r$) are approximately uncorrelated (Law and Carson (1979)). Therefore, $\bar{\bar{X}} = \frac{1}{k}\sum_{i=1}^{k} \bar{X}_i$ can be treated as the sample mean of a set of uncorrelated random variables and an approximate $100(1 - \alpha)$-percent confidence interval for $\mu = E(X_i)$ is given by $\bar{\bar{X}} \pm t_{\alpha/2;k-1} s_{\bar{\bar{X}}}$ where $s^2_{\bar{\bar{X}}} = \sum_{i=1}^{k} (\bar{X}_i - \bar{\bar{X}})^2/[k(k-1)]$.

One adaptation of the batch means method to multivariate estimation is to compute a $100(1 - \alpha_j)$-percent confidence interval for each μ_j individually, using the batch means method. These intervals will then be a set of simultaneous confidence intervals with confidence coefficient at least $100(1 - \alpha)$-percent by Bonferroni's inequality, where $\alpha = \sum_{j=1}^{h} \alpha_j$.

5.1 Multivariate Batch Means. In generalizing the batch means method to use multivariate data directly, one may encounter a synchronization problem. Consider, for example, the problem of estimating mean customer waiting time for each of two classes of customers in a queueing system, and suppose that, on average, ten class 1 customers pass through the system for each class 2 customer. If a batch is defined to consist of 100 waiting times each for class 1 customers and class 2 customers, then approximately 900 observations on waiting times for class 1 customers must be discarded during each batch while observations for class 2 customers are collected. This is clearly an undesirable situation, not only because it is wasteful of data, but also because the task of counting observations in each output process can become complex. If observations for all h output processes are produced simultaneously, then the output processes will be called synchronous; otherwise, they will be called asynchronous.

If the observation processes are synchronous, one can generalize the batch means method for estimation of the multivariate mean: Divide the run of n = mk observations from each process into k batches of m observations each. For each batch, compute the vector of sample means $\underline{\bar{X}}_i = (\bar{X}_{i1}, \bar{X}_{i2}, \ldots, \bar{X}_{ih})'$, where $\bar{X}_{ij}$ is the sample mean for observations in the jth output process. If $\sum_{r=-\infty}^{\infty} \mathrm{Cov}(X_{ij}, X_{i+r,j}) < \infty$, for all j, then the batch mean vectors are asymptotically uncorrelated as $m \to \infty$. Therefore, for sufficiently large m, the batch mean vectors $\underline{\bar{X}}_1, \underline{\bar{X}}_2, \ldots, \underline{\bar{X}}_k$ can be treated as a sequence of uncorrelated random vectors. If a central limit theorem applies to the output process, then the batch means will be approximately multivariate normally distributed, and the inference procedures in Section 2 can be applied to compute joint confidence regions or simultaneous confidence intervals.

5.2 Multivariate Batch-Ratios. When output processes are asynchronous, generalization of the batch means method is troublesome; however, there is an alternative. Define a "batch" to consist of all observations collected during an interval of length t simulation time units, rather than exactly m observations.

Using this definition of a batch, the batch sizes, i.e., the number of observations in each batch on each variable, is a random variable. Let $\underline{N}(t)$ be a vector whose j^{th} component, $N_j(t)$, is the number of observations on the jth variable during the interval (0,t]. If the batch duration is t units of time for each batch, then the batch size for the jth variable in the ith batch is $N_{ij}(t) = N_j(it) - N_j((i-1)t)$, $j = 1, 2, \ldots, h$; $i = 1, 2, \ldots, k$. Let $\underline{N}_i(t) = (N_{i1}(t), N_{i2}(t), \ldots, N_{ih}(t))$ be the vector of batch sizes for the ith batch. Define the batch-ratio for the jth output variable in the ith batch to be:

$$\hat{\mu}_{ij}(t) = \frac{1}{N_{ij}(t)} \sum_{r=N_j((i-1)t)+1}^{N_j(it)} X_{rj} ,$$

where X_{rj} is the rth observation on variable j, and let $\hat{\underline{\mu}}_i(t) = (\hat{\mu}_{i1}(t), \hat{\mu}_{i2}(t), \ldots, \hat{\mu}_{ih}(t))'$, $i = 1, 2, \ldots, k$. The batch ratio vectors $(\hat{\underline{\mu}}_1(t), \hat{\underline{\mu}}_2(t), \ldots, \hat{\underline{\mu}}_k(t))$ are analogous to the batch means vectors $(\bar{\underline{X}}_1, \bar{\underline{X}}_2, \ldots, \bar{\underline{X}}_k)$, except that $\hat{\underline{\mu}}_i(t)$ is a vector of ratio estimators because the denominator is a random variables. Since this gives the estimators an additional source of randomness, one would expect them to have different statistical properties than batch means. In particular, batch ratios are biased for finite samples. It has been shown, however, that if the batch means are consistent and asymptotically uncorrelated, then the batch ratios are also consistent and asymptotically uncorrelated (Seila (1982)). Therefore, multivariate batch ratios have the same second order asymptotic properties as batch means. This implies, in particular, that if the batch length, t, is sufficiently long, the sequence of batch ratio vectors, $(\underline{\mu}_1(t), \underline{\mu}_2(t), \ldots, \underline{\mu}_k(t))$, can be treated as a sequence of uncorrelated, identically distributed random vectors. If one is able to assure that these batch ratio vectors have an approximate multivariate normal distribution, then the inference procedures in Section 2 may be applied to test hypotheses and compute confidence intervals.

Although empirical results for batch ratios are not

presently available, other ratio estimators have been shown to be biased in finite samples (Law and Kelton (1979)) and one should therefore be cautious in using batch ratios. The jackknife (Law and Kelton (1982)) can be applied to reduce bias; however, this will generally inflate the variance of the estimator.

5.3 Implementation Considerations. Two decisions must be made in implementing the batch-means or batch-ratio methods for estimating the multivariate mean: When should data collection begin, and how long should each batch be? Both of these decisions are difficult when computing univariate estimates, more so when multivariate parameters are being estimated.

Data collection should not begin until the effects of initialization bias have disappeared. Schruben (1981) developed and evaluated a method for testing for initialization bias in multivariate response simulation when the observations are synchronous. This test, which is based upon a two-sample T^2 statistics, proved successful in the systems in which it was tested; however, it was recommended that the method be applied with care.

The validity of the batch-means and batch-ratio methods depends upon having batches large enough that the covariance between estimators in distinct batches is approximately zero. Univariate procedures for determining batch size have been given by Fishman (1978) and Law and Carson (1979). Both of these methods search for a batch size such that one would not reject the null hypothesis that the lag-1 serial covariance between batch means is zero. The circumstances in multivariate estimation, however, are more complex because one has matrices of serial covariances and cross-covariances. In order to test for the covariances being zero, one would have to adopt a norm for the matrix. It is known that, under appropriate conditions (Fishman (1979)), the estimators for the serial covariances are consistent and asymptotically normal. However, specific methods to compute batch sizes or batch lengths for multivariate estimation remain an open research question.

6. DISCUSSION

In Sections 3, 4, and 5 of this paper, it is clear that when computing simultaneous confidence intervals one has a choice between the Roy-Bose approach and using Bonferroni's inequality. In practice, these methods differ only in the distribution from which one obtains the percentage point that multiplies the standard error; see (7) and (9). In most practical situations, Bonferroni intervals are shorter than Roy-Bose intervals (Schruben (1981)) if the same confidence coefficient is used. This, however, is not the only consideration.

Studies have shown that finite sample variance estimator bias is a serious problem in analysis of simulation data which results in actual coverage probabilities being less than theoretical values (Law and Kelton (1979), Seila (1983)). If this is true for univariate intervals, the effect will be amplified when they are combined to form a simultaneous confidence interval. Consider the following example: Suppose that a 90-percent simultaneous confidence interval is to be computed for 5 parameters $\mu_1, \ldots, \mu_5$. In addition, suppose that the variance estimators have a negative bias such that the coverage probability of a 98-percent confidence interval is reduced to 95-percent. Finally, assume that observations on distinct variables are independent, so that the five univariate confidence intervals are independent, and that the sample size is very large. Then, if 98-percent confidence intervals are computed for each parameter, the simultaneous confidence coefficient would be at least $1 - \sum_{j=1}^{5} \alpha_j = 1 - 5(.02) = .90$ using Bonferroni's inequality. However, since the intervals are independent, the actual coverage probability would be $(.95)^5 = .7738$ instead of $(.98)^5 = .9032$. Using the Roy-Bose procedure, the confidence intervals would be $\hat{\mu}_j \pm 3.0414\ s(\hat{\mu}_j)$, where $3.0414 = T_{.10,5,\infty}$ is the appropriate percentage point of the Hotelling's T-square distribution and $\hat{\mu}_j$ and $s(\hat{\mu}_j)$ are the point estimate and standard error of $\hat{\mu}_j$. If a "98-percent" confidence interval has actual coverage probability .95, the bias in $s(\hat{\mu}_j)$ is $-.159\sigma(\hat{\mu}_j)$, where $\sigma(\hat{\mu}_j)$ is the standard error of $\hat{\mu}_j$. Using this, one can compute that $P(\mu_j \in [\hat{\mu}_j \pm 3.0414\ s(\hat{\mu}_j)] = .9896$, $j = 1, 2, \ldots, 5$. Therefore, the simultaneous confidence coefficient is $(.9896)^5 = .9491$. From these calculations, one can see that a three-percentage point error in the coverage probability of the univariate intervals reduced the coverage probability for Bonferroni simultaneous confidence intervals from above .90 to below .78; whereas, with Roy-Bose intervals, the actual coverage probability was reduced from .99 to .95. Clearly, Roy-Bose intervals are much more conservative; however, they are much less risky in the finite sample case when variance estimator bias might be a problem.

Very little research has been published in the area of multivariate output analysis in discrete event simulation, and even fewer empirical studies are available. Schruben (1981) studied the performance of a test for initialization bias in multivariate response simulation. Seila (1983) studied the performance of the multivariate regenerative approach given in Section 3 for estimation of conditional performance measures.

In this study, two systems were used: A loading dock model in which arriving customers independently request simultaneous service from a random number of servers, allocated from a fixed pool of s servers, and are served in strict first-come-first-served order; and a nonpreemptive priority queueing system with a single server and s priority classes. In the first system, mean customer queueing time was estimated for customers requesting exactly j servers, j = 1, 2, ..., s, and in the second system, mean queueing time was estimated for customers in priority class j = 1, 2, ..., s. In these tests, a procedure was considered to produce a valid confidence region or set of simultaneous confidence intervals if a confidence interval for the coverage probability, computed from the results of 100 independent replications, included the theoretical coverage probability. The runs showed that, in almost all cases, using 400 or more cycles, Roy-Bose simultaneous confidence intervals were valid over a range of numbers of variables, s, and levels of congestion; however, valid confidence regions could sometimes not be computed even if samples of 1600 cycles were used. Coverage probabilities did not seem to degrade with increasing numbers of variables, but there was some degradation with increasing congestion. Although there is some risk in generalizing the results of these studies, two conclusions seem clear: First, when compared to univariate estimation in discrete event simulation, multivariate procedures require larger sample sizes to achieve an equivalent level of reliability, as measured by the confidence coefficient or significance level of the test. Second, the methodology that has been tested has performed successfully in most experimental circumstances.

Multivariate output analysis seems to be a promising topic for research in simulation methodology. Empirical studies of the techniques that have been developed are also needed.

ACKNOWLEDGMENT.

This research was conducted in part while the author was at the University Computing Center, University of Zagreb, Yugoslavia, under the sponsorship of a Fulbright Research Grant. I wish to express my gratitude to the administration and staff of the University Computing Center, the Council for the International Exchange of Scholars, and the University of Georgia College of Business Administration for their encouragement and support.

REFERENCES

Anderson, T. W. (1958). An Introduction to Multivariate Statistical Analysis. John Wiley & Sons, Inc., New York, New York.

Billingsley, P. (1979). Probability and Measure. John Wiley & Sons, Inc., New York, New York.

Box, G. E. P. and Jenkins, G. M. (1970). Time Series Analysis Forecasting and Control. Holden-Day, San Francisco, California.

Crane, M. A. and Iglehart, D. L. (1975). Simulating stable stochastic systems, III: regenerative processes and discrete event simulations. Operations Research, 23, 33-45.

Crane, M. A. and Lemoine, A. J. (1977). An Introduction to the Regenerative Method for Simulation Analysis. Lecture Notes in Control and Information Sciences, Volume 4, Springer-Verlag: New York.

Feller, W. (1968). An Introduction to Probability Theory and Its Applications. John Wiley & Sons, Inc., New York, New York.

Feller, W. L. (1971). An Introduction to Probability Theory and Its Applications, Volume 2. John Wiley & Sons, Inc., New York, New York.

Fishman, G. S. (1973). Statistical analysis for queueing simulations. Management Science, 20, 363-369.

Fishman, G. S. (1978). Grouping observations in digital simulation. Management Science, 24, 510-521.

Fishman, G. S. (1979). Principles of Discrete Event Simulation. John Wiley & Sons, Inc., New York, New York.

Hannan, E. J. (1970). Multiple Time Series. John Wiley & Sons, Inc., New York, New York.

Heidelberger, P. and Welch, P. D. (1981). A spectral method for confidence interval generation and run length control in simulations. Communications of the ACM, 24, 233-245.

Iglehart, D. L. and Shedler, G. S. (1980). Regenerative Simulation of Response Times in Networks of Queues. Lecture Notes in Control and Information Sciences, Springer-Verlag: New York.

Iglehart, D. L. and Shedler, G. S. (1983). Simulation of non-Markovian systems. IBM Journal of Research and Development, 27, 472-480.

Law, A. M. (1980). Statistical analysis of the output data from terminating simulations. Naval Research Logistics Quarterly, 27, 131-143.

Law, A. M. and Carson, J. S. (1979). A sequential procedure for determining the length of a steady-state simulation. Operations Research, 27, 1011-1025.

Law, A. M. and Kelton, W. D. (1979). Confidence intervals for steady-state simulations, I: A survey of fixed sample size procedures. Operations Research 32, 1221-1239.

Law, A. M. and Kelton, W. D. (1982). Simulation Modeling and Analysis, McGraw-Hill: New York.

Morrison, D. F. (1982). Multivariate Statistical Methods, Second Edition. McGraw-Hill: New York.

Roy, S. N. and Bose, R. C. (1953). Simultaneous confidence interval estimation. Annals of Mathematical Statistics, 24, 513-536.

Rubinstein, R. Y. (1981). Simulation and the Monte Carlo Method. John Wiley & Sons, Inc.: New York. (For a review, see American Journal of Mathematical and Management Sciences, 2 (1982), 159-163.)

Scheffe, H. (1953). A method of judging all contrasts in analysis of variance. Biometrika, 40, 87-104.

Schruben, L. W. (1981). Control of initialization bias in multivariate simulation response. Communications of the ACM, 24, 246-252.

Seila, A. F. (1982). Multivariate estimation in regenerative simulation. Operations Research Letters, 1, 153-156.

Seila, A. F. (1983). Multivariate estimation of conditional performance measures in regenerative simulation. Technical Report, University of Georgia, Athens, Georgia.

Seila, A. F. (1984). Batch ratios in discrete event simulation. Technical report, University of Georgia, Athens, Georgia.

Siotani, M., Hayakawa, T., and Fujikoshi, Y. (1985). Modern Multivariate Statistical Analysis: A Graduate Course and Handbook. American Sciences Press, Inc., Columbus, Ohio.

Smith, W. L. (1955). Regenerative stochastic processes. Proceedings of the Royal Society, A 232, 6-31.

Received 2/15/84; Revised 3/11/85.

AMERICAN JOURNAL OF MATHEMATICAL AND MANAGEMENT SCIENCES

ON ASSESSING THE PRECISION OF SIMULATION ESTIMATES OF PERCENTILE POINTS

Edward J. Dudewicz
Department of Mathematics
Syracuse University
Syracuse, New York 13210, U.S.A.

and

Edward C. van der Meulen
Department of Mathematics
Katholieke Universiteit Leuven
Leuven, Belgium

SYNOPTIC ABSTRACT

A problem frequently solved by Monte Carlo methods is estimation of a percentile point of a random variable. In this paper we review the approaches available in the literature and give new complete procedures in a form ready for practical use. A numerical example from an actual instance is included.

Key Words and Phrases: simulation; estimation; percentiles; quantiles; Monte Carlo methods.

1984, VOL. 4, NOS. 3 & 4, 335-343
0196-6324/84/030335-9 $4.80

1. INTRODUCTION.

A problem frequently solved by Monte Carlo methods is estimation of a percentile point ξ_p of a random variable Z for some p $(0 < p < 1)$. If Z has a continuous cumulative distribution function $F(z)$, then ξ_p is a point such that

$$F(\xi_p) = P[Z \leq \xi_p] = p. \tag{1}$$

Complex methods, which are applicable only if a large sample size is available, were given by Schafer (1974). Simpler methods were given by Juritz, Juritz, and Stephens (1978). In Section 2 we complete those methods. In Section 3 a numerical example from actual use is given.

2. METHOD.

If $Z_1,\ldots,Z_N$ is a random sample from a continous distribution function $F(z)$ and $Z_{(1)},\ldots,Z_{(N)}$ denote the order statistics in increasing order, then for any integers $1 \leq r < s \leq N$ it is well-known (e.g., see p. 405 of Dudewicz (1976)) that the pth percentile ξ_p of the distribution of Z_1 satisfies

$$\begin{aligned} P[Z_{(r)} < \xi_p < Z_{(s)}] &= \sum_{k=r}^{s-1} \binom{N}{k} p^k (1-p)^{N-k} \approx P[V \leq s-1+0.5] - P[V \leq r-0.5] \\ &= \Phi\left(\frac{s-1+0.5-Np}{\sqrt{Np(1-p)}}\right) - \Phi\left(\frac{r-0.5-Np}{\sqrt{Np(1-p)}}\right) \end{aligned} \tag{2}$$

where V is a normal random variable with mean Np and variance $Np(1-p)$, Φ denotes the standard normal distribution function, and we have used a normal approximation (with continuity correction) to the binomial sum. To make this probability .95 (and hence find a 95% confidence interval for ξ_p), one may set the last two right-hand side terms equal to .975 and .025 respectively, which implies

$$\begin{cases} s-1+0.5 = 1.96\sqrt{Np(1-p)} + Np \\ r - 0.5 = -1.96\sqrt{Np(1-p)} + Np. \end{cases} \tag{3}$$

Here, r and s need not be integers, and if we simply replace them by [r] and [s] respectively (where [x] denotes the largest integer $\leq$ x) then the confidence coefficient of our interval on ξ_p may drop below .95. Hence we set

$$\hat{s} = [s]+1 = [1.96\sqrt{Np(1-p)} + Np + 1 + 0.5]$$

$$\hat{r} = [r] = [-1.96\sqrt{Np(1-p)} + Np + 0.5]$$

and (up to the normal approximation adequacy) obtain

$$P[Z_{(\hat{r})} < \xi_p < Z_{(\hat{s})}] - \sum_{k=\hat{r}}^{\hat{s}-1} \binom{N}{k} p^k(1-p)^{N-k} \geq .95.$$

Thus, after observing $Z_1,\ldots,Z_N$ we estimate their distribution's p^{th} quantile ξ_p by $Z_{([Np])}$ and assess the precision of the Monte Carlo estimate by giving the interval $(Z_{(\hat{r})},Z_{(\hat{s})})$ as an (at least) 95% confidence interval on ξ_p. (This method of assessing the precision of a Monte Carlo experiment, but without consideration of the problem beyond r and s, was proposed by Juritz, Juritz, and Stephens (1978). The other considerations above were first given by Dudewicz and van der Meulen (1981b), and thence partially (in a form which does not, however, preserve confidence $\geq$ .95) in Juritz, Juritz, and Stephens (1983).)

3. EXAMPLE.

Dudewicz and van der Meulen (1981a) performed a Monte Carlo study in order to determine the percentage points $H_p^*(m,n)$ of a statistic for testing the hypothesis of uniformity on the interval (0,1). The test statistic H(m,n) depends on the statistician's choice of m and the sample size n (not to be confused with the number of Monte Carlo replications N): Given a random sample $X_1,\ldots,X_n (n\geq 3)$ from a population with absolutely continuous density f, denote by $Y_1 \leq Y_2 \leq \ldots \leq Y_n$ the order statistics and define $Y_i = Y_1$ if $i < 1$, $Y_i = Y_n$ if $i > n$. Then

$$H(m,n) = \frac{1}{n} \sum_{i=1}^{n} \{\log \frac{n}{2m}(Y_{i+m} - Y_{i-m})\}, \tag{4}$$

where m is any positive integer smaller than $n/2$. The test procedure is then defined by the critical region

$$H(m,n) \leq H_p^*(m,n) \tag{5}$$

and the test has level p for given m and n.

For selected values of the sample size n (n=10, 20, 30, 40, 50, 100), N = 10,000 samples of size n were generated from a uniform distribution on (0,1), using pseudo-random number generator UNI with seeds IX = 524287 and JX = 654345465. This generator, which has a period of $2^{46} - 2^{29} \approx 7 \times 10^{13}$, has been found to have good properties in extensive previous testing (Dudewicz and Ralley (1981)).

For each sample, the statistic $H(m,n)$ was calculated for each m (m=1, 2, 3, 4, 5, 6, 7, 8, 9, 10, 15, 20, 30, 40) such that $m<n/2$. For each of a number of values of p (p = .40, .30, .20, .10, .05, .025, .01, .005), the percentage points $H_p^*(m,n)$ of the distribution of $H(m,n)$ under the null hypothesis were estimated from the 10,000 sample values of $H(m,n)$ generated by this Monte Carlo experiment; these values were reported in Dudewicz and van der Meulen (1981a).

For each value of p,m,n considered, a 95% confidence interval for $H_p^*(m,n)$ was calculated using the methods of Section 2, as we will now detail.

Suppose we denote the order statistics of the sample of N = 10,000 values of $H(m,n)$ (for fixed m,n) by $Z_1 \leq Z_2 \leq \ldots \leq Z_N$. Then as point estimate of $H_p^*(m,n)$ we have taken Z_j where j = (10,000)p. These estimates are given in Table 1 for the cases n = 10 and n = 20. For example, when n = 10, m = 4, p = .10, we estimated $H_p^*(m,n)$ by $Z_{1000} = -.6809$.

In order to assess the precision of the estimates of $H_p^*(m,n)$ we used the 95% confidence intervals $(Z_{(\hat{r})}, Z_{(\hat{s})})$ given in Table 1. (For n = 10 we also give $\hat{r}$ and $\hat{s}$, while for n = 20 these are omitted as they do not change.) For example, since the 95% confidence interval for $H_{.10}^*(4,10)$ goes from -.6884 to -.6726, we know that the point estimate -.6809 is accurate to at least ±.0083 (better than ±.01). In some instances (for example in power evaluation) the endpoints of this interval could be reasonably used in sensitivity studies of simulations relying on the estimated point $H_{.10}^*(4,10)$.

4. CONCLUSIONS.

Estimation of percentiles by Monte Carlo methods is a frequent problem. Accuracy of such estimates has been neglected due to lack of simple and accurate methods. The methods detailed in Section 2 (and illustrated in Section 3) are both simple and accurate and are recommended for standard use by all experimenters estimating percentile points by Monte Carlo. These methods allow assessment of the precision of the estimates, and can provide reasonable (rather than ad hoc) values for use in sensitivity studies.

TABLE 1. Monte Carlo Estimates of $H_p^*(m,n)$, n = 10.

m	p	$Z_{(\hat{r})}$	$H_p^*(m,n)$	$Z_{(\hat{s})}$	$\hat{r}$	$\hat{s}$
1	.40	-.549447	-.544029	-.537620	3904	4097
2	.40	-.431081	-.425992	-.420889	3904	4097
3	.40	-.436356	-.431368	-.427629	3904	4097
4	.40	-.470706	-.466429	-.462049	3904	4097
1	.30	-.623087	-.615368	-.606695	2910	3091
2	.30	-.486012	-.479871	-.474087	2910	3091
3	.30	-.483211	-.478341	-.473854	2910	3091
4	.30	-.518482	-.514644	-.510594	2910	3091
1	.20	-.714215	-.703476	-.695210	1922	2079
2	.20	-.557733	-.550679	-.543553	1922	2079
3	.20	-.550686	-.543545	-.537212	1922	2079
4	.20	-.581996	-.576937	-.570705	1922	2079
1	.10	-.855997	-.845020	-.834321	941	1060
2	.10	-.668003	-.659363	-.650901	941	1060
3	.10	-.654902	-.644935	-.638260	941	1060
4	.10	-.688367	-.680906	-.672582	941	1060
1	.05	-.991174	-.974181	-.960841	457	544
2	.05	-.777138	-.765613	-.752893	457	544
3	.05	-.756914	-.741442	-.733259	457	544
4	.05	-.786353	-.773908	-.761449	457	544
1	.025	-1.114470	-1.096749	-1.075422	219	282
2	.025	-.886398	-.870737	-.849100	219	282
3	.025	-.852256	-.836806	-.818132	219	282
4	.025	-.875621	-.863280	-.849252	219	282
1	.01	-1.252501	-1.228437	-1.197763	80	121
2	.01	-1.000996	-.978723	-.956059	80	121
3	.01	-.979956	-.950852	-.929872	80	121
4	.01	-1.006177	-.977331	-.954774	80	121
1	.005	-1.363396	-1.315088	-1.281399	36	65
2	.005	-1.098643	-1.046195	-1.012504	36	65
3	.005	-1.048275	-1.023903	-.999151	36	65
4	.005	-1.090305	-1.064271	-1.027395	36	65

TABLE 1 (continued). Monte Carlo Estimates of $H_p^*(m,n)$, n = 20.

m	p	$Z_{(\hat{r})}$	$H_p^*(m,n)$	$Z_{(\hat{s})}$
1	.40	-.419047	-.416042	-.412637
2	.40	-.284798	-.282126	-.279952
3	.40	-.264040	-.261874	-.259448
4	.40	-.270296	-.268382	-.266005
5	.40	-.285166	-.283409	-.280971
6	.40	-.306679	-.304341	-.302116
7	.40	-.330929	-.328868	-.326592
8	.40	-.358045	-.355977	-.353949
9	.40	-.385886	-.383713	-.381587
1	.30	-.459884	-.456712	-.452421
2	.30	-.316600	-.313229	-.309562
3	.30	-.291857	-.289099	-.286286
4	.30	-.296392	-.293994	-.291629
5	.30	-.311193	-.308702	-.306236
6	.30	-.331626	-.329505	-.327062
7	.30	-.355822	-.353219	-.350702
8	.30	-.382095	-.379521	-.377250
9	.30	-.410197	-.407485	-.405184
1	.20	-.509596	-.504488	-.499705
2	.20	-.355398	-.351840	-.348119
3	.20	-.329238	-.325343	-.321821
4	.20	-.331053	-.327383	-.324513
5	.20	-.343956	-.340563	-.337827
6	.20	-.363274	-.360503	-.357268
7	.20	-.386503	-.383707	-.381243
8	.20	-.412626	-.409726	-.407117
9	.20	-.441121	-.438447	-.435569
1	.10	-.593082	-.585424	-.578152
2	.10	-.416642	-.411760	-.406928
3	.10	-.382276	-.378327	-.374336
4	.10	-.382131	-.378062	-.373959
5	.10	-.395088	-.390740	-.387296
6	.10	-.413790	-.409922	-.405305
7	.10	-.437067	-.432727	-.428590
8	.10	-.463678	-.459855	-.455348
9	.10	-.493783	-.488623	-.484207
1	.05	-.667600	-.657822	-.649769
2	.05	-.472101	-.466107	-.458810
3	.05	-.435176	-.429018	-.423331
4	.05	-.432347	-.428204	-.422782
5	.05	-.444606	-.438376	-.433365
6	.05	-.464808	-.457936	-.452637
7	.05	-.487061	-.481219	-.476835

TABLE 1 (continued). Monte Carlo Estimates of H_p^* (m,n) n=20.

m	p	$Z_{(\hat{r})}$	$H_p^*(m,n)$	$Z_{(\hat{s})}$
8	.05	-.514806	-.508560	-.501801
9	.05	-.542550	-.536368	-.530370
1	.025	-.728171	-.716934	-.706858
2	.025	-.529557	-.520537	-.510302
3	.025	-.485763	-.473845	-.464612
4	.025	-.480219	-.471791	-.462024
5	.025	-.491822	-.482544	-.474462
6	.025	-.509033	-.500017	-.494834
7	.025	-.532850	-.525946	-.517346
8	.025	-.559816	-.551716	-.545084
9	.025	-.588130	-.580373	-.572822
1	.01	-.801596	-.787471	-.776562
2	.01	-.600395	-.588400	-.575058
3	.01	-.551230	-.536458	-.528227
4	.01	-.552986	-.535554	-.517928
5	.01	-.560784	-.543197	-.529733
6	.01	-.574291	-.557436	-.545199
7	.01	-.594912	-.580564	-.569422
8	.01	-.615902	-.604928	-.596369
9	.01	-.644403	-.631636	-.619936
1	.005	-.860409	-.836446	-.813554
2	.005	-.655577	-.634885	-.612777
3	.005	-.606792	-.580910	-.563508
4	.005	-.609411	-.573884	-.560356
5	.005	-.605411	-.586910	-.571718
6	.005	-.619216	-.596207	-.586319
7	.005	-.634863	-.619129	-.602664
8	.005	-.659279	-.643331	-.629499
9	.005	-.688957	-.671003	-.657505

ACKNOWLEDGMENTS

This research was supported by the NATO Research Grants Programme, NATO Research Grant No. 1674.

REFERENCES

Dudewicz, E.J. (1976). Introduction to Statistics and Probability. New York: Holt, Rinehart and Winston. (Currently published by American Sciences Press, Inc., Columbus, Ohio.)

Dudewicz. E.J. and Ralley, T.G. (1981) The Handbook of Random Number Generation and Testing with TESTRAND Computer Code. Columbus, Ohio: American Sciences Press, Inc.

Dudewicz, E.J. and van der Meulen, E. C. (1981a). Entropy-based tests of univormity. Journal of the American Statistical Association, 76, 967-974.

Dudewicz, E.J. and van der Meulen, E.C. (1981b). Assessing the precision of a Monte Carlo estimate of a percentile point. Mededelingen uit het Wiskundig Institut, No. 138. Katholieke Universiteit Leuven, Leuven, Belgium.

Juritz, J.M., Juritz, J.W.F., and Stephens, M.A. (1978). The use of order statistics to assess the precision of simulations. Unpublished manuscript, Statistics Department, Stanford University, Stanford, California.

Juritz, J.M., Juritz, J.W.F., and Stephens, M.A. (1983). On the accuracy of simulated percentage points. Journal of the American Statistical Association, 83, 441-444.

Schafer, R.E. (1974). On assessing the precision of sumulations. Journal of Statistical Computation and Simulation, 3, 67-69.

Received 7/29/83; Revised 6/14/84.

AMERICAN JOURNAL OF MATHEMATICAL AND MANAGEMENT SCIENCES

ARMA-BASED CONFIDENCE INTERVALS FOR SIMULATION OUTPUT ANALYSIS

Thomas J. Schriber

and

Richard W. Andrews

Graduate School of Business Administration

The University of Michigan

Ann Arbor, Michigan 48109

SYNOPTIC ABSTRACT

A method is presented for obtaining a confidence interval for the mean of a stationary stochastic process. The method fits an autoregressive moving average (ARMA) model to a sequence of sample outputs. The effectiveness of the confidence interval procedure is measured by applying the procedure to simulation output sequences generated by ARMA models and an M/M/1 queueing system model. Performance characteristics of the procedure are excellent for ARMA output sequences, and the coverage achieved with queueing data is promising.

Key Words and Phrases: autoregressive moving average; confidence interval; output analysis; simulation

1984, VOL. 4, NOS. 3 & 4, 345-373
0196-6324/84/030345-29 $8.80

1. INTRODUCTION.

Simulation output analysis often presents a confidence interval for the (stationary) mean of the process being simulated. The various alternative confidence interval procedures (CIP's) which have been proposed for this purpose fall into six classes: (1) replications (See Law (1977)); (2) batch means (See Schmeiser (1982)); (3) regeneration techniques (See Iglehart (1978)); (4) standardized time series (See Schruben (1983)); (5) model-based time series (See Fishman (1971)); and (6) spectral analysis (See Heidelberger and Welch (1981)). Methods in the first four classes are designed to circumvent the serial correlation structure present in a simulation output sequence. In contrast, methods in the last two classes explicitly allow for the presence of a serial correlation structure.

One approach to formulating a confidence interval procedure is to assume that a simulation output sequence has been produced by a theoretical output process (TOP) having known properties. These assumed properties can then be used to develop a corresponding confidence interval procedure. Such a CIP can be viewed as having been tailor made for the assumed theoretical output process and must, at a minimum, display satisfactory performance characteristics when used on output generated by the process on which it is based. The concept of tailor made CIP's, and their use in analyzing simulation output sequences, have been discussed by Schriber and Andrews (1981).

In this paper, we present a CIP which has been tailor made for use with output sequences produced by stationary autoregressive moving average (ARMA) processes, thereby providing for the first time an ARMA-based confidence interval procedure. This procedure falls into the category of model-based time series methods and allows for serial correlation by fitting a parametric model to a sequence of observations. The first step in fitting an ARMA model is to identify the autoregressive and moving average orders of the model. The model parameters are then estimated and the model is tested statistically for acceptability. If a model is acceptable, its parameter estimates can be used to estimate the variability of the estimator of the process mean and the applicable degrees of freedom of the t statistic. A confidence interval can then be built.

Apart from being of interest in its own right, an ARMA based confidence interval procedure is also of broader interest because of the potential it affords for analyzing output sequences produced by non-ARMA processes. This potential has been pointed out by Steudel and Wu (1977, p. 748), who state that "...any uniformly sampled wide sense stationary stochastic process can be adequately described by a discrete autoregressive moving average model of order n and n-1." (See also Pandit and Wu (1983).) This means that a CIP tailor made for a stationary ARMA process may perform effectively when applied to stationary processes of interest to simulation practitioners, and for which the theoretical form of the process at hand is unknown.

Discrete-time-parameter stationary processes can be adequately described by an ARMA model when the autoregressive and moving average orders are allowed to be appropriate nonnegative integers (e.g., see Cox and Miller (1965, p. 288)). As emphasized by the concept of parsimony in the time series literature (e.g., see Box and Jenkins (1976, p. 17)), small autoregressive and moving average orders can adequately fit many data sets. Therefore, the development and testing of an ARMA based CIP can focus on ARMA processes characterized by small, nonnegative autoregressive and moving average orders, as has been done in this research.

The effectiveness of a proposed confidence interval procedure can be assessed by subjecting the procedure to a series of appropriate tests. For CIP's presented in the literature, reported tests have largely been ad hoc and dissimilar, inhibiting cross-comparison of alternative procedures. Measures of effectiveness (MOE's) providing a basis for uniform testing of confidence interval procedures have been put forth (Schriber and Andrews

(1981)), and are used here to evaluate the effectiveness of the ARMA-based CIP. (More recently, additional measures of effectiveness have been suggested. One involves a measure of the probability of confidence interval coverage of values other than the true mean (Schmeiser, (1982).) Another includes a plot based on the distribution of the half-width in which the expected half-width and variation in the half-width are presented (Kang and Schmeiser, (1983)).

In Section 2, the stationary autoregressive moving average model is reviewed, and some of its pertinent properties are stated. Section 3 presents the details of the ARMA-based confidence interval procedure and provides a detailed numerical example. The testing environment used to measure the effectiveness of the CIP is presented in Section 4. Test results are presented in tabular form and discussed in Section 5. Recommendations for further research into the broader based utility of the ARMA based CIP are then offered in Section 6. Section 7 contains the conclusions.

2. AUTOREGRESSIVE MOVING-AVERAGE MODEL.

The stationary autoregressive moving-average model used is:

$$
\begin{aligned}
&X_t = \phi_1 X_{t-1} + \ldots\ldots + \phi_p X_{t-p} + \theta_0 + \varepsilon_t - \theta_1 \varepsilon_{t-1} - \ldots\ldots - \theta_q \varepsilon_{t-q} \\
&\varepsilon_i \sim N(0,\sigma_\varepsilon^2), \text{ for all } i \\
&E(\varepsilon_i \varepsilon_j) = \begin{cases} \sigma_\varepsilon^2 & \text{if } i = j \\ 0 & \text{if } i \neq j \end{cases} \qquad (1) \\
&\mathrm{Cov}(\varepsilon_t, X_s) = 0 \text{ if } t > s.
\end{aligned}
$$

Model (1) is referred to as ARMA(p,q), where p and q are the respective autoregressive and moving average orders of the model.

The ARMA(p,q) model has the following properties. The mean is

$$\mu_X = \theta_0 (1 - \sum_{i=1}^{p} \phi_i)^{-1} ,$$

while the variance is

$$\sigma_X^2 = \sigma_\varepsilon^2 R(\tilde{\phi},\tilde{\theta}),$$

where $\tilde{\phi}$ and $\tilde{\theta}$ are the (vector) autoregressive and moving average coefficients, respectively, and where the specific form of function R depends on (p,q). The spectral density function for model (1) (Fuller (1976, p. 146)) is

$$f(\omega) = \sigma_\varepsilon^2(2\pi)^{-1}\left|1-\sum_{j=1}^{q}\theta_j e^{-i\omega j}\right|^2\left|1-\sum_{j=1}^{p}\phi_j e^{-i\omega j}\right|^{-2}, \quad -\pi \leq \omega \leq \pi. \quad (2)$$

As will be seen (Section 3), the spectral density plays an integral role in estimating the variance of the sample mean when observations are taken on an ARMA process.

In most ARMA modeling applications, the objective is to find an adequate representation of the data under investigation. The procedures suggested in Box and Jenkins (1976) for finding an adequate ARMA model involve the well known steps of identification, estimation, and diagnostic checking. The order of the resulting model and the estimated parameters are of central importance. The fitted model is then used as a surrogate for the actual process, and provides a basis for forecasting.

This contrasts with our situation, in which fitting an ARMA model is a means to the end of forming an interval estimate on the mean of a stationary simulation output process. Of course, the important steps of identification, estimation, and diagnostic checking must be carried out, but the resulting model order and parameter values are not the end result; the success of our procedure is to be judged principally by characteristics of the confidence interval which it produces.

3. CONFIDENCE INTERVAL METHODOLOGY.

Figure 1 displays the six key steps involved in applying the ARMA based procedure for building a confidence interval. Detailed commentary on these steps follows.

Step 1. Compute the Sample Autocorrelations. For a sequence

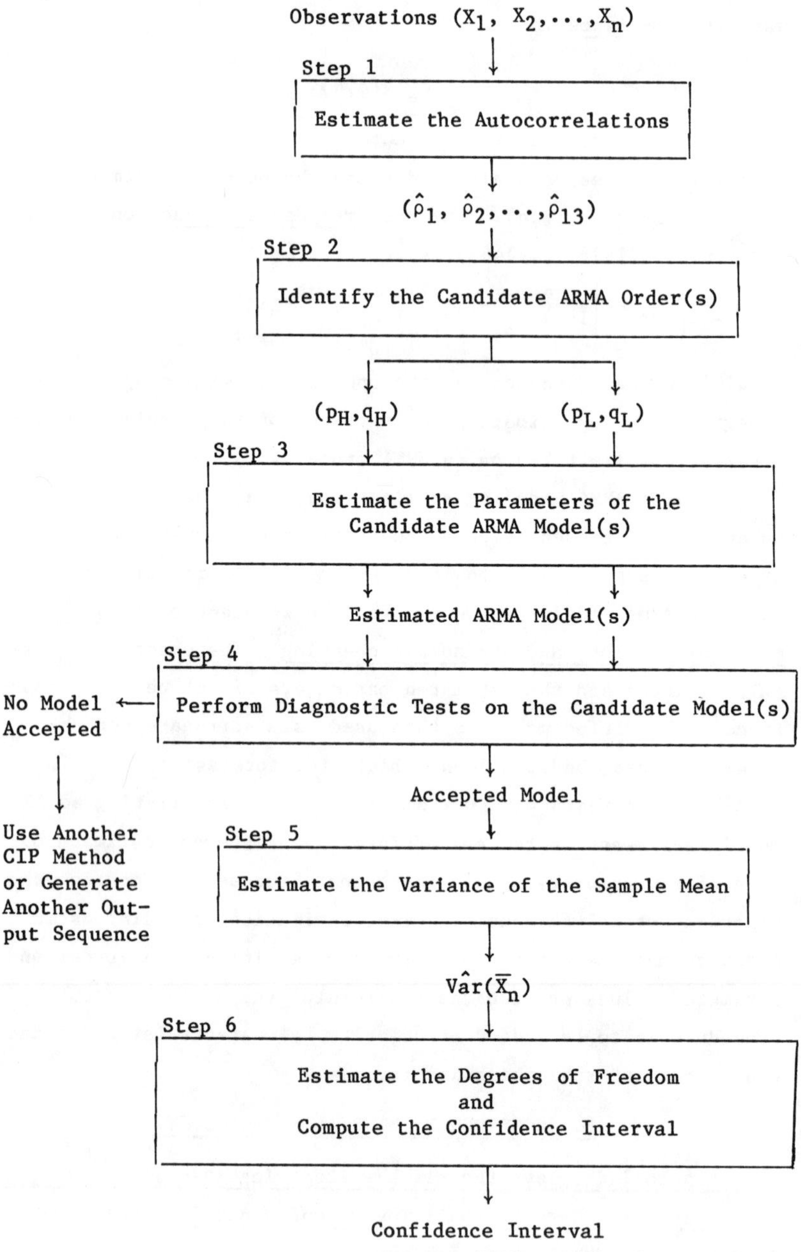

FIGURE 1. Overview of the ARMA-Based CIP.

of n observations $(X_1, X_2, \ldots, X_n)$, the first 13 sample autocorrelations $\hat{\rho}_s (s=1,\ldots,13)$ are calculated. The sample autocorrelation of lag s is

$$\hat{\rho}_s = \frac{\sum_{i=1}^{n-s} (X_i - \overline{X})(X_{i+s} - \overline{X})}{\sum_{i=1}^{n} (X_i - \overline{X})^2} .$$

For the 12 ARMA orders we tested (see Step 2), no autocorrelation lag larger than 13 was necessary (Gray, Kelley, and McIntire (1978, Appendix 2)). In this research, we used $n \geq 100$.

Step 2. Identify the Candidate ARMA Order(s). To automate the identification step we compute the D statistic proposed by Gray, Kelley, and McIntire (1978). There are two alternative D statistics, one based on the autocorrelation sequence $\{\hat{\rho}_s\}$, and one based on the switching autocorrelations $\{(-1)^s \hat{\rho}_s\}$. Gray, Kelley, and McIntire state that the D statistic based on $\{\hat{\rho}_s\}$ identifies better for high frequency data (as described by the spectral density function), whereas the D statistic based on $\{(-1)^s \hat{\rho}_s\}$ identifies better for low frequency data; they (and we) refer to the candidate ARMA orders resulting from use of the two alternative D statistics as the "high frequency case" (denoted (p_H, q_H) in Figure 1) and the "low frequency case" (denoted (p_L, q_L)), respectively.

We compute both D statistics for each of 12 ARMA orders corresponding to all combinations of p and q for p = 1, 2, and 3 and q = 0, 1, 2, and 3. The respective (p,q) combinations resulting in the largest D statistic for the high and low frequency cases are then candidate models. If the two (p,q) combinations are identical, there is only one candidate model.

Step 3. Estimate the Parameters of the Candidate ARMA Model(s). The p autoregressive coefficients, the q moving average coefficients, and the variance of the disturbance term σ_ε^2, are estimated for the candidate ARMA model(s). The estimation procedure uses the conditional likelihood method described in Box and Jenkins (1976, pp. 209-210).

Step 4. Perform Diagnostic Tests on the Candidate Model(s). Test statistics for the candidate model(s) are computed and evaluated to determine whether the model(s) adequately fit the data. Included among these statistics are the t statistic for each of the p autoregressive and q moving average coefficients in the model(s). Each t statistic is computed by dividing the corresponding estimated coefficient by its estimated standard error. The estimated standard error is found by using asymptotic maximum likelihood theory. The standard errors for the coefficients are the diagonal elements of the inverse of the information matrix. See Box and Jenkins (1976, pp. 226-227) for details. A model is judged unacceptable unless each t value is at least 1.96, which corresponds to a significance level of about 5% (Pankratz (1983, p. 82)).

In addition to the coefficient t statistics, the Ljung and Box (1978) Q statistic, which is an overall test for lack of fit, is calculated for the candidate model(s). The value of Q is given by

$$Q = n(n+2) \sum_{k=1}^{10} (n-k)^{-1} \hat{r}_k^2 ,$$

where $\hat{r}_k$ is the estimated autocorrelation of lag k of the residuals of the estimated model. Q has an approximate χ^2 distribution with 10 - p - q degrees of freedom. For a model to be acceptable, the achieved significance level of the Q statistic must be greater than .05.

In the case of two candidate ARMA models, it is possible that both models will pass the tests on the coefficient t statistics and on the Q statistic. If this occurs, we choose that model which has the largest minimum achieved significance level on the coefficients.

It is possible to come up empty in Step 4 if the model(s)

identified in Step 2 and estimated in Step 3 fail to pass the tests on the coefficient t and Q statistics. In this case, as shown in Figure 1, we recommend that another CIP method be used, or that another output sequence be generated.

Step 5. Estimate the Variance of the Sample Mean. If a model has been accepted, it is used to estimate $\mathrm{Var}(\bar{X}_n)$, the variance of the sample mean. If the spectral density function of a stationary time series X_t is continuous, then the variance is related to the spectral density by

$$\lim_{n\to\infty} n\ \mathrm{Var}(\bar{X}_n) = 2\pi f(0),$$

where f(0) is the spectral density of X_t evaluated at zero (Fuller (1976, p. 232)). The spectral density function in (2) is estimated by

$$\hat{f}(\omega) = \hat{\sigma}_\varepsilon^2\ (2\pi)^{-1} \left|1 - \sum_{j=1}^{q} \hat{\theta}_j\ e^{-i\omega j}\right|^2 \left|1 - \sum_{j=1}^{p} \hat{\phi}_j\ e^{-i\omega j}\right|^{-2}, \tag{3}$$

where $\hat{\phi}_j$, $\hat{\theta}_j$, and $\hat{\sigma}_\varepsilon^2$ are the respective estimates of the parameters. The variance of the sample mean can then be estimated by

$$\hat{\mathrm{Var}}\ (\bar{X}_n) = 2\pi\hat{f}(0)/n, \tag{4}$$

where (from (3)) $\hat{f}(0)$ is

$$\hat{f}(0) = \hat{\sigma}_\varepsilon^2\ (2\pi)^{-1}(1 - \sum_{j=1}^{q} \hat{\theta}_j)^2\ (1 - \sum_{j=1}^{p} \hat{\phi}_j)^{-2}.$$

Step 6. Determine the Degrees of Freedom and Compute the Confidence Intervals. The $100(1 - \alpha)\%$ confidence interval for μ is given by

$$\bar{X}_n \pm t_{\alpha/2,k}\ \hat{SD}\ (\bar{X}_n),$$

with $t_{\alpha/2,k}$ denoting the $1 - (\alpha/2)$ percentile of the t distribution with k degrees of freedom, and

$$\hat{SD}\ (\bar{X}_n) = \sqrt{\hat{\mathrm{Var}}\ (\bar{X}_n)}\ .$$

We estimate the degrees of freedom k in a manner similar to that suggested by Fishman (1971). For any stationary process it can be shown that

$$\mathrm{Var}(\bar{X}_n) = c_n \sigma_x^2/n , \tag{5}$$

$$\text{where} \quad c_n = 1 + 2 \sum_{i=1}^{n-1} (1 - i/n)\, \rho_i,$$

and ρ_i is the i-th lag correlation. If we have a sample of m independent observations from a distribution with mean μ and variance σ_x^2 identical to the mean and variance of the stationary process of interest, then

$$\mathrm{Var}(\bar{X}_m) = \sigma_x^2/m. \tag{6}$$

Equating the right-hand sides from (6) and (5), we have

$$n = mc_n.$$

This can be interpreted to mean that, in a degrees of freedom sense, each independent observation is equivalent to c_n correlated observations. We therefore specify the degrees of freedom (df) to be

$$df = (n/\hat{c}_n) - p - q - 1, \tag{7}$$

where we lose a degree of freedom for each estimated autoregressive and moving-average coefficient and for the estimated mean. The value $\hat{c}_n$ is calculated in the following manner. Taking the inverse transform, (3) is used to construct the autocovariance function (8)

$$\hat{\gamma}(s) = 2\int_0^{\pi} \hat{f}(\omega) \cos s\omega \, d\omega, \qquad s = 0, 1, \ldots, q. \tag{8}$$

The value of the integral in (8) is calculated using Simpson's rule, with the integrand evaluated at 40 uniformly spaced intervals ranging from 0 to π. For $i \geq q + 1$, $\hat{\gamma}(i)$ is then computed from the recursive relationship:

$$\hat{\gamma}(i) = \sum_{j=1}^{p} \phi_j \hat{\gamma}(i-j). \tag{9}$$

(See Box and Jenkins (1976, p. 75).) Then, using these estimated autocovariances,

$$\hat{c}_n = 1 + 2 \sum_{i=1}^{n-1} (1 - i/n) \hat{\gamma}(i)/\hat{\gamma}(0).$$

If $\hat{c}_n < 1$, meaning that $n/\hat{c}_n > n$, we set the degrees of free- freedom equal to $n - p - q - 1$. If (7) is less than 1, we set the degrees of freedom equal to 1.

The six steps will now be demonstrated by numeric example. All of the calculations are accomplished by FORTRAN subroutines. For each calculation, the source of the subroutine is specified. The resulting numbers are given so that the reader may explicitly follow the methodology.

Consider the sequence of 100 observations (n=100) given in Table I. These observations were generated from the theoretical output process (TOP) numbered 5 in the next section. It is an ARMA(2,1) process with $\phi_1 = 1.32$, $\phi_2 = -.68$, $\theta_1 = .8$, $\sigma_\varepsilon = 73.30$. The process mean is 1,000.

Step 1. The first 13 sample autocorrelations are calculated using the authors' subroutine. The resulting values for $\hat{\rho}_s$ (s=1, 2,...,13) are: .557, .011, -.438, -.614, -.467, -.142, .263, .387, .297, .048, -.133, -.231, and -.178, respectively.

Step 2. The FORTRAN subroutines given in Gray, Kelley, and McIntire (1978) are used to compute D statistics for the 12 (p,q) combinations. The computed D statistics for the high and low frequency cases are given in Tables II and III, respectively. Both tables indicate conclusively that the ARMA order is (2,1).

Step 3. Having identified the ARMA order as (2,1), the 100 observations are input into the International Mathematical and Statistical Libraries subroutine FTML (see the IMSL Reference

TABLE I.

100 Observations Generated from ARMA(2,1) Model

i	x_i	i	x_i	i	x_i	i	x_i
1	788.60	26	855.23	51	908.23	76	1011.72
2	886.06	27	874.97	52	1125.01	77	1004.87
3	1012.52	28	1068.71	53	1051.47	78	916.47
4	1177.32	29	1000.51	54	1059.21	79	1049.96
5	1159.23	30	1016.12	55	963.61	80	1029.17
6	1187.95	31	990.67	56	984.08	81	967.95
7	1061.53	32	847.30	57	1015.27	82	898.98
8	933.63	33	839.03	58	815.02	83	912.16
9	772.83	34	879.41	59	865.86	84	1032.50
10	758.12	35	1085.85	60	1023.08	85	1094.08
11	888.62	36	1108.78	61	1114.79	86	1231.64
12	1042.69	37	1047.05	62	1031.85	87	1120.28
13	1134.72	38	1087.96	63	979.72	88	966.88
14	1213.35	39	1030.56	64	934.90	89	913.73
15	1198.53	40	1079.79	65	900.01	90	862.02
16	997.94	41	1024.80	66	835.18	91	809.82
17	915.62	42	1040.78	67	973.90	92	1084.37
18	787.60	43	1075.33	68	1046.33	93	1198.17
19	846.89	44	974.10	69	930.68	94	1148.11
20	873.85	45	994.87	70	1122.68	95	1025.04
21	995.00	46	945.61	71	1105.18	96	858.31
22	1167.03	47	970.30	72	1092.07	97	984.69
23	1183.99	48	964.51	73	1022.71	98	976.48
24	1136.96	49	1011.96	74	986.43	99	1008.42
25	977.82	50	1004.85	75	925.87	100	998.91

TABLE II.

Values of D Statistic, High Frequency Case

p \ q	0	1	2	3
1	0.000	0.000	0.027	0.074
2	0.187	54.041	1.474	0.479
3	0.020	0.019	0.375	1.205

TABLE III.

Values of D Statistic, Low Frequency Case

p \ q	0	1	2	3
1	0.000	0.000	1.420	0.030
2	0.423	120.820	31.130	0.009
3	0.008	0.003	0.002	0.196

Manual (1982)). The parameter estimates are $\hat{\phi}_1 = 1.336$, $\hat{\phi}_2 = -.758$, $\hat{\theta}_1 = .797$, and $\hat{\sigma}_\varepsilon = 68.22$. The IMSL subroutine FTML calls other IMSL subroutines such as FTMA, which computes preliminary estimates of the θ's. All of the called subroutines are available in IMSL. Note that the estimates are close to the model values.

Step 4. An author-written subroutine is used to compute the estimated standard errors of the $\hat{\phi}$'s, the $\hat{\theta}$'s and the associated t values. For this example:

$$\hat{\phi}_1 = 1.336 \qquad \hat{SD}(\hat{\phi}_1) = .065 \qquad t = 20.55$$

$$\hat{\phi}_2 = -.758 \qquad \hat{SD}(\hat{\phi}_2) = .062 \qquad t = -12.23$$

$$\hat{\theta}_1 = .797 \qquad \hat{SD}(\hat{\theta}_1) = .060 \qquad t = 13.28$$

An author-written subroutine is also used to compute the residuals and their autocorrelations. The residuals for observations 3 through 100 are given in Table IV. Their autocorrelations are $\hat{r}_k(k=1,2,...,10)$: -0.070, 0.062, 0.069, -0.029, 0.068. -0.154, 0.184, -0.066, 0.006, and -0.145. For this example, Q is 11.135, which is a realization of a χ^2 random variable with 10-2-1 = 7 degree of freedom. The achieved significance level is 0.133. Based on the values of the t statistics and the achieved significance level of the Q statistic, the estimated model passes the diagnostic tests and consequently will be used to develop a confidence interval.

TABLE IV.

Residuals for Observations 3 through 100

i	Residual	i	Residual	i	Residual	i	Residual
1		26	-44.54	51	-97.54	76	88.75
2		27	16.71	52	174.10	77	4.44
3	5.16	28	139.97	53	-45.52	78	-76.91
4	79.04	29	-73.78	54	49.63	79	104.60
5	-4.42	30	9.41	55	-36.20	80	-16.80
6	106.86	31	-22.28	56	49.40	81	-45.84
7	17.07	32	-145.08	57	49.01	82	-71.94
8	8.20	33	-79.03	58	-177.69	83	-33.86
9	-84.66	34	-83.63	59	-16.42	84	46.96
10	-55.56	35	58.94	60	49.63	85	22.21
11	-4.11	36	-49.62	61	22.53	86	149.02
12	5.53	37	-72.01	62	-85.31	87	1.68
13	-1.62	38	50.88	63	-43.10	88	-16.16
14	65.19	39	-10.01	64	-47.53	89	36.95
15	68.35	40	98.36	65	-65.60	90	-17.72
16	-50.34	41	20.48	66	-132.20	91	-84.73
17	29.43	42	85.15	67	13.57	92	166.96
18	-77.12	43	108.22	68	-32.23	93	75.09
19	5.84	44	-8.66	69	-175.96	94	7.93
20	-77.31	45	80.35	70	110.83	95	-15.55
21	-13.49	46	-2.45	71	-22.18	96	-74.57
22	68.04	47	37.80	72	27.59	97	134.17
23	12.03	48	-6.23	73	2.16	98	-2.84
24	28.12	49	32.58	74	28.29	99	27.05
25	-42.54	50	-11.37	75	-15.55	100	-8.44

Step 5. An author-written routine is used to calculate $\overline{X} = 998.36$, $\hat{f}(0) = 171.22$, and $\hat{Var}(X_n) = 10.758$.

Step 6. Finally, an author-written routine is used to calculate the degrees of freedom and the confidence interval. Noting that $\hat{c}_n = .139 < 1$, the degrees of freedom given by (7) is $100 - 2 - 1 - 1 = 96$. The resulting confidence interval is $998.36 \pm (1.985)(3.28) = (991.85, 1004.87)$, which covers the process mean of 1000.

4. TESTING PROCEDURE.

Six theoretical output processes (TOP's) were chosen to test the ARMA based confidence interval procedure under tailor made conditions. In addition, an M/M/1 queueing system was simulated and the number in system was used as an output random variable on which to test the procedure. Fixed retained sample sizes of n = 100, 200, 300, and 400 were used. For each (TOP, sample size) combination, enough replications were generated to build 100 statistically acceptable ARMA models. For each replication all observations, including the first, were produced under stationary conditions. Hence, there was no need to delete nonstationary initial observations. For the purpose of arriving at a randomly determined starting point for each output sequence, however, the first 50 observations were deleted from each replication. Figure 2 shows the replication design for one TOP with the retained sample size set at 100. In Figure 2, X_i^j denotes the ith observed value in the jth replication. In general, more than 100 replica-

$X_1^1, X_2^1, \ldots X_{50}^1, \; X_{51}^1, \ldots X_{150}^1$

$X_1^2, X_2^2, \ldots X_{50}^2, \; X_{51}^2, \ldots X_{150}^2$

.
.
.
.

$X_1^N, X_2^N, \ldots X_{50}^N, \; X_{51}^N, \ldots X_{150}^N$

} Enough replications to build 100 statistically acceptable ARMA models

discarded observations (first 50) — retained observations (51–150)

FIGURE 2: Replication Design.

tions are needed to build 100 confidence intervals, because not every replication results in a statistically acceptable ARMA model. The number of replications needed to obtain 100 confidence intervals, denoted by N in Figure 2, is reported as a ratio in the measure of effectiveness table in Section 5.

The set of six ARMA TOP's was carefully chosen to include ARMA processes providing a representative range of behavior in terms of their autocorrelation functions and their limiting value of c_n.

TOP 1 (ARMA(1,0) is

$$X_t = .5X_{t-1} + .5 + \varepsilon_t, \quad \varepsilon_t \sim N(0,1). \tag{8}$$

For (8), $E(X_t) = 1$, $SD(X_t) = \sqrt{4/3}$, and $SD(\overline{X}_n) \approx 2/\sqrt{n}$. Furthermore, for any stationary ARMA(1,0) process it can be shown that

$$\lim_{n\to\infty} c_n = (1 + \phi_1)/(1 - \phi_1). \tag{9}$$

For (8), $c_n \to 3$, which can be thought of as a global measure of the degree of dependence inherent in this model when estimating $Var(\overline{X}_n)$. The ACF for this ARMA(1,0) process is given by

$$\rho_i = 0.5^i, \ i \geq 1.$$

The ACF for the process in (8) is consequently always positive, and decays exponentially. Such ACF behavior is representative of output from queueing system simulations (Steudel and Wu (1977)).

TOP 2 (ARMA(2,0)) is

$$X_t = .5X_{t-1} - .25\, X_{t-2} + .5 + \varepsilon_t, \ \varepsilon_t \sim N(0,1). \tag{10}$$

For (10), $E(X_t) = 2/3$, $SD(X_t) = 1.13$, and $SD\ (\overline{X}_n) \approx 1.31/\sqrt{n}$. For a stationary ARMA(2,0) process,

$$\lim_{n\to\infty} c_n = (1 + \phi_1 + \phi_1\phi_2 - \phi_2^2)/(1 - \phi_2)(1 - \phi_1 - \phi_2). \tag{11}$$

For (10), $c_n \to 1.4$.

The ACF for this ARMA(2,0) process is

$$\rho_1 = 0.4,$$

$$\rho_i = 0.5\ \rho_{i-1} - 0.25\ \rho_{i-2},\ i = 2, 3, 4, \ldots.$$

This ACF is of a damped sinusoidal form.

TOP 3 (ARMA(1,0)) is

$$X_t = .8\, X_{t-1} + 200 + \varepsilon_t,\ \varepsilon_t \sim N(0,3600). \tag{12}$$

This TOP was selected for test purposes because Steudel and Wu (1977) indicate that the behavior of an M/M/1 queueing system having a high server utilization can be modeled by an ARMA(1,0) process for which ϕ_1 approaches 1. For (12), $E(X_t) = 1000$, $SD(X_t) = 100$, and $SD(\overline{X}_n) \approx 300/\sqrt{n}$. From (9), $c_n \to 9$ for (12). The ACF (see TOP 1) decays exponentially.

<u>TOP 4 (ARMA(1,1))</u> is

$$X_t = .7X_{t-1} + 300 + \varepsilon_t + .4\varepsilon_{t-1},\ \varepsilon_t \sim N(0,2965.1). \tag{13}$$

For this process, $E(X_t) = 1{,}000$, $SD(X_t) = 100$, and $SD(\overline{X}_n) \approx 254/\sqrt{n}$. For any stationary ARMA(1,1) process,

$$\lim_{n\to\infty} c_n = 1 + 2\,\frac{(1 - \phi_1\theta_1)(\phi_1 - \theta_1)}{(1 - \phi_1)(1 + \theta_1^2 - 2\phi_1\theta_1)}. \tag{14}$$

For (13), $c_n \to 6.46$.

The ACF for this ARMA(1,1) process has

$$\rho_1 = 0.8186,$$

$$\rho_i = 0.7\, \rho_{i-1},\ i = 2, 3, 4, \ldots.$$

This ACF is always positive, and decays exponentially.

<u>TOP 5 (ARMA(2,1))</u> is

$$X_t = 1.32X_{t-1} - .68X_{t-2} + 360 + \varepsilon_t - .8\varepsilon_{t-1},$$

$$\varepsilon_t \sim N(0,\ 5373.1). \tag{15}$$

This model was used by Gray, Kelley, and McIntire (1978) to test their algorithm for automatic identification of an ARMA process. We use it here to support comparison with their results in terms of the ability of their algorithm to correctly identify an ARMA process.

For (15), $E(X_t) = 1{,}000$, $SD(X_t) = 100$, and $SD(X_n) \approx 40/\sqrt{n}$.

For a stationary ARMA(2,1) process,

$$\lim_{n\to\infty} c_n = \frac{\phi_2^2\theta_1^2-2\phi_2^2\theta_1+\phi_2^2-\phi_1\theta_1^2+2\phi_1\phi_2\theta_1-\phi_1\phi_2\theta_1^2+2\phi_1\theta_1-\phi_1\phi_2-\theta_1^2+2\theta_1-\phi_1-1}{(1-\phi_1-\phi_2)(2\phi_1\theta_1+\phi_2+\phi_2\theta_1^2-\theta_1^2-1)}. \quad (16)$$

For (15), $c_n \to 0.16$. This $c_n < 1$ indicates that the variance of the sample mean for this correlated process will be smaller than the variance of the sample mean for an independent process with the same underlying variance. This might contribute to the ability of Gray, Kelley, and McIntire algorithm to correctly identify data generated by (15) as coming from an ARMA(2,1) process (as reported by Gray, Kelley, and McIntire and as substantiated here in Section 5).

The ACF for this ARMA(2,1) process has

$$\rho_1 = 0.5299,$$

$$\rho_i = 1.32\ \rho_{i-1} - 0.68\ \rho_{i-2},\ i = 2, 3, 4,\ldots.$$

The ACF consequently shows damped sinusoidal behavior.

TOP 6 (ARMA(2,1)) is

$$X_t = .9X_{t-1} - .18X_{t-2} + 280 + \varepsilon_t + .9\varepsilon_{t-1},$$

$$\varepsilon_t \sim N(0,\ 1271.5). \quad (17)$$

$E(X_t) = 1{,}000$, $SD(X_t) = 100$, and $SD(\overline{X}_n) \approx 242/\sqrt{n}$. For (17), $c_n \to 5.85$.

The ACF is

$$\rho_1 = 0.8597,$$

$$\rho_i = 0.9\ \rho_{i-1} - 0.18\ \rho_{i-2},\ i = 2, 3, 4,\ldots.$$

This ACF is always positive and decreases exponentially.

With its $c_n > 1$ and its ACF properties, TOP 6 was designed to contrast with TOP 5. TOP 6 corresponds more closely to typical queueing system simulation output than does TOP 5.

TOP 7 (M/M/1 queueing system) models Poisson arrivals to an exponential server. The output random variable of interest is the number in system. Mean interarrival and service times of 10 and 9 were used, respectively, resulting in a .9 traffic intensity and a mean of 9 and variance of 90 for the number in system. A time-between-observations of 40 was used. This TOP was selectd to explore in preliminary fashion the potential applicability of the ARMA CIP to queueing-system output.

5. TEST RESULTS.

Results of using the ARMA based confidence interval procedure with the seven theoretical output processes are presented in Table V. The four horizontal sections in the table correspond to 100 replications consisting of 100, 200, 300, and 400 observations, respectively. Each horizontal section contains seven rows, labeled TOP 1 through 7. Each of the table columns corresponds to a particular measure of effectiveness (MOE) of the confidence-interval procedure. These MOEs will be described in general terms before the specific tabled results are discussed.

Table column 1 (MOE 1) reports the percentage of accepted ARMA models whose (p,q) order matched that of the known underlying ARMA process for TOPs 1 through 6. This MOE measures the ability of the Gray, Kelley, and McIntire algorithm to correctly identify the order of the ARMA process used to generate the time series being analyzed. (In the case of TOP 7 this MOE is not applicable.)

Table column 2 (MOE 2) provides a measure of the coverage properties of the confidence intervals built for the accepted ARMA models. In particular, the number reported in column 2 is the achieved significance level of a χ^2 test for uniformity in the distribution of the random variable

$$\eta^* = \inf\{\eta : \theta \in C(X_1, X_2, \ldots, X_n; \eta)\},$$

where

θ = the process parameter of interest,

η = a confidence level,

and

$C(X_1, X_2, \ldots, X_n; \eta)$ = a confidence interval based on the sequence $X_1, X_2, \ldots, X_n$ at confidence level η.

The random variable η^* is the confidence level that just succeeds in covering the parameter of interest, which in our case is the process mean. (The distribution of η^* is referred to as the coverage function.) For a theoretically perfect confidence interval procedure, η^* follows a uniform (0,1) distribution (Schruben (1980)).

We conducted the χ^2 goodness of fit test by dividing the (0,1) interval into 10 cells of equal width and then computing the corresponding test statistic. Low values of the achieved significance level of this statistic would indicate that the observed η^*'s do not conform to the theoretically correct uniform (0,1) distribution.

Table column 3 (MOE 3) provides the estimated coefficient of variation ($\hat{CV}$) of the standard error of the mean, which is a measure of the degree of variability in the half-widths of the confidence intervals. This estimate is computed as follows:

$$\hat{CV} = \hat{SD}(\hat{SD}(\overline{X}_n))/\overline{\hat{SD}(\overline{X}_n)},$$

where

$$\overline{\hat{SD}(\overline{X}_n)} = 100^{-1} \sum_{j=1}^{100} \hat{SD}_j(\overline{X}_n);$$

$$\hat{SD}(\hat{SD}(\overline{X}_n)) = \{99^{-1} \sum_{j=1}^{100} (\hat{SD}_j(\overline{X}_n) - \overline{\hat{SD}(\overline{X}_n)})^2\}^{1/2};$$

and $\hat{SD}_j(\overline{X}_n)$ is the estimated standard error for the jth replication. For independent and identically distributed (iid) observations taken from a normal distribution, Schmeiser (1982) derived

$$CV = \{\frac{2}{n-1}\,\Gamma^2(\frac{n+1}{2}) - \Gamma^2(\frac{n}{2})\}^{1/2}/\Gamma(\frac{n}{2}).$$

In this case the CV depends only on the sample size, n. For iid normal samples of size 100, 200, 300, and 400, the corresponding CV values are 0.071, 0.050, 0.041, and 0.035. These numbers provide a benchmark for MOE 3.

Table column 4 (MOE 4) provides the conventional measures for reporting the properties of a confidence interval procedure. Column 4(a) indicates the average relative half-width (i.e., the half-width divided by the estimate of the mean) of the confidence intervals built for statistically acceptable models at a 95% confidence level. Column 4(b) gives the coverage percentage for the 100 replications which resulted in a statistically acceptable ARMA model. Column 4(c) gives the coverage percentage for all the replications, whether or not they resulted in a statistically acceptable ARMA model.

Table column 5 (MOE 5) indicates how many replications had to be generated to obtain 100 usable replications. A usable replication is one to which an ARMA model can be fitted acceptably in the statistical sense described in Section 4. This measure is reported as the ratio of replications generated to replications used.

We now discuss the performance of the ARMA based confidence interval procedure in light of the test results reported in Table V. Referring to MOE 1 (% Correct Identification), we see that the procedure performed extremely well in its ability to correctly identify the order of the ARMA process for TOPs 1 through 5 in the cases of 300 and 400 observations per accepted replication. (This high percentage of correct identifications for TOP 5 is consistent with the findings of Gray, Kelley, and McIntire when they used this same TOP to test their identification algorithm.) For example, 95% of the replications were correctly identified for TOP 5 in the case of 300 observations per replication. The smallest percentage of correctly identified replications for these TOP/

TABLE V

Measures of Effectiveness for Analysis of Six ARMA Models and an M/M/1 Model.

n		% Correct Identification (MOE 1)	Achieved Significance for Coverage Function (MOE 2)	Coefficient of Variation of the Standard Error (MOE 3)	Average Relative Half-Width (MOE 4(a))	% Coverage for Statistically Acceptable Models (MOE 4(b))	% Coverage for All Models (MOE 4(c))	Replication Ratio (MOE 5)
100	TOP 1	83	0.437	0.247	0.409	93	92	1.47
	TOP 2	64	0.005	0.403	0.376	85	83	2.02
	TOP 3	98	0.514	0.281	0.059	87	87	1.08
	TOP 4	44	0.029	0.296	0.053	93	94	1.26
	TOP 5	81	0.046	0.613	0.009	86	84	1.66
	TOP 6	11	0.514	0.338	0.058	94	92	1.74
	TOP 7	N/A	0.000	0.950	1.912	71	73	1.22
200	TOP 1	88	0.401	0.219	0.284	90	88	1.21
	TOP 2	85	0.225	0.179	0.272	89	89	1.52
	TOP 3	97	0.494	0.254	0.042	93	93	1.15
	TOP 4	76	0.851	0.208	0.036	93	94	1.41
	TOP 5	92	0.024	0.353	0.005	82	82	1.40
	TOP 6	10	0.419	0.252	0.038	97	92	1.77
	TOP 7	N/A	0.000	1.055	1.617	75	76	1.17
300	TOP 1	86	0.534	0.174	0.223	90	90	1.21
	TOP 2	86	0.154	0.128	0.227	93	91	1.40
	TOP 3	98	0.419	0.176	0.033	89	88	1.08
	TOP 4	84	0.154	0.174	0.029	95	95	1.18
	TOP 5	95	0.086	0.249	0.005	89	90	1.39
	TOP 6	5	0.225	0.169	0.031	99	99	1.57
	TOP 7	N/A	0.000	1.542	1.667	75	76	1.13
400	TOP 1	98	0.964	0.101	0.199	95	94	1.12
	TOP 2	89	0.122	0.131	0.190	86	88	1.46
	TOP 3	100	0.534	0.166	0.030	98	98	1.13
	TOP 4	88	0.779	0.129	0.025	97	97	1.19
	TOP 5	96	0.494	0.188	0.004	91	90	1.26
	TOP 6	12	0.616	0.204	0.005	95	97	2.03
	TOP 7	N/A	0.000	0.974	0.887	81	81	1.19

sample size combinations was 84% (TOP 4, sample size 300). These results indicate good to excellent performance on the part of the identification algorithm.

With only 100 or 200 observations per replication, the percentage of correct identifications for TOPs 1 through 5 was also large in most instances, but not all, with 44% being the lowest achieved percentage (TOP 4, sample size 100). This leads to the conclusion that large sample sizes are to be preferred, which is not surprising.

The percentage of correct identifications for the TOP 6 ARMA(2,1) model is very low at all sample sizes. An explanation for this misidentification lies with the choice of the coefficient of the second order autoregressive term, ϕ_2, which for this process has a value of -0.18. This relatively small value results in data adequately fitted by ARMA(1,1) models. In fact, of the 100 statistically acceptable ARMA models for the various TOP 6 sample sizes, 62, 66, 62, and 63, respectively, were misidentified to be of (1,1) order. (In spite of these misidentifications, most of the coverage properties for TOP 6 are satisfactory, as discussed further below.)

As for <u>MOE 2 (Achieved Significance for Coverage Function)</u>, results for this measure of effectiveness are acceptable to excellent for TOP's 1 through 6 at sample sizes of 300 and 400, ranging in value from 0.086 (TOP 5, sample size 300) to 0.964 (TOP 1, sample size 400). Even at sample size 200, this measure is excellent for all ARMA TOPs except TOP 5, where the achieved significance of 0.024 results in rejection of the hypothesis regarding uniformity of η^* at a 0.05 significance level. For samples of size 100, the hypothesis regarding uniformity of η^* at a 0.05 significance level would be rejected for three of the ARMA TOPs.

For TOP 7 the uniformity hypothesis is rejected at all 4 sample sizes. Investigation of the values of η^* for TOP 7 showed that too many η^*'s were greater than .90, and this led to a large value of the χ^2 statistic. This is consistent with the lower coverage achieved for this queueing-system TOP (MOE 4(b)).

The MOE 3 (Coefficient of Variation of the Standard Error) results in Table V are larger than the iid normal benchmark values reported above. At samples of size 400, for example, the test results range from 0.101 (TOP 1) to 0.974 (TOP 7), as compared with the benchmark figure of 0.035. The fact that the MOE 3 measures exceed the iid benchmarks reflects the dependencies in the ARMA and M/M/1 queueing system observations.

The (a) component of MOE 4 (Average Relative Half-Width) is useful when it is of interest to estimate the sample size required to achieve a specified relative half-width in a confidence interval. There are no standards against which to compare these measures. Simply by changing the process mean for which the data are generated, the relative half-widths can be changed without either improving or degrading the confidence interval procedure. Average relative half-widths consequently are not comparable across TOP's having nonidentical means.

The (b) component of MOE 4 (% Coverage for Statistically Acceptable Models) in Table V indicates that the coverage rate of confidence intervals at a 95% confidence level was highly satisfactory for all six ARMA TOP's at sample sizes of 300 and 400, ranging from 82% (TOP 5, sample size 200) to 99% (TOP 6, sample size 300). The average coverage rate for all 24 ARMA TOP/sample size combinations was 91.6%.

The coverage for TOP 7 (M/M/1 queueing system) is considerably less than for the ARMA TOPs. However, the sample sizes required for the ARMA based CIP methodology to perform satisfactorily on non-ARMA output sequences might be much greater than the sample sizes of 100, 200, 300, and 400 used in this work. (See Section 6.) For example, the authors made a preliminary run using TOP 7 for samples of size 1000 and found that the coverage increased to 85%.

The (c) component of MOE 4 (% Coverage for All Models) gives the coverage for all replications, not just those resulting in a statistically acceptable ARMA model. As can be seen, there is little difference in the column 4(b) and 4(c) entries. This suggests that users of the ARMA CIP who fail to conduct or choose to ignore the diagnostic checks will nevertheless obtain confidence intervals which cover as effectively as those based on acceptable ARMA models.

MOE 5 (Replication Ratio) is a measure of the ability of the confidence interval procedure to fit a statistically acceptable ARMA model to an output sequence from a stationary process. The larger the replication ratio, the larger the number of replications which had to be discarded because no acceptable model would fit them. In the worst case (TOP 6, sample size 400), the replication ratio of 2.03 indicates that slightly more than half of the replications had to be discarded. In the best cases (TOP 3, sample sizes 100 and 300), an acceptable ARMA model could be fitted to over 90% of the replications. As might be expected, the replication ratio tends to decrease with increasing sample size in most cases, the major exception being TOP 6.

TOP 2 for 100 observations and TOP 6 for 400 observations stand out in Table V because their replication ratios exceed 2. For the TOP 2 ARMA(2,0) process, many of the replications were overfitted with (2,1) models which then proved to be statistically unacceptable (Figure 1, Step 4) because the t statistic for the moving average term had a value less than 1.96. At larger sample sizes, more (2,0) models were fitted to the TOP 2 output sequences, and these proved to be statistically acceptable in terms of the t and Q statistics, as MOE 5 in Table V shows.

The TOP 6 ARMA(2,1) process produced output sequences which were often fitted with (1,1) models at sample size 400. These (1,1) models were then rejected on statistical grounds, because the achieved significance level of the Q statistic had a value less than 0.05.

The replication ratios need to obtain 100 statistically acceptable ARMA models for queueing system TOP 7 were among the smallest replication ratios realized. Most of the accepted ARMA models for TOP 7 were of order (1,0). (There were 96, 96, 98, and 98 ARMA(1,0) models accepted for TOP 7 at sample sizes of 100, 200, 300, and 400, respectively. For the TOP 7 sample size of 1000, 92 of the accepted models were of order (1,0).) Our findings are consistent with the findings of Steudel and Wu (1977), who concluded on the basis of their limited empirical results that the number-in-system output variable for an M/M/1 queueing system is adequately modeled by an ARMA(1,0).

6. FUTURE RESEARCH DIRECTIONS.

Future research in confidence interval methodology should include a comprehensive investigation of use of the ARMA based confidence interval procedure with non-ARMA stochastic processes. Such processes might take the form of a variety of queueing models or of inventory models for which analytic results are available. The means of the selected non-ARMA processes would have to be known so that MOE's 2 and 4(b) and (c) could be evaluated.

As indicated by TOP 7, the sample sizes required if the ARMA based CIP is to perform satisfactorily on non-ARMA output sequences might have to be much greater than the sample sizes of 100, 200, 300, and 400 used in this work. For example, it has been reported that sample sizes of about 75,000 are required when a sequential batch-means CIP is used to analyze the delay-in-queue output from an M/M/1 queueing system (Law (1983, p. 1006)).

Finally, if the ARMA based CIP shows good performance characteristics when used to process qualifying non-ARMA output sequences of known form, then its application potential for use on output of unknown form, but of practical interest to simulation practitioners, warrants investigation. Briefly, this research would involve developing and using classification criteria for estimating the extent to which output from a variety of processes of unknown form is similar to output from ARMA processes (Schriber and Andrews (1981)).

7. CONCLUSIONS.

AN ARMA based confidence interval procedure has been developed and described, and results of applying the procedure to produce 2,800 confidence intervals based on simulation output sequences generated by six ARMA models and one M/M/1 queueing system model have been presented. For the ARMA output sequences, the procedure results in confidence intervals which have characteristics ranging from good to excellent, with ARMA output sequences consisting of 300 or 400 observations leading to consistently excellent results. Confidence interval coverages fall short of expectation for the queueing system output sequences with small sample sizes, but improve with increasing sample size. Reasons why the ARMA based procedure is of potential utility for any stationary output process are cited, and the directions which further research might take toward extending the procedure's domain of application are suggested.

8. ACKNOWLEDGMENTS.

This research was supported by the Office of Naval Research under Contract N00014-81-K-0120. The authors acknowledge the helpful comments of Clifford Ball, E. Philip Howrey, Joseph A. Machak, Robert G. Sargent, and Bruce Schmeiser. The insightful comments of editor Edward J. Dudewicz and of two anonymous referees are also acknowledged with thanks.

REFERENCES

Box, G. E. P. and Jenkins, G. M. (1976). Time Series Analysis: Forecasting and Control, Revised Edition. Holden-Day, San Francisco, California.

Cox, D. R. and Miller, H. D. (1965). The Theory of Stochastic Processes. Halstead Press, New York.

Fishman, G. S. (1971). Estimating sample size in computing simulation experiments. Management Science, 18, 21-38.

Fuller, W. A. (1976). Introduction to Statistical Time Series. John Wiley & Sons, Inc., New York.

Gray, H. L., Kelley, G. D., and McIntire, D. D. (1978). A new approach to ARMA modeling. Communications in Statistics, B7, 1-77.

Heidelberger, P. and Welch, P. D. (1981). A spectral method for confidence interval generations and run length control in simulation. Communications of the Association of Computing Machinery 24, 233-245.

Iglehart, D. L. (1978). The regenerative method for simulation analysis. In Current Trends in Programming Methodology; Vol. III. Software Engineering, pp. 52-71, Chandry, K. M. and Yeh, R. T. (eds). Prentice-Hall, Englewood Cliffs, New Jersey.

International Mathematical and Statistical Libraries Inc. Library Reference Manual, 9th Ed. 1982. Houston, Texas.

Law, A.M. (1977). Confidence intervals in discrete event simulation: a comparison of replication and batch means. Naval Research Logistics Quarterly, 24, 667-678.

Law, A. M. (1983). Statistical analysis of simulation output data. Operations Research, 31, 983-1029.

Ljung, G. M. and Box, G. E. P. (1978). On a measure of lack of fit in time series models. Biometrika, 65, 297-303.

Pandit, S. M. and Wu, S. M. (1983). Time Series and Systems Analysis with Applications. John Wiley & Sons, Inc., New York.

Pankratz, A. (1983). Forecasting with Univariate Box-Jenkins Models. John Wiley & Sons, Inc., New York.

Schriber, T. J. and Andrews, R. W. (1981). A conceptual framework for research in the analysis of simulation output. Communications of the Association for Computing Machinery, 24, 218-232.

Schmeiser, B. (1982). Batch size effects in the analysis of simulation output. Operations Research, 30, 556-568.

Schruben, L. W. (1980). A coverage function for interval estimators of simulation responses. Management Science, 26, 18-27.

Schruben, L. W. (1983). Confidence interval estimation using standardized time series. Operations Research, 31, 1090-1108.

Steudel, H. J. and Wu, S. M. (1977). A time series approach to queueing systems with applications for modeling job-shop in-process inventories. Management Science, 23, 745-755.

Received 10/83; Revised 8/10/84.

AMERICAN JOURNAL OF MATHEMATICAL AND MANAGEMENT SCIENCES

VALIDATION OF SIMULATION MODELS VIA SIMULTANEOUS CONFIDENCE INTERVALS

Osman Balci
Department of Computer Science
Virginia Polytechnic Institute and State University
Blacksburg, Virginia 24061

Robert G. Sargent
Department of Industrial Engineering and Operations Research
Syracuse University
Syracuse, New York 13210

SYNOPTIC ABSTRACT

The purpose of this paper is to present state-of-the-art and new research results on the use of simultaneous confidence intervals (and joint confidence regions) for determining the operational validity of a multivariate response simulation model of an observable system. A methodology is presented which allows the use of different types of statistical procedures and provides for a tradeoff analysis among sample sizes, confidence levels, sizes of confidence intervals (or regions), and, if desired, cost of data collection. The methodology is illustrated for the validation of mean behavior.

Key Words and Phrases: confidence intervals; modeling; operational validity; simulation; tradeoff analysis; validation

1984, VOL. 4, NOS. 3 & 4, 375-406
0196-6324/84/030375-32 $9.40

1. INTRODUCTION

One of the most important issues in the development of a simulation model is determining whether, within its domain of intended application, it does or does not have sufficient accuracy for its intended purpose. This determination is usually referred to as model validation (see, e.g., Schlesinger et al. (1979)).

The amount of accuracy required for a simulation model to be valid for its intended purpose is usually given by an acceptable range of accuracy (see, e.g. Schlesinger et al. (1979)), which usually consists of a range that each model response (output) variable must lie within in order for the model to be considered valid. For example, the range that the mean of response variable j must satisfy would usually be given by $L_j \leq \mu_j^m - \mu_j^s \leq U_j$, where L_j and U_j are the lower and upper bounds of the acceptable difference between the means of the jth model (μ_j^m) and system (μ_j^s) response variable.

Validity should be evaluated over sets of experimental conditions (Sargent (1982, 1984a, 1984b); also called the experimental frame by Zeigler (1976)) which cover the total domain of the model's intended application, since a model may be valid for one set of experimental conditions and invalid for another. Unfortunately, it is sometimes not feasible to determine whether a model is valid or not for each set of experimental conditions in the domain of intended application (Sargent (1982, 1984a, 1984b), Shannon (1975)). In these situations, tests and evaluations are conducted until sufficient confidence is obtained that a model can be considered valid for its intended application (for further discussion, see Gass (1983) and Sargent (1984a, 1984b)).

Recent research, e.g. by Gass and Thompson (1980) and Sargent (1981,1982, 1984a), has related the validation process to specific steps of the model development process. We are concerned in this paper with operational validity, i.e.

determining that the model's output data has sufficient accuracy for the model's intended purpose over its intended domain of application. As discussed by Sargent (1984a, 1984b), two major attributes of operational validity are (i) whether the problem entity (system) being modeled is observable or not and (ii) whether subjective or objective approaches are used in determining the model's operational validity. (If an entity is observable, then data on its output behavior can be used in validation, otherwise it cannot.) The objective approach for evaluation uses formal statistical tests and procedures while the subjective approach does not. There are three major statistical approaches used with observable entities in operational validity (Balci (1981), Balci and Sargent (1984), Sargent (1984a, 1984b)): statistical hypothesis tests, confidence intervals, and graphical comparison of the output data. For discussions on using statistical hypothesis tests, including the necessity of considering type II error, see Balci and Sargent (1981, 1982a, 1982b, 1983). For a statistical test that can be used when comparing model and system graphical data, see Schruben (1980).

The purpose of this paper is to present the use of simultaneous confidence intervals (and joint confidence regions) for testing the operational validity of a multivariate response simulation model of an observable system (entity) under a given set of experimental conditions. A methodology is presented in Section 2 which allows the use of different types of statistical procedures and provides for a tradeoff analysis among sample sizes, confidence levels, sizes of confidence intervals (or regions), and, if desired, cost of data collection. The methodology is illustrated in Section 3 for validation of mean behavior.

2. METHODOLOGY

The operational validity of a multivariate response simulation model of an observable system under a given set of experimental conditions can usually be evaluated by examining the differences between the corresponding parameters (e.g. means and variances), distributions, and time series of the model and system response variables. The range of accuracy of the jth model response variable can be represented by the jth confidence interval (c.i.) for the differences between the parameters and distributions of the jth model and system response variables. The simultaneous confidence intervals (s.c.i.) formed by these c.i.'s or the joint confidence regions (j.c.r.) obtained for the differences will be referred to as the model range of accuracy.

2.1. Validity Decision. With respect to determining the validity of a simulation model under a set of experimental conditions, an acceptable range of accuracy is either specified, or it is not. If it is not specified, then a judgment decision must be made as to whether the model range of accuracy is sufficiently accurate for its intended application at one or more confidence levels. We will assume an acceptable range of accuracy is specified, given as ranges for the differences between the population parameters of the corresponding model and system response variables, e.g. $L_j \leq \mu_j^m - \mu_j^s \leq U_j$.

There are two approaches to using a specified range of accuracy in determining model validity. The first approach (i) is to determine if the model range of accuracy is contained in the specified acceptable range of accuracy for each set of experimental conditions at one or more confidence levels. If it is, then the model is accepted as being valid with the appropriate confidence level for this set of experimental conditions; otherwise it is not. The second approach (ii) is to use the specified acceptable range of accuracy as the model range of accuracy and determine the confidence level over each interval of each set of parameters (e.g., means or variances) and distributions of interest; then a decision must be made as to whether the confidence levels are satisfactory to consider the model as valid under this set of experimental conditions.

2.2. Statistical Procedure. To construct the model range of accuracy, a statistical procedure (i.e., a statistical approach, a statistical technique, and a method of data collection) must be developed. There are two basic statistical approaches, namely, univariate and multivariate approaches (see, e.g. Miller (1981), Morrison (1976), and Siotani, Hayakawa, and Fujikoshi (1985)). In approach I, univariate statistical techniques and the Bonferroni inequality are used to develop s.c.i. In approach II, multivariate statistical techniques are used to develop s.c.i. (or j.c.r.).

Within each of the two approaches, there are three different ways of obtaining the model range of accuracy. The first way is to use statistical techniques which require independence between the model and system observations and which can be used to directly obtain the s.c.i. (or j.c.r.) of the differences in the parameters or distributions. The second way is to use statistical techniques which use paired observations from the model and system to obtain the s.c.i. (or j.c.r.). The third way is to develop a c.i. of each model and system parameter or distribution separately and then combine them to develop s.c.i. of the differences by the use of the Bonferroni inequality (see Kleijnen (1975), p. 466.). Examples of using these different ways within the two basic approaches are given in Section 3 for determining validity with respect to mean behavior.

There are many statistical techniques that can be used. These include both parametric and nonparametric (Gibbons (1985), Lehmann (1975), and Miller (1981)) techniques. The data collection method selected for a given statistical technique must satisfy its underlying assumptions. The standard statistical techniques and data collection methods of simulation output analysis can be used: (1) replication, (2) batch means, (3) regenerative, (4) spectral, (5) time series, and (6) standardized time series. (See Banks and Carson (1984), Crane and Lemoine (1977), Fishman (1978), Goldsman and Schruben (1984),

Heidelberger and Lewis (1981), Kleijnen (1975), Law (1983), Law and Kelton (1982), Sargent (1979a), Schriber and Andrews (1981, 1984), Schruben (1983), and Seila (1982, 1984) for descriptions and details.) Examples of univariate statistical techniques are the classical t-statistic and the new standardized time series technique of Schruben (1983), both for means, and the F-statistic for variances. Examples of multivariate techniques are the Roy-Bose (Morrison (1976)) and the new multivariate regeneration technique of Seila (1982), both for means.

In developing the statistical procedure, it is necessary to consider whether the simulation model is self-driven (also called distribution-driven) or trace-driven (also called retrospective-driven) (Kobayashi (1978), Rubinstein (1981), and Sherman (1976)) and whether it is a steady-state or terminating simulation (Law and Kelton (1982)). In order to have the same set of experimental conditions for the model and the real system, the simulation model must be driven with the "same" input data that drives the system. If the simulation model is self-driven, then the "same" indicates that the model input data are coming independently (by the use of random numbers) from the same populations or stochastic processes of the system input data. Since the model and system input data are independent of each other, the model and system output (response) data are expected to be independent and identically distributed. If the model is trace-driven, then the "same" indicates that the model input data are exactly the same as the system input data. In this case, the model and system output data are expected to be dependent and identically distributed.

If the simulation is a terminating simulation, the data collection method of replication would usually be used in order to produce model output observation data vectors that are independent of each other. If the simulation is a steady state simulation, then any of the standard techniques and methods used in simulation output analysis noted above can be used. Whether the model output observation data vectors are independent of each other or not depends upon the data collection method used. Regarding data collection methods and statistical techniques for the system, the same methods, techniques, and results apply as for the simulation models.

2.3 Tradeoff Analysis. It is usually desirable to construct the model range of accuracy with the sizes of the s.c.i. (or j.c.r.) as small as possible: the smaller the sizes, the more useful and meaningful the specification of the model range of accuracy will usually be. The sizes are affected by the values of confidence levels, variances of the model and system response variables, and sample sizes. The sizes can be made smaller by decreasing the confidence levels. Variance reduction techniques (Fishman (1978), Law and Kelton (1982)) can be used in some cases when collecting observations from a simulation model to decrease the variances and thus obtain a smaller size. The sizes can also be decreased by increasing the sample sizes. However, such increases may significantly raise the cost of data collection. Thus, it may be desirable to perform a tradeoff analysis among the sample sizes, confidence levels, estimates of the sizes of the model range of accuracy, and, if appropriate, the data collection budget and method of data collection.

A tradeoff analysis can be performed by using graphs which show the relationships among the estimated size of the model range of accuracy, confidence levels, and either cost of data collection or sample size (e.g. see Figure 2). If the cost of data collection is considered, it is determined from the sample sizes and the data collection method(s). Therefore, the sample size and data collection method are indirectly determined in the tradeoff analysis. The graphs can be examined and judgment decisions can be made to determine the appropriate confidence levels and sample sizes for a given data collection method (either directly or indirectly) to produce a model range of accuracy with a satisfactory size considering, if appropriate, the cost of data collection. The graphs are constructed from data contained in schedules which are discussed below. (An example in Section 3 illustrates the graphs and tradeoff analysis.)

To consider the cost of data collection, a cost model must be developed. For a system represented by a simulation model with k response variables, let $\underline{n}' = [n_1, n_2, \ldots, n_k]$ and $\underline{N}' = [N_1, N_2, \ldots, N_k]$ be the respective k dimensional vectors of the sample sizes of observations on the model and system response variables. Let $\underline{c}' = [c_1, c_2, \ldots, c_k]$ and $\underline{C}' = [C_1, C_2, \ldots, C_k]$ be the respective k dimensional vectors of the unit costs of collecting one observation from the model and system response variables. Let $\underline{c}_0' = [c_{01}, c_{02}, \ldots, c_{0k}]$ and $C_0' = [C_{01}, C_{02}, \ldots, C_{0k}]$ be the respective k dimensional vectors of the overhead data collection costs for the model and system response variables. Total cost of data collection on the model (Tc) and on the system (TC) can usually be evaluated as a linear function of the sample sizes and overhead costs. One would usually simultaneously collect observations from a simulation model with equal sample sizes (n). In this case, Tc would be evaluated as

$$Tc = c_t + c_m n \equiv \underline{c}_0'\underline{1} + \underline{c}'\underline{1}n = (c_{01}+c_{02}+\ldots+c_{0k}) + (c_1+c_2+\ldots+c_k)n.$$

In those cases where the real system is observed simultaneously with equal sample sizes (N), TC would be evaluated as

$$TC = C_t + C_s N \equiv \underline{C}_0'\underline{1} + \underline{C}'\underline{1}N = (C_{01}+C_{02}+\ldots+C_{0k}) + (C_1+C_2+\ldots+C_k)N.$$

If unequal system sample sizes ($\underline{N}$) are desired, then the linear cost model would be $TC = \underline{C}_0'\underline{1} + \underline{C}'\underline{N}$ if the data collection is done independently for each response variable. Other types of cost models can be developed depending on what is appropriate and desired. The total cost of data collection is CDC = Tc + TC.

The unit and overhead data collection costs should be estimated with respect to the data collection method (and statistical technique) employed. Alternative values of the model and system unit and overhead costs may correspond to alternative methods of data collection. The analyst may wish to make a tradeoff analysis with respect to alternative methods of data collection, and rely upon this analysis in deciding which data collection method to employ in validation.

For a given data collection budget B, it is possible to select different values for the sample sizes n and $\underline{N}$. (Unequal system sample sizes are considered for the purpose of generality.) It is desirable to select the sample sizes in such a way that the size of the model range of accuracy will be minimized for a given data collection budget. A function, $f(n, N_j; j = 1,2,...,k)$, of the s.c.i. half lengths expression (H_j, $j = 1,2,...,k$) or the area expression(A) of the j.c.r. must be determined for the statistical procedure of interest such that the (expected) half lengths or area of the model range of accuracy decrease as the value of this function decreases. (For example, for s.c.i. (2) in Section 3.1, $f(n,N) = 1/n + 1/N$ where $f(n,N)$ indicates a decrease in the half lengths when its value decreases.) Then the sample sizes n and $\underline{N}$ can be found, to produce the model range of accuracy with minimum lengths or area for a given data collection budget, by solving the optimization problem:

$$\begin{aligned} &\text{Minimize:} \quad f(n,N_j;\ j = 1,2,...,k) \\ &\text{Subject to:} \quad c_t + c_m n + \sum_{j=1}^{k} (C_j + C_j N_j) \le B \qquad (1) \\ &\qquad kn + \sum_{j=1}^{k} N_j \ge q \\ &\qquad n \ge r, \\ &\qquad N_j \ge R, \qquad j = 1,2,...,k \\ &\qquad n,\ N_j \text{ integer} \qquad j = 1,2,...,k \end{aligned}$$

where q is the minimum total sample size requirement and r and R are the minimum sample size requirements for the statistical procedure used in constructing the s.c.i. (or j.c.r.).

Estimates of the s.c.i. half lengths (or area of the j.c.r.) can be made for a specific statistical procedure by using estimates of the variances of the response variables obtained from a pilot run (or other data), a value for the confidence level, and a set of values for the sample sizes n and $\underline{N}$. When the optimal sample sizes n^* and $\underline{N}^*$, obtained from (1) for a given data collection budget, are used, we will let H_j^*, j = 1,2,...,k, represent the estimates of the s.c.i. half lengths (or A^* represent the estimate of the area of the j.c.r.) for that data collection budget.

Schedules - systematic tabulation of data - should be constructed to develop graphs for the tradeoff analysis. The first step in developing schedules is to determine what relationships are to be contained in them. For example, the validity decision determines whether different sizes of model ranges of accuracy are to be considered in the tradeoff analysis or if the acceptable range of accuracy is to be used as the model range of accuracy. Another example is whether the data collection costs are to be considered in the tradeoff analysis. The second step in developing the schedules is to determine what range each of the controllable variables are to be considered over. For example, what confidence levels are to be considered, and, if the data collection costs are included, how many different data collection methods are to be considered and what range of data collection costs are of interest. The third step is to generate the data for the schedules. This requires a procedure to be developed which satisfies the methodology. Usually it is desirable to write a computer program and use it to generate the data. In summary, a schedule is developed to contain the appropriate data of the desired relationships among the unit and overhead data collection costs ($\underline{c}$, $\underline{C}$, $\underline{c}_0$, $\underline{C}_0$), data collection budget (B), optimal sample sizes (n^*, $\underline{N}^*$), total cost of data collection (CDC), confidence level ($1-\gamma$), and the estimates of the model range of accuracy (H_j^*, j=1,2,...,k or A^*).

C_m, c_t	C_s, C_t	B	n^*	N^*	CDC	Y	H_1^*	...	H_k^*
C_{m1}, c_{t1}	C_{s1}, C_{t1}	B_{11}	n^*_{11}	N^*_{11}	CDC_{11}	Y_1	H^*_{1111}	...	H^*_{k111}
						⋮	⋮	...	⋮
						Y_c	H^*_{111c}	...	H^*_{k11c}
		⋮	⋮	⋮	⋮	⋮	⋮	...	⋮
		B_{1b}	n^*_{1b}	N^*_{1b}	CDC_{1b}	Y_1	H^*_{11b1}	...	H^*_{k1b1}
						⋮	⋮	...	⋮
						Y_c	H^*_{11bc}	...	H^*_{k1bc}
⋮	⋮	⋮	⋮	⋮	⋮	⋮	⋮	...	⋮
C_{ma}, c_{ta}	C_{sa}, C_{ta}	B_{a1}	n^*_{a1}	N^*_{a1}	CDC_{a1}	Y_1	H^*_{1a11}	...	H^*_{ka11}
						⋮	⋮	...	⋮
						Y_c	H^*_{1a1c}	...	H^*_{ka1c}
		⋮	⋮	⋮	⋮	⋮	⋮	...	⋮
		B_{ab}	n^*_{ab}	N^*_{ab}	CDC_{ab}	Y_1	H^*_{1ab1}	...	H^*_{kab1}
						⋮	⋮	...	⋮
						Y_c	H^*_{1abc}	...	H^*_{kabc}

FIGURE 1. The Schedules.

An example of a schedule is given in Figure 1. This schedule assumes that various values of H_j^*'s are of interest, $N_j = N$ for j=1,2,...,k, and the data collection cost is to be considered. The schedule shown is for "a" values of c_m, c_t, C_s, and C_t; for "b" values of B; and for "c" values of γ. The specific values used depend upon the ranges of interest. For example, the values of B depend upon the range of the data collection budget desired to be considered in the trade-off analysis. (Additional schedules and details are given in Balci (1981)).

2.4. Steps of the Methodology. We now present the methodology for using simultaneous confidence intervals (or joint confidence regions) as a series of steps:

Step 1. Determine the set of experimental conditions under which the validity of the model is to be made.

Step 2. Select the validity approach to be used if an acceptable range accuracy is specified, or determine who is to make the validity decision if none is specified.

Step 3. Select the statistical approach to be used.

Step 4. Select the statistical technique(s) and the method(s) of data collection to be used (or considered).

Step 5. Estimate the necessary parameters from pilot runs or available data.

Step 6. Determine if cost is to be considered in the tradeoff analysis. (If not, go to Step 8.)

Step 7. Formulate and solve the sample size optimization problem.

Step 8. Develop the schedules and generate the data for them.

Step 9. Develop the tradeoff curves.

Step 10. Perform the tradeoff analysis to determine sample sizes and any other required information, e.g. confidence level(s).

Step 11. Collect data for the validation.

Step 12. Analyze the data and determine the validity of the model with respect to set of parameters or distributions under consideration for the specified set of experimental conditions.

3. ILLUSTRATION OF THE METHODOLOGY FOR VALIDATING MEAN BEHAVIOR.

The purpose of this section is to illustrate the methodology, using classical statistical techniques requiring independent and normally distributed observations for evaluation of the mean behavior of the response variables. We present seven statistical techniques for developing s.c.i., and two techniques for developing j.c.r. (Some of these techniques will be used in an example later in this section.)

Assume that there are k response variables (performance measures) from the model and from the system. Let $(\underline{\mu}^m)' = [\mu_1^m, \mu_2^m, \ldots, \mu_k^m]$ and $(\underline{\mu}^s)' = [\mu_1^s, \mu_2^s, \ldots, \mu_k^s]$ be the k dimensional vectors of the population means of the model and system response variables, respectively. Let $\underline{\bar{x}}' = [\bar{x}_1, \bar{x}_2, \ldots, \bar{x}_k]$ and $\underline{y}' = [\bar{y}_1, \bar{y}_2, \ldots, \bar{y}_k]$ be the k dimensional vectors of sample means of observations on model and system response variables, respectively. Let the 100(1-γ)% s.c.i. for $\underline{\mu}^m - \underline{\mu}^s$ be $[\underline{\ell}, \underline{u}]$ where $\underline{\ell}' = [\ell_1, \ell_2, \ldots, \ell_k]$ and $\underline{u}' = [u_1, u_2, \ldots, u_k]$. Let $(1-\gamma_j)$ be the confidence level for $(\mu_j^m - \mu_j^s) \in [\ell_j, u_j]$, and a superscript of either m or s be added to γ or γ_j if we are concerned only with the model or system s.c.i. or c.i. Let $\underline{L}' = (L_1, L_2, \ldots, L_k)$ and $\underline{U}' = (U_1, U_2, \ldots, U_k)$ be the k dimensional vectors of the lower and upper bounds of the acceptable range of accuracy for the differences of $(\underline{\mu}^m)'$ and $(\underline{\mu}^s)'$.

The independence of the data observation vectors collected on the model (and on the system) can be satisfied by using either the replication or batch means method of data collection. The model and system output data will be independent if the simulation model is self-driven, dependent if trace-driven. The statistical procedure and the value of the confidence level must be selected by taking into account whether the model and system output data are independent or not.

3.1. Statistical Techniques for Simultaneous Confidence Intervals. We first present four statistical techniques using the univariate approach. The t-statistic (Walpole and Myers (1985)) will be used. The first two techniques require independence between the model and system observations, and directly give the c.i.; s.c.i.'s can be obtained from these c.i.'s by using the Bonferroni inequality. Technique I assumes the variances of the model and system response variables are equal and unknown. The s.c.i. are given as follows with a confidence level of at least $(1-\sum_{j=1}^{k}\gamma_j) = (1-\gamma)$:

$$(\bar{x}_j-\bar{y}_j) \pm t_{\gamma_j/2,n+N-2} S_j \sqrt{\frac{1}{n}+\frac{1}{N}}, \quad j = 1,2,\ldots,k \tag{2}$$

where $t_{\gamma_j/2,n+N-2}$ is the upper $\gamma_j/2$ percentage point of the t distribution with degrees of freedom n+N-2 and S_j is the pooled standard deviation of the jth response variables.

Technique II assumes the variances of the model and system response variances are unknown and unequal. This technique should be used in place of technique I if variance reduction techniques are used in collecting the data on the simulation model or if the variances of the model and system response variables are expected to be unequal. The s.c.i. are the following with a confidence level of at least $(1-\sum_{j=1}^{k}\gamma_j) = (1-\gamma)$:

$$(\bar{x}_j - \bar{y}_j) \pm t_{\gamma_j/2,\nu} \sqrt{\frac{S^2_{mj}}{n}+\frac{S^2_{sj}}{N}}, \quad j=1,2,\ldots,k \tag{3}$$

where $t_{\gamma_j/2,\nu}$ is the upper $\gamma_j/2$ percentage point of the t distribution with ν degrees of freedom, S^2_{mj} and S^2_{sj} are the estimates of the variances of the model and system response variable j using the n and N observations, respectively, and

$$\nu = \frac{(S_{mj}^2/n + S_{sj}^2/N)}{[(S_{mj}^2/n)^2/(n-1)] + [(S_{sj}^2/N)^2/(N-1)]} .$$

Technique III uses paired observations between the model and the system. The technique to be given should be used only for dependent model and system output data (it is less efficient than techniques I and II when the data is independent). Let $\underline{\bar{d}}' = [\bar{d}_1, \bar{d}_2, \ldots, \bar{d}_k]$ be the k dimensional vector of sample means of differences between the paired observations on the model and system response variables. The s.c.i. are given as follows with an overall confidence level of at least $(1 - \sum_{j=1}^{k} \gamma_j) = 1-\gamma$:

$$\bar{d}_j \pm t_{\gamma_j/2,N-1} \sqrt{S_{dj}^2/N} , \qquad j = 1,2,\ldots,k \tag{4}$$

where S_{dj}^2 is the sample variance of the differences of the paired observations of the jth response variable.

For Technique IV, the s.c.i. are given as follows with an overall confidence level of at least $(1 - \sum_{j=1}^{k} \gamma_j^m - \sum_{j=1}^{k} \gamma_j^s) = (1-\gamma^m-\gamma^s) = (1-\gamma)$ when the model and system output data are dependent and with a level of at least $(1-\gamma^m-\gamma^s + \gamma^m\gamma^s) = (1-\gamma)$ when the data are independent:

$$(\bar{x}_j - \bar{y}_j) \pm (t_{\gamma_j^m/2,n-1} \sqrt{S_{mj}^2/n} + t_{\gamma_j^s/2,N-1} \sqrt{S_{sj}^2/N}), \tag{5}$$

$$j = 1,2,\ldots,k$$

where S_{mj}^2 and S_{sj}^2 are the sample variances of observations on the jth model and system response variables.

We now present three statistical techniques using the multivariate approach. The Roy-Bose statistical method (Morrison (1976)) will be used. This method requires multivariate normal populations, independent observation vectors, equal sample sizes

(n) of the model response variables, and equal sample sizes (N) of the system response variables. Statistical Technique V also requires independence between the model and system output data and gives the s.c.i. directly. It is given as follows with a confidence level of (1-γ):

$$\underline{a}'(\bar{\underline{x}} - \bar{\underline{y}}) \pm \sqrt{\underline{a}'S\underline{a}\,\frac{n+N}{nN}}\; T_{\gamma;k,n+N-k-1} \tag{6}$$

where $\underline{a}$ is a k dimensional vector which is defined to obtain the range of accuracy of the jth model response variable by specifying 1 in the jth element and zeroes in the others, $j = 1,2,\ldots,k$; S is the pooled variance-covariance matrix; and $T^2_{\gamma;k,n+N-k-1}$ is the upper γ percentage point of Hotelling's T^2 distribution with degrees of freedom k and n+N-k-1.

Technique VI uses paired observations between the model and system response variables. The s.c.i. are given as follows with a confidence level of (1-γ):

$$\underline{a}'\bar{\underline{d}} \pm \sqrt{\frac{1}{N}\,\underline{a}'S_d\underline{a}}\;\; T_{\gamma;k,N-k} \tag{7}$$

where S_d is the variance-covariance matrix of the differences.

For Technique VII, the s.c.i. are constructed first for the model response variables as

$$\underline{a}'\bar{\underline{x}} \pm \sqrt{\frac{1}{n}\,\underline{a}'S_m\underline{a}}\;\; T_{\gamma^m;k,n-k} \tag{8}$$

and then for the system response variables as

$$\underline{a}'\bar{\underline{y}} \pm \sqrt{\frac{1}{N}\,\underline{a}'S_s\underline{a}}\;\; T_{\gamma^s;k,N-k} \tag{9}$$

where S_m and S_s are the model and system variance-covariance matrices. The following s.c.i. as the model range of accuracy are then constructed by using (8) and (9) with a confidence level of at least $(1-\gamma^m-\gamma^s) = (1-\gamma)$ when the model and system output data are dependent and with a level of at least $(1-\gamma^m-\gamma^s + \gamma^m\gamma^s) = (1-\gamma)$ when the output data are independent:

$$\underline{a}'(\bar{\underline{x}}-\bar{\underline{y}}) \pm \left(\sqrt{\frac{1}{n}\,\underline{a}'S_m\underline{a}}\; T_{\gamma^m;k,n-k} + \sqrt{\frac{1}{N}\,\underline{a}'S_s\underline{a}}\; T_{\gamma^s;k,N-k} \right). \tag{10}$$

<u>3.2. Discussion of Techniques for s.c.i.</u> The purpose of this subsection is to make some comparisons between the statistical techniques given in Section 3.1. A comparison between the univariate statistical techniques and the multivariate techniques shows that much more is known about using the univariate techniques for analyzing simulation output data.

The univariate techniques have the advantage of specifying a different confidence level for each of the k ranges of accuracy and controlling the length depending upon the importance of a response variable to a model user whereas multivariate techniques usually do not have this capability. However, univariate techniques have the disadvantage of the multiple-comparisons problem (Kleijnen (1975) and Law and Kelton (1982)), due to the fact that $\gamma \leq \sum_{j=1}^{k} \gamma_j$. Suppose that five c.i.'s are constructed with $\gamma_j = 0.2$, $j = 1,\ldots,5$. Then, the probability that all five c.i.'s are simultaneously correct can only be claimed to be greater than or equal to zero. This is naturally not a meaningful conclusion. Hence, γ_j's should be chosen by considering the value of k. For example, if the five c.i.'s could be constructed with $\gamma_j = 0.01$, $j = 1,\ldots,5$, the probability could be claimed to be greater than or equal to 0.95. However, the c.i.'s lengths would be much longer.

Univariate techniques allow the use of unequal sample sizes for different response variables, whereas multivariate techniques usually do not. The univariate techniques however do not have exact confidence levels because of the use of Bonferroni inequality.

Comparisons regarding the use of the t-statistic and the Roy-Bose multivariate method show that the lengths of the s.c.i. are smaller when using the t-statistic for the same sample size and confidence level (Balci (1981) and Morrison (1976)). The exact differences in length can usually be readily calculated (Morrison (1976)).

In summary, the selection of the specific statistical technique to be used should be based upon consideration of: (1) the satisfaction of underlying assumptions, (2) the size of the s.c.i. (or j.c.r.), (3) the exactness of the confidence levels (i.e., $= 1-\gamma$ rather than $\geq 1-\gamma$), (4) the equality or inequality of confidence levels for the ranges of accuracy, (5) the equality or inequality of sample sizes, and (6) the tradeoffs revealed by the schedules and graphs.

3.3 Joint Confidence Regions. When an acceptable range of accuracy is not specified, a j.c.r. is usually desired as the model range of accuracy. Joint confidence regions require the use of multivariate statistical techniques. We present two statistical techniques for developing ellipsoidal joint confidence regions using the Hotelling's T^2 statistic (Morrison (1976)). Both techniques require independent multivariate normal observations. (For robust versions, see Nath and Duran (1983).)

The first technique, (Technique VIII) requires independence between the model and system output data. The $100(1-\gamma)\%$ joint confidence region is specified by those vectors $\underline{\delta} = (\underline{\mu}^m - \underline{\mu}^s)$ satisfying the inequality

$$(\bar{\underline{x}}-\bar{\underline{y}}-\underline{\delta})' S^{-1} (\bar{\underline{x}}-\bar{\underline{y}}-\underline{\delta}) \leq \frac{n+N}{nN} T^2_{\gamma;k,n+N-k-1}. \tag{11}$$

The other technique (Technique IX), requires paired observations. The $100(1-\gamma)\%$ joint confidence region consists of the vectors $\underline{\mu}^d$ satisfying the inequality

$$N(\bar{\underline{d}}-\underline{\mu}^d)' S_d^{-1} (\bar{\underline{d}}-\underline{\mu}^d) \leq T^2_{\gamma;k,N-k} . \tag{12}$$

Comparison of (11) with (6) and (12) with (7) reveals that the projections of the joint confidence region determine the lengths of the corresponding Roy-Bose s.c.i. Therefore, the sizes of joint confidence regions constructed by (11) and (12) can easily be controlled by the lengths of (6) and (7), respectively. Hence, the tradeoff analysis can be performed for the lengths of (6) or (7) to obtain a reasonable size for the corresponding joint confidence region. (Alternatively, areas or volumes of the ellipse or ellipsoidal could be used.)

When k=2, the joint confidence region can easily be presented visually as shown in Figure 6 in Section 3.4.2, and can be used to evaluate the model accuracy with an exact level of confidence. As k increases, interpretation of j.c.r. becomes difficult, but not impossible. An approach that can be used is to visually examine two dimensions of the j.c.r. (as in Figure 6) at a time while simultaneously enumerating $\underline{\delta}$ or $\underline{\mu}^d$ over the ranges of interest; an interactive computer program with graphics aids in using this approach. Resorting to the statistical techniques given in Section 3.1 would usually be suboptimal in case of nonspecified acceptable range of accuracy for the means.

3.4. Examples.

A simulation model of an M/M/1 queueing system (see, e.g. Law and Kelton (1982) for details of the model) serves as an example for illustrating the tradeoff analysis and the validation methodology (section 3.4.1) as well as construction of the confidence region (section 3.4.2).

3.4.1. Tradeoff Analysis and Validation Methodology: Example.

The simulation model is represented by a computerized self-driven model of an M/M/1 queue with arrival rate $a_r = 1$ and service rate $s_r = 1/0.76$. Similarly, the real system is represented by a self-driven simulation model of an M/M/1 queue with $a_r = 1$ and $s_r = 1/0.75$. (Note: A simulator of an M/M/1 queue is used to generate the output data for both the simulation model and the real system by using service rates of $s_r = 1/0.76$ and $s_r = 1/0.75$, respectively.) The random variate generation is done on an IBM 370 using the Inverse Transform Method (Fishman (1978), Law and Kelton (1982)) and the multiplicative congruential random number generator $W_n = 7^5 W_{n-1} (\text{mod } 2^{31}-1)$. The initial conditions in the simulations are assumed to be an empty system, with the first arrival at time zero. The methodology in Section 2 will be followed to illustrate the sample size selection with a tradeoff analysis and the construction of the model range of accuracy.

There are two response variables of interest, namely the utilization of the server (response variable 1) and the average time in the system (i.e., waiting time plus service time). The set of experimental conditions under which the model range of accuracy is to be constructed (step 1 of the methodology) is determined by the Poisson arrival process with rate a_r, exponential service times with rate s_r, and the first-come, first-served queue discipline. Assuming that the intended application of the model is to analyze the mean behavior of the system with respect to the performance measures chosen, the acceptable range of accuracy for the population means is specified as

$$\begin{aligned} -0.035 &\leq \mu_1^m - \mu_1^s \leq 0.035 \\ -0.450 &\leq \mu_2^m - \mu_2^s \leq 0.450 \ . \end{aligned} \qquad (13)$$

The validity approach to be used (Step 2 of the Methodology) is to compare the model range of accuracy to the specified acceptable range of accuracy.

Statistical Technique IV (Steps 3 and 4 of the methodology) using (5) is chosen for purposes of illustration. The method of batch means (Step 4) is used as the method of data collection, with batch size of 5,000 customers; the first 10,000 are deleted to remove the effect of the transient period. Supposing that a tradeoff analysis is desired, estimates of variances are obtained from five independent (batch) observations in pilot runs (Step 5).

Thus, we obtained $S^2_{m1} = 0.00058$, $S^2_{m2} = 0.093834$, $S^2_{s1} = 0.000311$, and $S^2_{s2} = 0.071064$.

Assume that $c_t = \$150$, $C_t = \$250$, $c_m = \$6$, and $C_s = \$8$ (Step 6). Noting that the half lengths of the s.c.i. for $\underline{\mu}^m$ can be shortened in terms of the sample size by minimizing 1/n, the optimization problem (1) is given (Step 7) as:

$$\text{Minimize } \{1/n \mid c_m n + c_t \leq B^m;\ n \geq 2;\ n \text{ integer}\}$$

where B^m is the data collection budget for the model. Denoting the largest integer less than or equal to x by $\lfloor x \rfloor$, the optimal sample size n^* is obtained as $\lfloor (B^m - c_t)/c_m \rfloor$ if $\lfloor (B^m - c_t)/c_m \rfloor \geq 2$. Similarly, N^* can be found.

Schedules are constructed next (Step 8 of the methodology). Three steps are given in Section 2.3. for this construction. The first step is to determine the relationships to be contained in them. Separate schedules are used here for the model and the system because the statistical technique chosen has the statistical analysis done separately for the model and system. (Since the separate schedules are similar, we will only discuss the schedules for the model.) The relationships of interest are the data collection costs (c_t, c_m), the budget (B), the optimal sample size (n^*), total data collection cost (Tc), confidence level (γ), and estimates of the model range of accuracy -- the minimum half lengths (H_1^{m*}, H_2^{m*}). The second step is to determine the range for each of the controllable variables (c_t, c_m, B, and γ). We are considering only one data collection method and its cost. The range of interest for the budget is \$200 to \$500 with \$25 increments. The values of the confidence level of interests are 0.0025, 0.005, 0.0125, 0.025, and 0.05. The third step is to generate the data for the schedules. We first solve the optimization problem to find the optimal sample size, n^*, for each value of the budget, B. For each specific value of the budget and n^*, the total data collection cost (Tc) can be determined and the minimum half lengths (H_1^{m*}, H_2^{m*}) for each confidence level can be determined by using the estimates of variances S_{m1}^2 and S_{m2}^2, in the half length expression (from (5)) $t_{\gamma_j^m/2, n^*-1}\sqrt{S_{mj}^2/n^*}$.

Figures 2, 3, 4 and 5 are developed (Step 9 of the methodology) by plotting the data contained in the schedules. It is desirable to choose the sample sizes and the overall confidence level, at a reasonable cost, in such a way that the model range of accuracy that will be determined will have half lengths that are no longer than the half lengths of the acceptable range of accuracy (13). We analyze the tradeoffs among the minimum half length estimates, data collection cost, and confidence levels by considering the acceptable range of accuracy and variances of the response variables. Depending upon the importance of a response variable to model user, a different confidence level can be chosen for each variable. The importance may also be reflected upon the shortness of the interval. Therefore, a balance needs to be established between the confidence level and the interval length depending upon the response variable's importance to model user and the values of other parameters. Assume that, as a result of the tradeoff analysis (Step 10), the following has been found satisfactory for the intended application of the model: $n^* = 25$, Tc = \$300, $\gamma_1^m = \gamma_2^m = 0.025$, $H_1^{m*} = 0.0117$, $H_2^{m*} = 0.1483$, $N^* = 20$, TC = \$410, $\gamma_1^s = \gamma_2^s = 0.025$, $H_1^{s*} = 0.0097$, and $H_2^{s*} = 0.1469$.

The simulation model and the system are run for 25 and 20 batches in steady-state (Step 11), respectively, for 5,000 customers in each batch after deleting the first 10,000 customers in the transient period. The model and system outputs are independent. The following results (Step 12) are obtained: $\bar{x}_1 = 0.7626$, $\bar{x}_2 = 3.1767$, $S_{m1}^2 = 0.00028$, $S_{m2}^2 = 0.05546$, $\bar{y}_1 = 0.7504$, $\bar{y}_2 = 3.0401$, $S_{s1}^2 = 0.00021$, and $S_{s2}^2 = 0.05922$. The univariate normality of the observations collected is tested by

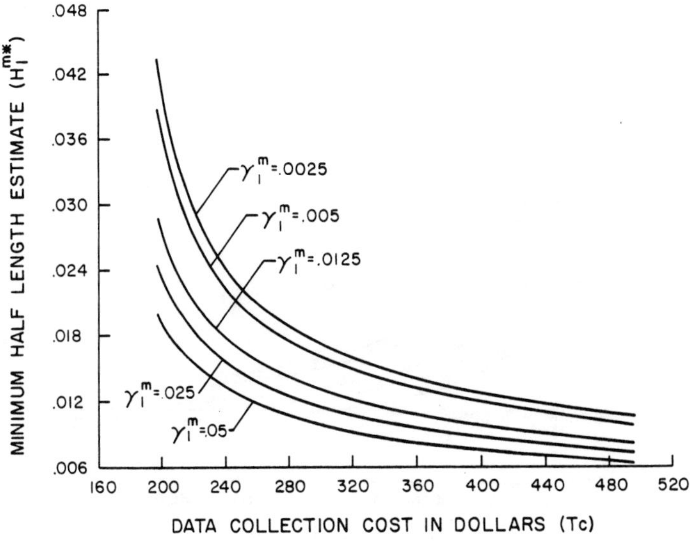

FIGURE 2: Cost Curves for H_1^{m*}

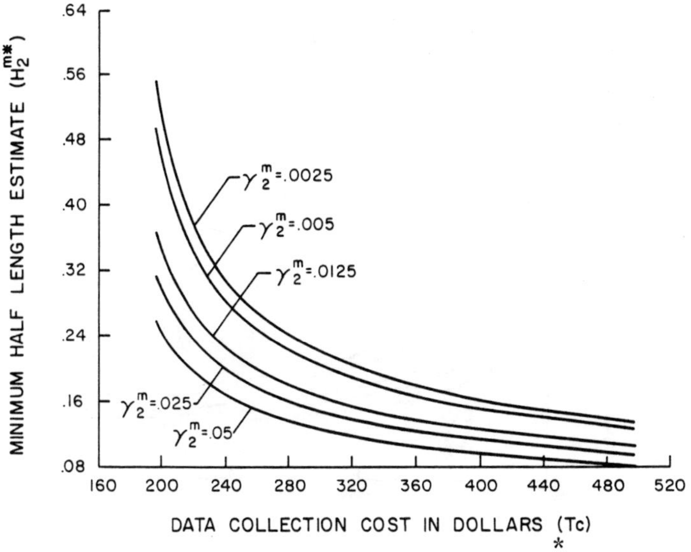

FIGURE 3: Cost Curves for H_2^{m*}

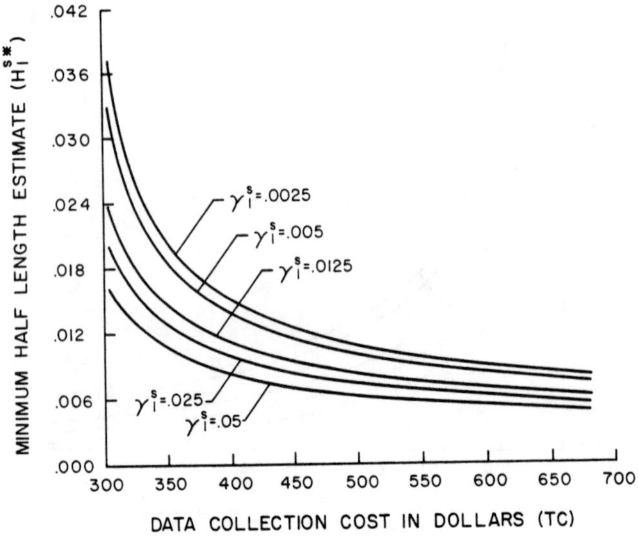

FIGURE 4: Cost Curves for H_1^{s*}

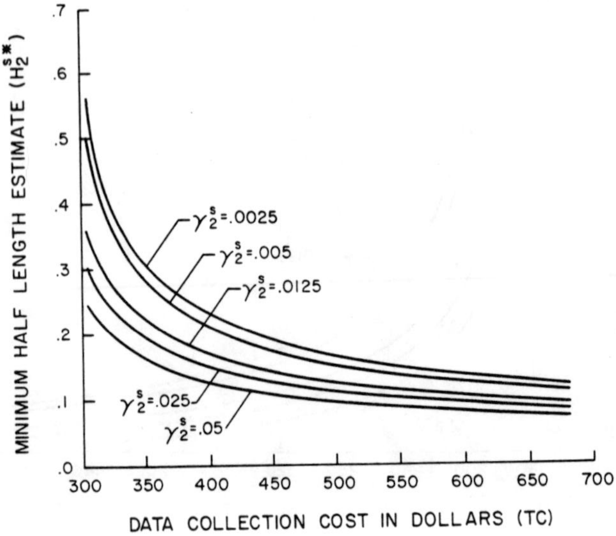

FIGURE 5: Cost Curves for H_2^{s*}

using the Box-Cox transformation test. This test uses the power transformation to determine whether the data are nonnormal or not. A step-by-step description of it can be found in Andrews, Gnanadesikan, and Warner (1973) and Balci and Sargent (1982a). The univariate normality is accepted for $\underline{x}_1$, $\underline{x}_2$, $\underline{y}_1$, and $\underline{y}_2$, with approximate significance levels of 0.66, 0.65, 0.78, and 0.86, respectively. (Alternatively, the W test (Royston (1982a, 1982b, 1983a, 1983b)) can be used to test for normality).

The range of accuracy of the simulation model is constructed for several values of overall confidence level ($\geq 100(1-\gamma^m-\gamma^s+\gamma^m\gamma^s)$ percent where $\gamma^m=\gamma^s= 0.1, 0.05, 0.025, 0.005$) by using (5) and is presented in Table 1. (The model range of accuracy at all overall confidence levels shown in Table 1 contain the true differences $(\mu_1^m-\mu_1^s, \mu_2^m-\mu_2^s) = (0.01, 0.167)$.) Since the 81%, 90%, and 95% model range of accuracy is completely contained within the acceptable one (13), it is concluded (Step 12) that we are at least 95% confident that the model is valid with respect to the acceptable range of accuracy under the set of experimental conditions.

3.4.2. Illustration of the Joint Confidence Region. Suppose that (13) is not given and Statistical Technique V is chosen for validating the model of Section 3.4.1. To evaluate the validity, we can construct an ellipsoidal joint confidence region which is usually the preference in the case of a nonspecified acceptable range of accuracy. Assume that a tradeoff analysis is preformed for (6) and a reasonable size is expected for the confidence region at a moderate cost of \$710 for $n^* = 25$, $N^* = 20$, and $\gamma = 0.1$. The data collected by the method of batch means in Section 4.1 is then tested by using the multivariate normality transformation test (Andrews, Gnanadesikan, and Warner (1973) and Balci and Sargent (1982a)). Multivariate normality of the model and the system response variables is achieved at an approximate significance level of 0.17 and 0.82, respectively. Then, the confidence region is constructed by using (11) and is shown in Figure 6. The validity of the model can be evaluated by an

TABLE 1. Range of Accuracy of the Self-Driven Steady-State Simulation Model.

M/M/1 Model $(a_r = 1,\ s_r = 1/0.76,\ n^* = 25)$ M/M/1 System $(a_r = 1,\ s_r = 1/0.75,\ N^* = 20)$	
Confidence	Model Range of Accuracy
$\geq$ 81%	$(\mu_1^m-\mu_1^s)\ \varepsilon\ [-0.0015,\ 0.029]$ $(\mu_2^m-\mu_2^s)\ \varepsilon\ [-0.0745,\ 0.3477]$
$\geq$ 90%	$(\mu_1^m-\mu_1^s)\ \varepsilon\ [-0.0039,\ 0.0283]$ $(\mu_1^m-\mu_2^s)\ \varepsilon\ [-0.1115,\ 0.3847]$
$\geq$ 95%	$(\mu_1^m-\mu_1^s)\ \varepsilon\ [-0.0059,\ 0.0303]$ $(\mu_2^m-\mu_2^s)\ \varepsilon\ [-0.1428,\ 0.4160]$
$\geq$ 99%	$(\mu_1^m-\mu_1^s)\ \varepsilon\ [-0.0118,\ 0.0362]$ $(\mu_2^m-\mu_2^s)\ \varepsilon\ [-0.2344,\ 0.5076]$

examination of this region.

If the Roy-Bose technique (6) given in Section 3.1 for Statistical Technique V were used, the model range of accuracy would be given at $\gamma = 0.1$ as

$$\begin{aligned} &(\mu_1^m-\mu_1^s)\ \varepsilon\ [0.0016,\ 0.0228] \\ &(\mu_2^m-\mu_2^s)\ \varepsilon\ [-0.02399,\ 0.297]. \end{aligned} \tag{14}$$

As shown in Figure 6, s.c.i. (14) are the projections of the joint confidence region. If Statistical Technique I with the

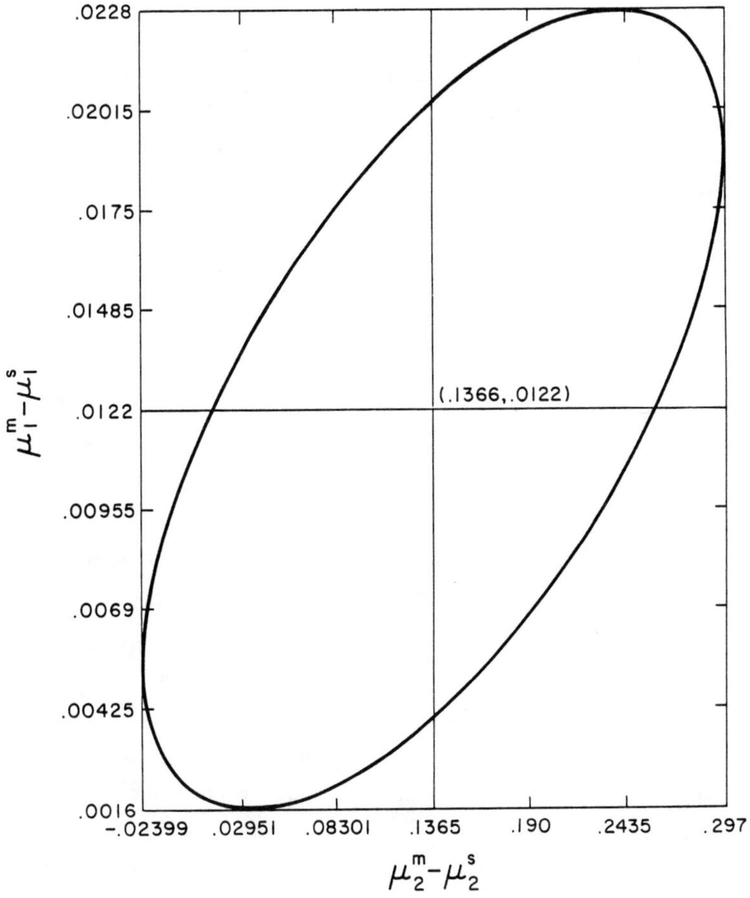

FIGURE 6: Joint Confidence Region.

t-statistic (2) of Section 3.1 were used, the model range of accuracy would be given at $\gamma \leq 0.1$ as

$$\begin{aligned} (\mu_1^m - \mu_1^s) &\in [0.00265,\ 0.02175] \\ (\mu_2^m - \mu_2^s) &\in [-0.00808,\ 0.28128]. \end{aligned} \tag{15}$$

The s.c.i. (15) are shorter than (14) as expected. (Also note that the lengths of (14) and (15) are shorter than those given in Table 1 for confidence level of at least 90% using Statistical Technique IV and the t-statistic.)

4. CONCLUSIONS.

A methodology is presented for using s.c.i. and j.c.r. for testing the operational validity of a multivariate response simulation model of an observable system for a given set of experimental conditions. The methodology allows the use of different types of statistical procedures. Factors to be considered in selecting one of the seven statistical techniques for s.c.i. are given.

This methodology includes the use of graphs to show the relationships among the cost of data collection, size estimates of the model range of accuracy, the confidence levels, and data collection methods (and statistical techniques). The model sponsor, model user, and model builder, individually or together, can use these graphs to perform a tradeoff analysis and to make judgment decisions as to what data collection budget to allocate, what data collection method (and statistical technique) to use, and what confidence level(s) to use to produce a satisfactory size for the model range of accuracy. The results of these decisions readily yield the number of observations (sample sizes) to collect on each model and system response variable.

The methodology can be applied to only one type of population parameters (e.g. means or variances) or for the population distributions using one set of experimental conditions at a time. The methodology must be repeated for each set of experimental conditions and for each different type of population parameters or distribution.

Additional research is needed in the use of multivariate techniques to better understand their applicability in simulation. Also, the use of multivariate times series models and methods for validation (and output analysis) is an open area for research.

REFERENCES

Andrews, D.F., Gnanadesikan, R, and Warner, J.L. (1973). Methods for assessing multivariate normality. Multivariate Analysis III, edited by P.R. Krishnaiah, Academic Press, New York, 95-116.

Balci, O. (1981). Statistical Validation of Multivariate Response Simulation Models. Ph.D. Dissertation, Syracuse University. Syracuse, New York.

Balci, O. and Sargent, R.G. (1981). A methodology for cost-risk analysis in the statistical validation of simulation models. Communications of the ACM, 24, 190-197.

Balci, O. and Sargent, R.G. (1982a). Validation of multivariate response models using Hotelling's two-sample T^2 test. Simulation, 39, 185-192.

Balci, O. and Sargent, R.G. (1982b). Some examples of simulation model validation using hypothesis testing. Proceedings of the 1982 Winter Simulation Conference, edited by H.J. Highland, Y.W. Chao, and O.S. Madrigel, San Diego, California, 620-629,

Balci, O. and Sargent, R.G. (1983). Validation of multivariate response trace-driven simulation models. Performance 83, edited by A.K. Agrawala and S.K. Tripathi, North Holland, Publishing Company, Amsterdam, The Netherlands, 309-323.

Balci, O. and Sargent, R.G. (1984). A bibliograph on the credibility assessment and validation of simulation and mathematical models. Simuletter, 15, 3, 15-27.

Banks, J. and Carson II, J.S. (1984). Discrete-Event System Simulation. Prentice-Hall, Englewood, New Jersey.

Crane, M.A. and Lemoine, A.J. (1977). An Introduction to the Regenerative Method of Simulation. Lecture Notes in Control and Information Sciences, Vol. 4, Springer-Verlag, New York.

Fishman, G.S. (1978). Principles of Discrete Event Simulation. Wiley-Interscience, New York.

Gass, S.I. (1983). Decision-aiding models: validation, assessment, and related issues for policy analysis. Operations Research, 31, 603-631.

Gass, S.I. and Thompson, B.W. (1980). Guidelines for model evaluation: an abridged version of the U.S. General Accounting Office exposure draft. Operations Research, 28, 431-479.

Gibbons, J.D. (1985), Nonparametric Methods for Quantitative Analysis, Second Edition, American Science Press, Inc., Columbus, Ohio.

Goldsman, D. and Schruben, L.W. (1984). Asymptotic properties of some confidence interval estimators. Management Science, 30, 1217-1225.

Heidelberger, P. and Lewis, P.A.W. (1981). Regression-adjusted estimates for regenerative simulations with graphics. Communications of ACM, 24, 260-273.

Kleijnen, J.P.C. (1975). Statistical Techniques in Simulation. Marcel Dekker, New York, Vol. 2.

Kobayashi, H. (1978). Modeling and Analysis: An Introduction to System Performance Evaluation Methodology. Addison-Westley, Reading, Massachusetts.

Law, A.M. (1983). Statistical analysis of simulation output data. Operations Research, 31, 983-1029.

Law, A.M. and Kelton, W.D. (1982). Simulation Modeling and Analysis. McGraw-Hill, New York.

Lehmann, E.L. (1975). Nonparametrics: Statistical Methods Based on Ranks. Holden-Day, San Francisco, California.

Miller, R.G., Jr. (1981). Simultaneous Statistical Inference, 2nd edition. Springer-Verlag, New York.

Morrison, D.F. (1976). Multivariate Statistical Methods. McGraw-Hill, New York.

Nath, R. and Duran, B.S. (1983). A robust test in the multivariate two-sample location problem. American Journal of Mathematical and Management Sciences, 3, 225-249.

Royston, J.P. (1982a). An extension of Shapiro and Wilk's W test for normality to large samples. Applied Statistics, 31, 115-124.

Royston, J.P. (1982b). Algorithm AS 181: The W test for normality. Applied Statistics, 31, 176-180.

Royston, J.P. (1983a). Correction to Algorithm AS 181: The W test for normality. Applied Statistics, 32, 224.

Royston, J.P. (1983b). Some techniques for assessing multivariate normality based on the Shapiro-Wilk W. Applied Statistics, 32, 121-133.

Rubinstein, R.Y. (1981). Simulation and the Monte Carlo Method John Wiley & Sons, New York.

Sargent, R.G. (1979a). An introduction to statistical analysis of simulation output data. Proceedings of the NATO AGARD Symposium on Modeling and Simulation of Avionics Systems and Command, Control, and Communication Systems, No. 268, Paris, France, 3-1/3-13.

Sargent, R.G. (1979b). Validation of simulation models. Proceedings of the 1979 Winter Simulation Conference, edited by H.J. Highland, M.G. Spiegel and R.E. Shannon, San Diego, California, 497-503.

Sargent, R.G. (1981). An assessment procedure and a set of criteria for use in the evaluation of computerized models and computer-based modelling tools. Final Technical Report RADC-TR-80-409.

Sargent, R.G. (1982). Verification and validation of simulation models. Progress in Modeling and Simulation, edited by F.E. Cellier, Academic Press, London, 159-169.

Sargent, R.G. (1983). Validating simulation models. Proceedings of the 1983 Winter Simulation Conference, edited by S. Roberts, J. Banks, and B. Schmeiser, Arlington, Virginia, 333-337.

Sargent, R.G. (1984a). Simulation model validation. Simulation and Model-Based Methodologies: An Integrative View, edited by T.I. Oren, B.P. Ziegler and M.S. Elzas, Springer-Verlag, 537-555.

Sargent, R.G. (1984b). A tutorial on verification and validation of simulation models. Proceedings of the 1984 Winter Simulation Conference, edited by S. Sheppard, U.W. Pooch, and C.D. Pegden, Dallas, Texas, 115-121.

Schlesinger, S., Crosbie, R.E., Gagne, R.E., Innis, G.S., Lalwani, C.S., Loch, J., Sylvester, R.J., Wright, R.O., Kheir, N., and Bartos, D. (1979). Terminology for model credibility. Simulation, 32, 3, 103-104.

Schriber, T.J. and Andrews, R.W. (1981). A conceptual framework for research in the analysis of simulation output. Communications of the ACM, 24, 218-232.

Schriber, T.J. and Andrews, R.W. (1984). ARMA-based confidence-intervals for simulation output analysis. American Journal of Mathematical and Management Sciences, 4, 345-373.

Schruben, L.W. (1980). Establishing the credibility of simulaitions. Simulation, 34, 101-105.

Schruben, L.W. (1983). Confidence intervale estimation using standardized time series. Operations Research, 30, 1090-1108.

Seila, A.F. (1982). Multivariate estimation in regenerative simulation. Operations Research Letters, 1, 153-156.

Seila, A.F. (1984). Multivariate simulation output analysis. American Journal of Mathematical and Management Sciences, 4, 313-334.

Shannon, R.E. (1975). Systems Simulation: The Art and Science. Prentice-Hall, New Jersey.

Sherman, S.W. (1976). Trace-driven modeling: an update. Proceedings of the Symposium on the Simulation of Computer Systems IV, 87-91.

Siotani, M., Mayakawa, T., and Fujikoshi, Y. (1985). Modern Multivariate Statistical Analysis, A Graduate Course and Handbook. American Sciences Press, Inc., Columbus, Ohio.

Walpole, R.E. and Myers, R.H. (1985). Probability and Statistics for Engineers and Scientists, third edition. Macmillan, New York.

Zeigler, B.P. (1976). Theory of Modelling and Simulation. John Wiley & Sons, Inc., New York.

Received 1983; Revised 3/15/85.

ANNOUNCEMENT

THE 1984 THOMAS L. SAATY AND JACOB WOLFOWITZ PRIZES

The 1984 Jacob Wolfowitz Prize has been awarded to Professor Edward J. Dudewicz (Syracuse University, Syracuse, New York) and Dr. Siddhartha R. Dalal (Bell Communications Research, New Jersey) for their paper "Multiple-Comparisons With A Control When Variances Are Unknown and Unequal."

Typical of evaluation of this paper were the comments: "...deserves the Wolfowitz Prize, because it deals with statistical problems that statisticians face in just about every data analysis," "This is a complex case...and...the article is well written, lucid," and "This paper solves an important practical problem that has traditionally been (inadequately) handled."

The 1984 Thomas L. Saaty Prize has been awarded to Professor Rand R. Wilcox (University of Southern California, Los Angeles) for his paper "Measuring Mental Abilities With Latent State Models."

Typical evaluation of this paper included such comments as "...represents a new approach to mental test theory that solves a whole family of problems that were previously impossible to address," "...an achievement of applied psychometrics facing real-world problems," and "...concise and understandable...clarifie[s] the nature of Latent State Models...."

Evaluation Chairman for the 1984 Prizes was Dr. Young Jack Lee (National Institutes of Health, Bethesda, Maryland). Dr. Lee has also been Evaluation Chairman for the TECHNOMETRICS Prizes.

The Thomas L. Saaty Prize for Applied Advances in the Mathematical and Management Sciences, and The Jacob Wolfowitz Prize for Theoretical Advances in the Mathematical and Management Sciences, were established in honor of those whose contributions epitomize excellence in their respective areas. The Prizes are awarded annually and consist of a monetary award and suitably engraved certificate. The goal of the Prizes is to recognize and stimulate excellence in these fields.

Both Prize winning articles were published in the AMERICAN JOURNAL OF MATHEMATICAL AND MANAGEMENT SCIENCES, published by the American Sciences Press, Inc., Columbus, Ohio, U.S.A.

THE THOMAS L. SAATY AND JACOB WOLFOWITZ PRIZES

The Thomas L. Saaty Prize for Applied Advances in the Mathematical and Management Sciences, and The Jacob Wolfowitz Prize for Theoretical Advances in the Mathematical and Management Sciences, were established in 1981 to recognize and encourage high quality work in these fields (which, due to their youth, did not have associated with them prizes covering these important modern areas of achievement). The Prizes are awarded annually, the first Prizes having been awarded in 1982.

The Prizes consist of a monetary award and suitably engraved certificate, and are awarded yearly to the author(s) of the respective best Applied/Theoretical Advances paper appearing in the previous year. (The monetary component varies yearly, depending on contributions received by The Thomas L. Saaty Prize Fund and The Jacob Wolfowitz Prize Fund. Contributions may be sent to the Funds at P.O. Box 21161, Columbus, Ohio 43221-0161, U.S.A.)

Authors of past Prize-winning articles, and the contributions for which they were honored, are:

	Thomas L. Saaty Prize	*Jacob Wolfowitz Prize*
1982	*William R. Fairweather* "A Distribution-Free Comparison of Multiple Tumor Incidence in the Presence of Unrelated Censoring"	*Samuel Kotz & Norman L. Johnson* "Dependent Relevations: Time-to-Failure Under Dependence"
1983	*Umed Singh and K.P. Singh* "Improved Models for Fertilizer Nutrient Experiments"	*Michael R. Chernick* "The Influence Function and Its Application to Data Validation"
1984	*Rand R. Wilcox* "Measuring Mental Abilities With Latent State Models"	*Edward J. Dudewicz & S.R. Dalal* "Multiple-Comparisons With a Control When Variances Are Unknown and Unequal"

THE AMERICAN SCIENCES PRESS
SERIES IN MATHEMATICAL AND MANAGEMENT SCIENCES

American Sciences Press, Inc., P.O. Box 21161, Columbus, Ohio 43221-0161, U.S.A.

VOLUME 1: Introduction to Statis
Edward J. Dudewicz

VOLUME 2: Nonparametric Me
Jean D. Gibbons

VOLUME 3: Solutions in Stat
Edward J. Dud

VOLUME 4: The Handbook of Ra
and Testing with TESTRAN
Edward J. Dudewicz & Thomas G. R

VOLUME 5: The Sequential Statistical Analysis of Hypothesis Testing, Point and Interval Estimation, and Decision Theory
Z. Govindarajulu

VOLUME 6: The Complete Categorized Guide to Statistical Selection and Ranking Procedures
Edward J. Dudewicz & Joo O. Koo

VOLUME 7: The Chronological Annotated Bibliography of Order Statistics, Volume I: Pre-1950 (Revised Edition)
H. Leon Harter, with a Foreword by H.A. David

VOLUME 8: The Chronological Annotated Bibliography of Order Statistics, Volume II: 1950-1959
H. Leon Harter, with a Foreword by Lionel Weiss

VOLUME 9: Modern Multivariate Statistical Analysis: A Graduate Course and Handbook
Minoru Siotani, T. Hayakawa, and Y. Fujikoshi

VOLUME 10: The Frontiers of Modern Statistical Inference Procedures, Proceedings and Discussions of the IPASRAS Conference
Ed. Edward J. Dudewicz

VOLUME 11: Statistics and Optimization
Ed. Bruce L. Golden, Arjang A. Assad, & Stelios H. Zanakis

VOLUME 12: Modern Digital Simulation Methodology: Input, Modeling, and Output
Ed. Pandu R. Tadikamalla